DAVID G. DELKER
Kansas State University

Experiments in 8085 Microprocessor Programming and Interfacing

Merrill Publishing Company
A Bell & Howell Information Company
Columbus Toronto London Melbourne

Cover Photo: Courtesy Intel Corporation

Published by Merrill Publishing Company
A Bell & Howell Information Company
Columbus, Ohio 43216

This book was set in Century Schoolbook
Administrative Editor: Steve Helba
Production Coordinator: Julie Higgins
Art Coordinator: Vincent Smith
Cover Designer: Cathy Watterson

Library of Congress Catalog Card Number: 88-63026
International Standard Book Number: 0-675-20663-4
Printed in the United States of America
1 2 3 4 5 6 7 8 9—92 91 90 89

To my loving wife, Shawn,
and our wonderful children,
Ryan, Collin, and Kelsey—

Thank you for sacrificing so much
to make this book a reality.

PREFACE

This laboratory manual of experiments in 8085 microprocessor programming and interfacing was designed to provide the student with *practical* laboratory experiences to reinforce the concepts covered in most 8085 microprocessor courses. I emphasize the word *practical,* as each experiment relates specific microprocessor programming or interfacing techniques to realistic industrial applications. These experiments go well beyond the usual "bit-shuffling" exercises to include applications such as

- bidirectional DC motor control
- DC load control using pulse-width modulation
- serial and parallel data communications with a personal computer
- stepper motor control
- software-controlled keyboard scanning and display multiplexing
- temperature measurement
- waveform synthesis

The manual also contains five major programming and interfacing projects, each a suitable capstone activity to integrate important microprocessor concepts.

The manual complements the textbook *Microprocessor Architecture, Programming, and Applications with the 8085/8080A,* 2nd edition, by Ramesh S. Gaonkar, but it can be used with other texts as well. Each experiment is suitable for use in two- and four-year engineering technology courses, undergraduate engineering courses, and continuing education courses and seminars. The organization of the book allows for flexibility in a variety of curricular structures, including a one-semester course in 8085 programming and interfacing applications, a second-semester course including advanced programming and interfacing applications, and a two-semester sequence of courses, in which the first course emphasizes programming and the second course emphasizes interfacing. The manual contains more experiments than are needed for many course structures. Thus, the instructor can select those exercises that best meet specific educational goals in his or her particular course.

Overall Organization of the Book

The experiments are arranged in two major categories. Part One includes activities that emphasize programming applications of the 8085, while Part Two emphasizes interfacing applications. The first experiment in Part One introduces the single-board computer; students load and run a simple program during their first laboratory session. The Intel SDK-85 is the computer used for the activities in the manual, although many other types of computers are equally suited.

Other experiments in Part One emphasize the architecture of the 8085 and the use of status flags in binary and BCD arithmetic, decision making, and array-processing applications. The stack and subroutines are explored, and lookup tables are used in data conversion applications. Instruction cycle timing concepts are used to calculate program execution time and to generate precision time delays. The 8355 and the 8155 peripheral devices are introduced to connect the microprocessor to external hardware, including matrix keyboards and multiplexed LED displays.

The capstone activities in Part One are the two software-intensive programming projects: a digital alarm clock and a four-function integer calculator. Both projects require a systematic approach to the problem definition, software design, coding, and debugging phases of a microprocessor-based product. My students have found these two projects to be very challenging and rewarding.

Part Two of the manual emphasizes microprocessing interfacing. It begins by introducing the logic analyzer, which is used to trace instructions, I/O operations, and subroutine linkages. The 8085 interrupt structure is explored, and actual interrupt-driven applications are developed. Several digital systems are interfaced to the 8085 computer; these include memory circuits, TTL I/O ports, a stepper motor, the 8255A programmable peripheral device, the 8253 interval timer, the 8251A USART, a D/A converter, and an A/D converter. Software to drive each of these digital systems is developed to satisfy specific design objectives.

A personal computer is interfaced to an 8085-based microcomputer in Part Two to demonstrate parallel and serial interfacing techniques. The Intel HEX file protocol is used for transferring blocks of data from one machine to the other.

The culminating activities in Part Two are the three major interfacing projects that integrate all important programming and interfacing concepts. The slide gate controller project provides valuable experience in controlling a mechanical system with a microcomputer. The digital storage oscilloscope project ties together data acquisition, data processing, and waveform synthesis concepts into the design of a microprocessor-based test instrument. The last project in Part Two is a complete microcomputer built around the 8085 microprocessor. Students must propose, design, construct, test, and fully document a complete microprocessor-based product.

The six appendices contain an ASCII code table, an 8085 instruction set summary, a list of required equipment and supplies, connector pin assignment tables for the SDK-85 microcomputer, and a summary of the frequently used subroutines available in the SDK-85 monitor program. Appendix D contains a description of a typical 8085 cross assembler, including instruction syntax, assembler directives, and data types. Although a cross assembler program is not required for most experiments, it is a highly recommended tool to use *after* the students can proficiently hand-assemble a program. Students can accomplish far more in the laboratory if they do not have to use most of their time hand-assembling programs.

Organization of Each Experiment

The *Objectives* at the beginning of each experiment tell students what they will accomplish.

The *Reference Reading* section lists related reading material in the Gaonkar textbook or in Intel's *MCS-80/85 Family User's Manual*.

The *Materials Needed* section lists the test equipment, circuit components, and other supplies needed in the experiment.

The *Discussion* reviews important concepts. Example programs, flowcharts, schematic diagrams, and other relevant material are discussed.

The *Procedure* describes *what* is to be accomplished and may also suggest how to accomplish it. Guidelines for interpreting the experimental results are also included.

The *Additional Activities* provide optional laboratory work to challenge the more advanced student. These can also be used as alternative experiments so that the instructor does not have to use the same material each term.

The *Review Questions* at the end of each experiment briefly review the important concepts covered in the experiment.

Acknowledgments
I am indebted to the following reviewers who provided many constructive comments as the manual was developed: David Hata, Portland Community College, Portland, Oregon; Gene Singleton, DeVry Institute of Technology, Decatur, Georgia; Ronald Way, Muskegon Community College, Muskegon, Mississippi; Jim Pannell, DeVry Institute of Technology, Irving, Texas; and Bernard McIntyre, University of Houston, Houston, Texas.

My appreciation also goes to several individuals at Merrill Publishing Company. Steve Helba, administrative editor, offered guidance and encouragement that made this sometimes tedious task enjoyable. Julie Higgins, associate production editor, efficiently coordinated the production of the manual. Janet Greenblatt, copy editor, offered many valuable suggestions as she carefully edited the manuscript.

A final word of thanks must go to all of my former and current students at Kansas Technical Institute (now Kansas College of Technology) and Kansas State University. In sharing my fascination with microprocessor applications, they have given me the incentive to design and present the experiments in a practical application approach.

Notice to the Reader

The publisher and the author(s) do not warrant or guarantee any of the products and/or equipment described herein nor has the publisher or the author(s) made any independent analysis in connection with any of the products, equipment, or information used herein. The reader is directed to the manufacturer for any warranty or guarantee for any claim, loss, damages, costs, or expense, arising out of or incurred by the reader in connection with the use or operation of the products and/or equipment.

The reader is expressly advised to adopt all safety precautions that might be indicated by the activities and experiments described herein. The reader assumes all risks in connection with such instructions.

CONTENTS

PART TWO
8085 Microprocessor Peripheral Interfacing

Experiments in 8085 Microprocessor Programming and Interfacing

PART ONE

8085 Microprocessor Programming Applications

EXPERIMENT 1

Introduction to the 8085 Single-Board Computer

Objectives

A single printed circuit board consisting of an 8085 microprocessor, a few memory components, and some input/output circuitry is powerful enough to control a variety of industrial processes. Also, this type of single-board computer offers the ideal way to learn about microprocessor programming and interfacing. After completing this experiment, you will be able to use your single-board computer to

- Examine and modify information in memory
- Examine and modify the contents of the registers in the 8085
- Enter and execute machine language programs
- Design and test simple data transfer programs

Reference Reading

Gaonkar, Ramesh S. *Microprocessor Architecture, Programming, and Applications with the 8085/8080A*. 2nd ed. Columbus, OH: Merrill, 1989. Sections 1.1, 1.2, and 2.1 and Appendices B and F.

The MCS-80/85 Family User's Manual. Santa Clara, CA: Intel Corp., 1986. Pages 1–1 to 1–5, 2–1 to 2–2, and 5–1 to 5–6.

Materials Needed

8085 single-board computer with user's manual

Discussion

In future experiments, you will use an 8085-based single-board microcomputer to develop and debug 8085 machine language programs. You will also interface this microcomputer to several peripheral integrated circuits and other devices. By actually programming and interfacing the 8085, you will gain a thorough understanding of the architecture and capabilities of a typical microprocessor.

This experiment describes the basic operating modes of the Intel SDK-85 microcomputer. Refer to the material in the *SDK-85 User's Manual* for detailed descriptions of these operating modes and other features. If you are using a different type of microcomputer, your instructor can supply the necessary operating instructions.

8085 Programming Overview

Before we discuss the operation of the SDK-85 microcomputer, a brief overview of the 8085's architecture is appropriate. Refer to the Reference Reading material for additional 8085 details.

The 8085 uses a group of registers for most data manipulation tasks. These registers play a very important role in programming the 8085. Figure 1.1 shows the 8085 registers that can be accessed by the user.

Here is a brief description of each 8085 register:

Accumulator (A) register: This 8-bit register is used in many logical, arithmetic, and data transfer operations.

Flag (F) register: This 8-bit register indicates the current status of the 8085. The flag bits show, for example, whether or not a previous operation produced a negative result, generated a carry bit, or resulted in an even parity condition.

B, C, D, E, H, and L registers: These general-purpose 8-bit registers are used for temporary data storage, counting, and various other purposes. These registers are also used in pairs to form the 16-bit register pairs BC, DE, and HL.

Program counter (PC) register: This 16-bit register points to the next instruction to be executed.

Stack pointer (SP) register: This 16-bit register is used to control access to a special memory area known as the stack. The stack allows a subroutine to

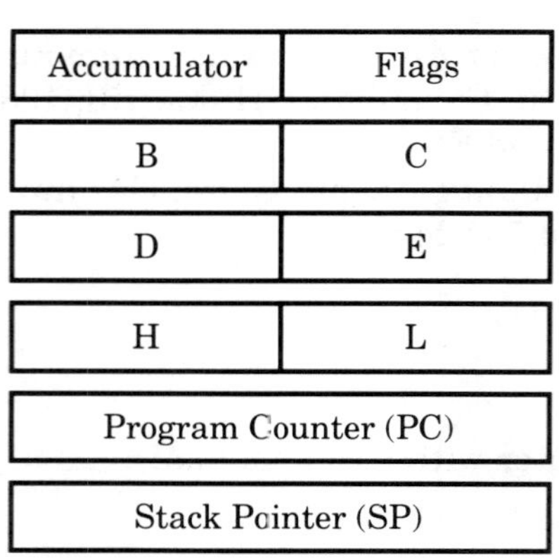

FIGURE 1.1
8085 Registers

return to its calling program. The stack is also used as an easily accessible data storage area.

Interrupt mask (I) register: This 8-bit register contains status and control bits used by the interrupt logic in the 8085.

Two major types of semiconductor memory are used in a microcomputer. The first type of memory is known as *Read-Only Memory,* or ROM. The microprocessor can read from the ROM, but it cannot write to it. The bits of information stored in a ROM are normally built into the device at the factory, although some types of ROM devices can be "programmed" with information by the user. The data bits stored in a ROM are maintained, even when no power is connected to the device. Memory that permanently maintains data in this manner is known as *nonvolatile* memory.

The second major category of memory in a microcomputer is *Random-Access Memory,* or RAM. RAM is sometimes referred to as Read/Write Memory(R/WM) because the microprocessor can read from it or write to it. RAM is used to store data, programs, and other information in a microcomputer. RAM is usually *volatile* in nature, meaning that it will lose its data when power is removed.

The ROM in the SDK-85 contains the *monitor program,* which is the program that controls the operation of the SDK-85. Part of the RAM in the SDK-85 is available for storage of user programs. The remaining RAM space is reserved for use by the monitor program. Additional space in the memory map of the machine is used for user-supplied memory and input/output devices. These memory areas are addressed as follows:

Memory Area	*Address Range*
Monitor ROM (IC A14)	0000H–07FFH
User RAM (IC A16)	2000H–20C1H
Expansion RAM (IC A17)	2800H–28FFH
Buffered Expansion Space	8000H–FFFFH

8085 Data Transfer Instructions

The 8085 moves data from place to place in the system using simple data transfer instructions. Data transfer instructions allow the 8085 to

- Place a data constant directly into a register
- Move data from one register to another
- Move data from memory to a register
- Move data from a register to memory

Here is a summary of several 8085 data transfer instructions:

Instruction	*Description*
MOV r1,r2	Move register r2 contents into register r1.
MVI r,8-bit data	Move immediate 8-bit data value into register r.
LXI rp,16-bit data	Move immediate 16-bit data value into register pair rp.
STA 16-bit address	Store accumulator contents in memory location specified.
LDA 16-bit address	Load accumulator from memory location specified.

LHLD 16-bit address	Load L with contents of memory location specified. Load H with contents of next memory location
SHLD 16-bit address	Store L contents in memory location specified. Store H contents in next memory location.
XCHG	Exchange contents of register pair HL with contents of register pair DE.

Program Testing and Debugging

Each user-written program must end with the RST 1 instruction. This instruction stops the user's program and returns control of the computer to the monitor program. The user may then examine the contents of memory and registers to determine the program results.

WARNING: Register contents are modified when the RESET key on the SDK-85 is used to stop a program or terminate any SDK-85 operation. RESET does not affect memory contents.

The following exercises demonstrate some of the basic features and capabilities of the SDK-85 microcomputer. Step-by-step procedures are given to demonstrate how to examine and modify memory and register contents and also how to enter and execute 8085 programs. You will use some additional SDK-85 debugging features in Experiment 2.

Procedure

1. Initializing the SDK-85

Turn on the SDK-85 power supply. The LED display should show this sign-on message:

- 80 85

If this message does not appear, press the RESET key on the keyboard.

Note that there are six 7-segment LED display digits. The group of four digits on the left form the *address field* of the display, and the two digits on the right form the *data field*.

2. Examining Memory Contents

Examine the contents of memory locations 2000H–2003H by pressing the RESET key and then the SUBST MEM (Substitute Memory) key. Now, enter the 4-digit hexadecimal address (2000H) of the first location to be examined. Press the NEXT key to show the contents of that location in the data field of the display.

Press the NEXT key three more times to view the contents of locations 2001H, 2002H, and 2003H. Finally, press the "." key to exit the memory-examine mode.

3. Modifying Memory Contents

Place the values 12H, 34H, 56H, and 78H into locations 2000H, 2001H, 2002H, and 2003H, respectively, by examining the first location (2000H) to be modified using the procedure that was described in step 2. Next, enter the number 12H into location 2000H by pressing the 1 key, then the 2 key. Press the NEXT key, which will store the 12H in location 2000H and display the address of the next location (2001H).

Enter the value 34H into location 2001H, 56H into location 2002H, and 78H into location 2003H. Finally, press the "." key to terminate the memory-modify mode. Examine memory locations 2000H–2003H to verify that these locations contain the correct values.

Turn off the power supply, wait a few moments, then turn the power supply back on. Examine locations 2000H–2003H and note what has happened. Does this observation indicate that this memory area is volatile or nonvolatile?

Examine location 005BH. You should see the number 21H, which is located in the monitor ROM. Try changing this value to 3FH. The display should produce an error message. Since ROM is read-only in nature, the SDK-85 cannot modify its contents. Whenever the SDK-85 Substitute Memory function attempts to modify a memory location, the 8085 writes the data to that address, then reads it back to check the results. The error message on the SDK-85 display indicates that the attempt to modify that location failed.

Turn off the power supply, wait a few moments, then turn the power back on. Examine location 005BH again. What does this observation show concerning the nature of the memory addressed at location 005BH? Is it volatile or nonvolatile?

4. Examining and Modifying 8085 Registers

The 8085 registers can be examined or modified using the Examine Register function. A register can be examined by pressing the EXAM REG key followed by the name of the register. For example, examine the accumulator contents by pressing the EXAM REG (Examine Register) key and then the A key. The displayed accumulator value can be modified at this time by entering a 2-digit hexadecimal number.

Press the "." key to terminate the register-examine mode, or press the NEXT key to examine/modify the other 8085 registers. Note that the 16-bit program counter and stack pointer registers are displayed eight bits at a time. PCH and PCL are the high and low portions of the program counter, while SPH and SPL are the high and low bytes of the stack pointer.

5. Executing a Demonstration Program

You are now ready to enter and execute your first machine language program. Put the following hexadecimal bytes into the SDK-85 memory locations specified. Enter each value carefully, because each number is an important part of a machine language program.

Addresses	*Hexadecimal Data*			
2000H–2003H	31	C2	20	11
2004H–2007H	FF	FF	13	D5
2008H–200BH	CD	63	03	11
200CH–200FH	00	80	CD	F1
2010H–2013H	05	D1	C3	06
2014H	20			

Run the program by pressing the GO key, followed by the 4-digit program starting address of the program (2000H). This step initializes the program counter register to the beginning location in the program. Press the EXEC (Execute) key to execute the program. You should see the address field LEDs on the SDK-85 count in hexadecimal sequence.

Stop the program by pressing the RESET key. Change the contents of location 200DH to 20H. Run the program again and observe the results. Change the contents of location 2006H to 1BH, then run the program. As you can see, changing only one byte has a very noticeable effect on the operation of this program.

6. Data Transfer Instruction Applications

For each of the following cases, manually assemble and execute the given program. Check the results by examining appropriate registers or memory locations. Each program should begin at memory location 2000H. Document your results as shown in the following example:

Given Program

```
MVI A,5FH        ;PLACE A CONSTANT INTO REGISTER A
STA 2050H        ;STORE THE CONSTANT IN MEMORY
RST 1            ;STOP
```

Assembled Program

Address	*Contents*	*Instruction*	*Comments*
2000H	3E 5F	MVI A,5FH	;PLACE A CONSTANT INTO REGISTER A
2002H	32 50 20	STA 2050H	;STORE THE CONSTANT IN MEMORY
2005H	CF	RST 1	;STOP

Observed Results

Accumulator contains 5FH.
Memory location 2050H contains 5FH.

```
a. MVI B,2DH        ;PUT DATA CONSTANT INTO REGISTER B
   MOV A,B          ;TRANSFER IT TO ACCUMULATOR
   RST 1            ;STOP

b. LDA 05F4H        ;GET A BYTE FROM MONITOR ROM
   MOV D,A          ;STORE IT IN REGISTER D
   STA 2080H        ;AND ALSO IN RAM
   RST 1            ;STOP

c. LHLD 05F4H       ;LOAD H AND L FROM MONITOR ROM
   SHLD 2070H       ;STORE H AND L IN RAM
   RST 1            ;STOP

d. LXI H,1234H      ;PUT 12H INTO REGISTER H, 34H INTO REGISTER L
   LXI D,5678H      ;PUT 56H INTO REGISTER D, 78H INTO REGISTER E
   XCHG             ;SWAP DE WITH HL
   RST 1            ;STOP
```

7. A Simple Data Transfer Instruction Problem

Write a program that will exchange the contents of registers A and B. Manually enter values into registers A and B, then execute the program. Record your observations.

Additional Activities

1. Study the listing of your single-board computer's monitor program. Display some of the contents of these memory locations with your computer. Note the similarities between some of the 8085 instructions and instructions in typical "high-level" languages, such as FORTRAN, BASIC, or Pascal.

2. *Disassemble* the demonstration program code given in procedure step 5. Convert the machine language code into assembly language mnemonics using the instruction set table in Appendix B. With your instructor's guidance, study the resulting assembly language program and see if you can understand in general terms how the program works.

Review Questions

1. What is the difference between nonvolatile memory and volatile memory?
2. How do the data retention characteristics of RAM and ROM storage devices differ?
3. What is the purpose of the program counter register?
4. How many bytes of RAM are available to the SDK-85 user? What range of addresses is occupied by this RAM?

EXPERIMENT 2

Binary Arithmetic

Objectives

The instruction set of the 8085 microprocessor includes instructions to add and subtract 8-bit binary quantities. Arithmetic operations are performed on multibyte quantities by cascading these simple 8-bit operations. After completing this experiment, you will be able to

- Add or subtract 8-bit binary quantities
- Add or subtract multibyte binary quantities
- Inspect and interpret the contents of the flag register
- Use single-stepping and breakpoint debugging techniques

Reference Reading

Gaonkar, Ramesh S. *Microprocessor Architecture, Programming, and Applications with the 8085/8080A*. 2nd ed. Columbus, OH: Merrill, 1989. Sections 3.15 and 6.2, Chapter 5, and Appendices A, B, and F.

The MCS-80/85 Family User's Manual. Santa Clara, CA: Intel Corp., 1986. Pages 2–1 to 2–2 and 5–1 to 5–9.

Materials Needed

8085 single-board computer with user's manual

Discussion

8085 Arithmetic Instructions

You will use many of the following 8085 arithmetic instructions in this experiment. Refer to the Reference Reading material for additional details.

Instruction	*Description*
ACI 8-bit data	Add immediate with carry 8-bit data to accumulator.
ADD r	Add contents of register r to accumulator.
ADI 8-bit data	Add immediate 8-bit data value to accumulator.
ADC r	Add contents of register r with carry to accumulator.
DAD rp	Add register pair contents to register pair HL.
SUB r	Subtract contents of register r from accumulator.
SBI 8-bit data	Subtract immediate with borrow 8-bit data from accumulator.
SUI 8-bit data	Subtract immediate 8-bit data from accumulator.
SBB r	Subtract with borrow contents of register r from accumulator.

Each of these instructions affects one or more flags in the processor status register. The Carry (CY) and Zero (Z) flags are of particular interest in arithmetic processing. Figure 2.1 illustrates the position of each flag in the status register. You may observe or modify the flags in the F register of the SDK-85 using the Examine Register function.

Multibyte Addition and Subtraction

Addition of multibyte quantities must be performed one byte at a time using the 8-bit addition instructions. As an example, the following program adds the 16-bit contents of register pairs BC and DE and places the sum in register pair HL:

```
MOV A,C  ;GET LEAST SIGNIFICANT BYTE OF FIRST OPERAND
ADD E    ;ADD IT TO L.S. BYTE OF SECOND OPERAND
MOV L,A  ;THEN STORE THE L.S. SUM BYTE
MOV A,B  ;GET MOST SIGNIFICANT BYTE OF FIRST OPERAND
ADC D    ;ADD IT WITH CY TO M.S. BYTE OF SECOND OPERAND
MOV H,A  ;THEN STORE THE M.S. SUM BYTE
RST 1    ;STOP
```

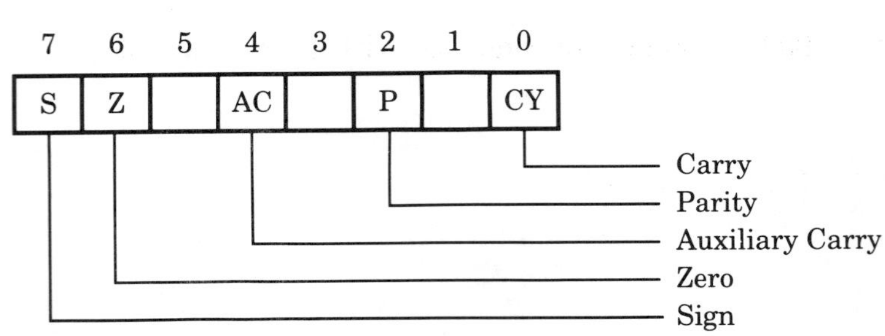

FIGURE 2.1
8085 Flag Register

Notice that the two least significant bytes are added first, using the ADD instruction. The addition of these two bytes may produce a carry, which the ADC instruction then adds with the two most significant bytes.

This example program could be expanded to handle operands containing three or more bytes. When doing multibyte addition with operands larger than two bytes, add the two least significant bytes first with the ADD instruction. Add all more significant pairs of bytes using ADC instructions.

When doing multibyte subtraction, subtract the two least significant bytes with the SUB instruction. Subtract all more significant pairs of bytes using SBB (subtract with borrow) instructions. In the previous example program, register pair DE can be subtracted from register pair BC by simply replacing the ADD instruction with SUB and the ADC instruction with SBB.

Program Debugging

The SDK-85 provides a debugging feature that allows the user to execute a program one instruction at a time. This technique, known as single stepping, is accomplished on the SDK-85 using this procedure:

1. Press the SINGLE STEP key on the SDK-85.
2. Enter the 4-digit address of the first program instruction.
3. Press the NEXT key to execute the first instruction. The SDK-85 display shows the program counter contents and the data contained at that address. You may press the NEXT key repeatedly to single-step through several instructions.
4. Press the "." key to terminate the single-step mode. You may now examine or modify the contents of memory and registers.
5. You may resume single-stepping the program by pressing the SINGLE STEP key, followed by the NEXT key. You do not need to enter an address before resuming; the program counter is still pointing to the next instruction in the program.
6. Instead of resuming program execution in the single-step mode, you may choose to execute the remaining instructions at full speed. Do this by pressing the GO key followed by the "." key.

One final debugging technique involves the RST 1 instruction. This instruction may be inserted anywhere in a program to serve as a "breakpoint." A breakpoint stops the program and allows the user to examine or modify the contents of memory and registers. When debugging a long program, place RST 1 instructions at strategic locations so that you can observe intermediate results. After your program debugging is completed, you may replace each RST 1 instruction with a NOP (no operation) instruction and execute the program without breakpoint interaction.

Procedure

1. Write a program to add the contents of registers B and C. The program should place the result in register H. Test your program by manually placing values into registers B and C using the Examine Register function of your computer. Execute the program. Record the contents of registers B, C, and H and note the status of the CY and Z flags. Test your program for each of the following cases; then verify your results with manual calculations before proceeding.

a. (B) = 4EH, (C) = 97H
b. (B) = D2H, (C) = 5EH
c. (B) = 2FH, (C) = D1H

2. Write a program to subtract the contents of memory location 2050H from the contents of location 2051H, and store the difference in location 2052H. Try your program for each of the following cases; record the difference and the status of the CY and Z flags for each case.

   a. (2050H) = 47H, (2051H) = 8EH
   b. (2050H) = 8EH, (2051H) = 47H
   c. (2050H) = F7H, (2051H) = F7H

3. Write a program to perform the following multibyte addition operation:

```
 91986FH
+2E6794H
--------
```

   Test the program by manually placing the two 3-byte numbers into consecutive memory locations. Design your program to add the values together and store the sum in three other memory locations. Execute the program using the single-step debugging mode. Record the sum and the CY flag and Z flag values after the program adds each pair of bytes. Verify these observations with manual computations.
4. Write a program to subtract one 3-byte number from another. The procedure is very similar to the addition program you developed in step 3. Test the program with these values:

```
  91086FH
- 2E3714H
---------
```

   Verify the results of your program by manually subtracting the two numbers.
5. Exchange the minuend (top number) and subtrahend (bottom number) values as shown:

```
  2E3714H
- 91086FH
---------
```

   Execute the subtraction program again and record the results. Verify the results manually, paying particular attention to the CY flag. How does the CY flag indicate the sign of the result?
6. In an automobile manufacturing plant, an assembly line conveyer belt is used to transfer components from one assembly work station to another. A photosensor mounted above the conveyer belt senses the components that pass; each time an object passes, the sensor sends a pulse to a 16-bit binary counter circuit. An 8085-based microcomputer reads the output from this counter periodically and adds the 16-bit counter value to a 32-bit total.

   Write the 8085 assembly language program to add the 16-bit output number from the counter to the 32-bit total. Test your program with these values:

```
  79B7EF24H
+     5D2FH
-----------
```

Additional Activities

1. Write and test a program to 2's complement the value in register B. Use the arithmetic instructions described in this experiment, plus any necessary data transfer instructions.
2. Write a program to perform the following subtraction operation by forming the 2's complement of the subtrahend and then adding it to the minuend. Verify your results.

$$\begin{array}{r} 91086FH \\ -\underline{2E3714H} \end{array}$$

3. Write a program to add the following 32-bit numbers. Use the DAD, LHLD, and SHLD instructions where appropriate. Assume that the two numbers are initially stored in RAM.

$$\begin{array}{r} 1F2CD43AH \\ +\ \underline{B7248D6CH} \end{array}$$

Review Questions

1. The following program is supposed to add the contents of memory location 2050H to the accumulator. The program works correctly only part of the time. Show what is wrong with the program and how to correct it.

```
MOV B,A      ;SAVE ACCUMULATOR CONTENTS
LDA 2050H    ;GET SECOND OPERAND
ADC B        ;ADD THEM TOGETHER
RST 1        ;STOP
```

2. In a multibyte addition program, when must you use the ADD instruction? When must you use the ADC instruction?
3. Assume that register pair HL contains the value 1234H. What does it contain after executing the instruction DAD H?

EXPERIMENT 3

Branching and Decision Making

Objectives

The microprocessor can read and interpret thousands of pieces of information every second. This high-speed decision-making capability is the key element in many microprocessor applications. In this exercise, you will explore several 8085 decision-making applications. After completing this experiment, you will be able to

- Test the 8085 status flags with the conditional jump instructions
- Mask individual data bits with the logical AND instruction
- Compare binary quantities with the comparison instructions
- Write programs that include simple looping structures

Reference Reading

Gaonkar, Ramesh S. *Microprocessor Architecture, Programming, and Applications with the 8085/8080A*. 2nd ed. Columbus, OH: Merrill, 1989. Chapter 5, Sections 6.3, 6.4, 7.1, and 7.5, and Appendices B and F.

The MCS-80/85 Family User's Manual. Santa Clara, CA: Intel Corp., 1986. Pages 5–1 to 5–13.

Materials Needed

8085 single-board computer

Discussion

8085 Decision-Making Instructions

You will use many of the following decision-making instructions in this experiment. Refer to the Reference Reading material for additional details.

Instruction	*Description*
ANI 8-bit data	AND immediate data with accumulator.

CMP r	Compare register with accumulator: (A)−(r).
	If (A) < (r), CY = 1, Z = 0.
	If (A) = (r), CY = 0, Z = 1.
	If (A) > (r), CY = 0, Z = 0.

CPI data8	Compare immediate with accumulator: (A)−data8.
	If (A) < data8, CY = 1, Z = 0.
	If (A) = data8, CY = 0, Z = 1.
	If (A) > data8, CY = 0, Z = 0.

INR r	Increment register r.
DCR r	Decrement register r.
JMP 16-bit address	Jump to address specified.
JC 16-bit address	Jump on carry (CY = 1).
JNC 16-bit address	Jump on no carry (CY = 0).
JZ 16-bit address	Jump on zero (Z = 1).
JNZ 16-bit address	Jump on not zero (Z = 0).

Decision-making programs rely on the proper use of the 8085 flags. As you develop 8085 programs, carefully consider the effect that each instruction has on the flags. Note that some 8085 instructions do not affect any flags, while other instructions modify several of them.

Bit Masking

Bit masking involves isolating one or more bits in a binary quantity while hiding, or masking, the unwanted bits. Masking is usually done with the logical AND instructions. The following program segment illustrates the masking concept. In this program, if bit 5 of location 2050H is 1, the program jumps to location 2020H. If bit 5 is 0, the program jumps to location 2040H.

```
LDA 2050H       ;RETRIEVE BYTE TO BE TESTED
ANI 20H         ;MASK ALL BITS, EXCEPT BIT 5
JNZ 2020H       ;JUMP TO 2020H IF BIT 5 = 1
JMP 2040H       ;ELSE, GO TO 2040H
```

Simple Looping Structures

Program loops are designed to repeat a group of instructions. In addition to the *body* of the loop (the instructions that are repeated), each loop includes a *loop counter* to control the number of repetitions and a *flag* to indicate when to stop the looping process.

The following program implements a simple repeated-addition multiplication technique to multiply two 8-bit numbers. The flowchart for this program is given in Figure 3.1. In this algorithm, the multiplier (register B) serves as the loop counter, the multiplicand resides in register C, and the product is contained in register pair HL.

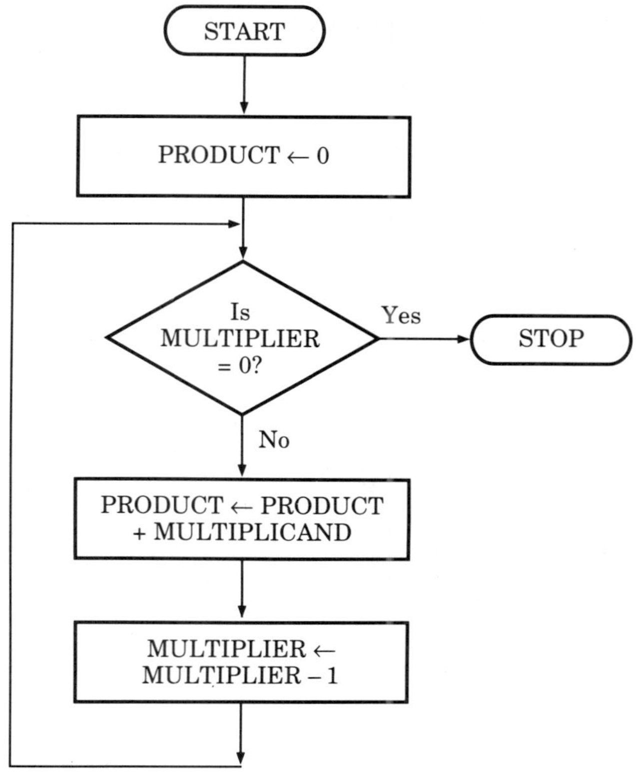

FIGURE 3.1
Flowchart for Multiplication Using Repeated Addition

```
        LXI H,0000H     ;CLEAR PRODUCT REGISTER PAIR
LOOP:   MOV A,B         ;GET MULTIPLIER
        CPI 00H         ;COMPARE MULTIPLIER WITH ZERO
        JNZ OVER        ;IF NOT ZERO, CONTINUE
        RST 1           ;ELSE, QUIT
OVER:   MOV A,L         ;GET LS BYTE OF PRODUCT
        ADD C           ;ADD MULTIPLICAND
        MOV L,A         ;SAVE THE LS PRODUCT BYTE
        MOV A,H         ;ADD CARRY AND MS PRODUCT BYTE
        ACI 00H
        MOV H,A         ;SAVE MS PRODUCT BYTE
        DCR B           ;DECREMENT MULTIPLIER
        JMP LOOP        ;REPEAT
```

8085 Program-Debugging Techniques

Debugging machine language programs on a single-board computer sometimes is a very difficult task. However, we can make this job easier by using some of the built-in features of our single-board computer. The SDK-85 monitor program contains two subroutines that can display data produced by a program. One subroutine displays a 16-bit value on the address field of the display, and the other displays an 8-bit value on the data field. The following information describes these two SDK-85 subroutines:

Subroutine Name: UPDAD
Calling Address: 0363H

Description: Updates address field of display.
Inputs: Contents of DE are displayed. Register B controls decimal point (DP) at right edge of field. (B) = 01 turns on DP, (B) = 00 turns off DP.
Outputs: None
Registers Modified: A, B, C, D, E, H, L, and flags

Subroutine Name: UPDDT
Subroutine Calling Address: 036EH
Description: Updates data field of display.
Inputs: Contents of accumulator are displayed. Register B controls decimal point (DP) at right edge of field. (B) = 01 turns on DP, (B) = 00 turns off DP.
Outputs: None
Registers Modified: A, B, C, D, E, H, L, and flags

NOTE: If you are using a single-board microcomputer other than the SDK-85, your instructor can supply specific details about similar monitor subroutines available in your computer.

The following program demonstrates the use of the UPDAD and the UPDDT subroutines. This program displays the contents of memory locations 2051H and 2050H on the address field of the display. The contents of memory location 2075H are produced on the data field of the display. Note that the LXI SP,20C2H instruction should be placed at the beginning of any program that includes a subroutine call or other stack operation. (The LXI SP operand may be different if you are using a microcomputer other than the SDK-85.) You will learn more about the LXI SP instruction and subroutines in Experiment 8.

```
        LXI SP, 20C2H   ;INITIALIZE THE STACK POINTER
        LDA 2051H       ;GET MS BYTE TO BE DISPLAYED
        MOV D,A
        LDA 2050H       ;GET LS BYTE TO BE DISPLAYED, THEN
        MOV E,A
        CALL 0363H      ;DISPLAY DE CONTENTS IN ADDRESS FIELD
        LDA 2075H       ;GET BYTE TO BE DISPLAYED, THEN
        CALL 036EH      ;DISPLAY IT IN DATA FIELD
LOOP:   JMP LOOP        ;STAY HERE FOREVER
```

The JMP instruction at the end of the program creates an endless loop, which prevents the usual RST 1 instruction from stopping the program and returning control to the monitor program of the machine. If we replaced the JMP instruction with RST 1, the monitor program would write the "-80 85" prompting message over any previously displayed information.

One precaution must be observed when using these two monitor subroutines: The contents of *all* registers are modified by the execution of either subroutine. Registers containing important data values should be saved temporarily in memory before calling either subroutine and then restored after the subroutine ends.

Procedure

1. Write a program that will perform the tasks described by the flowchart in Figure 3.2. Document your program by including appropriate comments in the program listing.

   Check the program by manually placing a test value into the accumulator. (Note that bit 0 of the accumulator is the least significant bit, while bit 7 is the

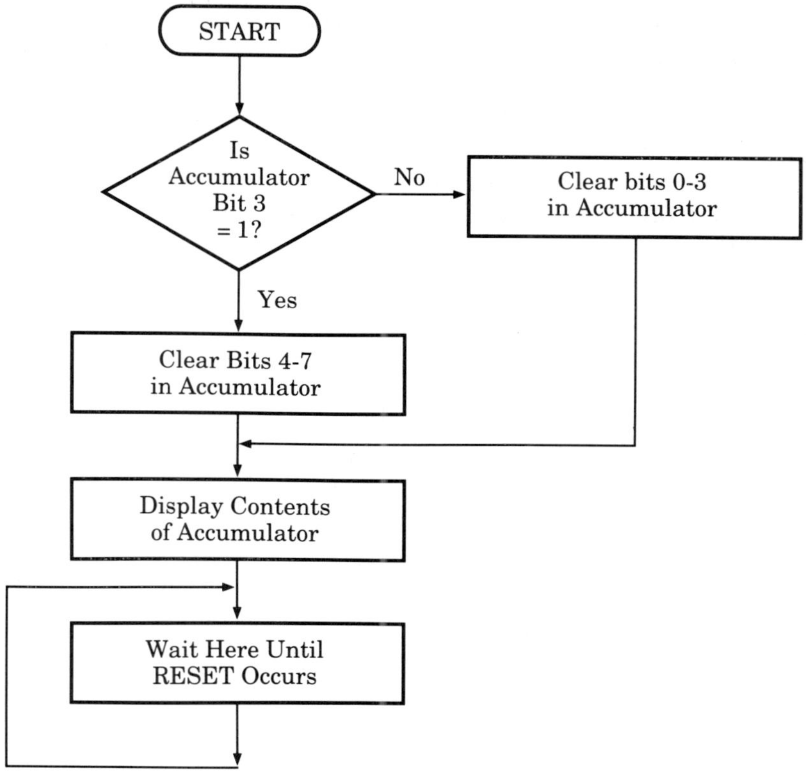

FIGURE 3.2
Flowchart for Procedure Exercise 1

most significant bit.) Execute the program and record the results. Check the program performance by trying several different test values.

2. A hexadecimal number between 00H and 0FH is to be converted to ASCII before being transmitted to a remote video terminal. As an example, 00H must be converted to 30H in ASCII, 0BH must be converted to 42H, etc.

   Develop a flowchart, then write and test a program that will convert the number contained in the accumulator into its corresponding ASCII code. (Refer to the ASCII chart in Appendix A.) The program should display the original number on the left two digits and the ASCII value on the right two digits of the address field of the SDK-85 display. If the number in the accumulator is 05H, for example, the program should display 0535. If the value in the accumulator is 0AH, the program should display 0A41.

3. An 8085-based microcomputer monitors eight limit switches on an automated machine tool. The microcomputer reads the status of these switches periodically and stores this 8-bit value in memory location 2080H. The system uses these bits to determine the appropriate message to display on the control console of the machine tool. If sensor bits 7, 3, and 2 are each logic 1, the display shows the number AAAA. If this condition is not present, bits 0 and 1 are tested. If *either* of these two bits is logic 1, the number 0000 is displayed. The display shows 1111 for all other sensor conditions.

   Draw a flowchart, then write and test an 8085 program to implement this logic. Produce the three messages on the address field of the SDK-85 display.

Additional Activities

1. Draw a flowchart, then write and test an 8085 program that will compare register B with register C. If (B) is less than (C), display CCCC in the address field of the display. If (B) is greater than (C), display BBBB, and if (B) equals (C), display 0000.
2. A microcomputer monitors the temperature of the oil in an experimental engine. The microcomputer reads data from two 8-bit temperature transducer modules periodically and stores these readings in memory. Write an 8085 program that will compare the two numbers, which reside in locations 2080H and 2081H. Display the larger number on the most significant two digits of the address field of the SDK-85 display, and display the smaller number on the least significant two digits.

Review Questions

What value remains in the accumulator after executing each of the following program segments? What are the states of the CY and Z flags?

1.
```
MVI A,57H
ANI 08H
```

2.
```
MVI A,FFH
INR A
```

3.
```
MVI A,FFH
ADI 01H
```

4.
```
MVI A,80H
CPI F0H
```

5.
```
MVI A,F0H
CPI 80H
```

EXPERIMENT 4

Array Processing

Objectives

Computers use arrays to allow efficient manipulation of large quantities of data. The 8085 instruction set includes several instructions that facilitate efficient array processing. After completing this experiment, you will be able to

- Apply indexing techniques to solve array-processing problems
- Develop a program to search a data array for a specific value
- Develop a program to sort a data array into ascending order

Reference Reading

Gaonkar, Ramesh S. *Microprocessor Architecture, Programming, and Applications with the 8085/8080A*. 2nd ed. Columbus, OH: Merrill, 1989. Chapter 5, Sections 7.1, 7.2, and Appendix F.

The MCS-80/85 Family User's Manual. Santa Clara, CA: Intel Corp., 1986. Pages 5–1 to 5–13.

Materials Needed

8085 single-board computer

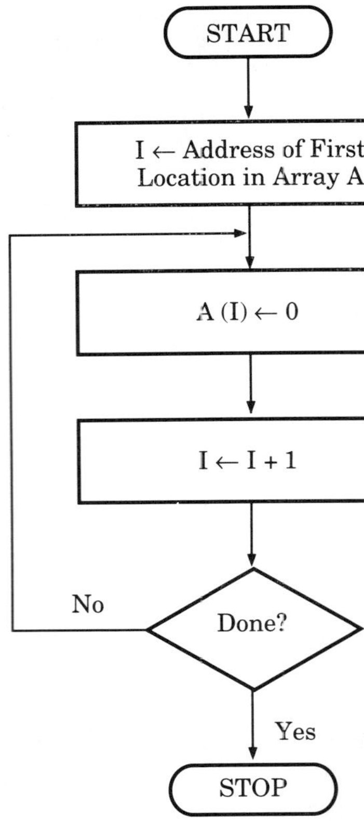

FIGURE 4.1
Flowchart for Array-Clearing Technique Using Indexing

Discussion

8085 Array-Processing Instructions

Data array processing generally uses a subscript to identify a specific array element. In assembly language programming, this subscript is known as an index or pointer. Typically, a register or register pair serves as a pointer. Here are several 8085 instructions that can manipulate this index and access memory values referenced by the index:

Instruction	*Description*
LDAX rp	Load A from location specified by rp contents.
STAX rp	Store A in location specified by rp contents.
MOV M,r	Move data from register r to location specified by register pair HL.
MOV r,M	Move data from locations specified by register pair HL to register r.
INX rp	Increment register pair rp by 1.
DCX rp	Decrement register pair rp by 1.

Indexing Example

Consider the flowchart in Figure 4.1. This logic shows how to clear an array using an indexing technique.

The following program implements the logic illustrated in Figure 4.1. The program clears memory locations 2050H–206FH. Study the action of register pair HL (the index pointer) for each pass through the body of the loop.

```
      LXI H,2050H   ;INITIALIZE POINTER
MORE: MVI A,00H     ;CLEAR ACCUMULATOR
      MOV M,A       ;STORE ZERO IN MEMORY POINTED TO BY RP HL
      INX H         ;POINT TO NEXT LOCATION
      MVI A,70H     ;SEE IF PAST THE END OF THE ARRAY
      CMP L         ; BY COMPARING (L) WITH 70H
      JNZ MORE      ;IF NOT DONE YET, JUMP BACK FOR MORE
      RST 1         ;ELSE, QUIT
```

The loop repetition in this program is controlled by comparing the value in register L with 70H at the end of each pass through the loop. When register L reaches 70H, the program stops. The program does not need to check the most significant byte of the index pointer, because it will always be 20H. Notice that the program would stop one location prematurely if it compared the contents of register L with the number 6FH.

Procedure

1. A bar code scanner reads the product code labels on cartons in a warehouse and sends these 8-bit binary codes to an 8085-based microcomputer, where they are stored in an array. The warehouse manager uses this microcomputer to search this array of numbers for all occurrences of a particular product code number.

   Write an 8085 program that will count the occurrences of a given code number in the array. Test your program by searching locations 0000H–07FFH for the target value C3H. Display the total on the data field of the SDK-85 display. NOTE: The area of memory being searched is occupied by the SDK-85 monitor ROM; there are less than 256 C3H values in this range, so the total will fit satisfactorily in the 8-bit data field.

   Testing a program of this type requires some special techniques. Since there are too many ROM locations to examine manually, you must test the performance of your program with a smaller array of numbers. Try modifying your program temporarily so that it will search through a small range of RAM locations. Manually place some C3H bytes in this memory space, then run the program. If the program works properly for this small array, it *probably* will work correctly for the larger array as well. Make sure the program works properly if it encounters the target value in the first or the last location in the array.
2. An 8085-based microcomputer in a chemical plant reads an 8-bit value from a temperature sensor circuit once each minute. The microcomputer stores each reading in an array in memory. At the end of each day, the computer sorts these readings into ascending order, then prints the daily summary report.

   You are responsible for writing an 8085 program to sort the array of readings into ascending order. The flowchart in Figure 4.2 describes a simple exchange sort algorithm that you can use for this purpose.

   The exchange sort method compares the magnitude of adjacent items in the array. If the first array item is greater than the second one, the two values are exchanged; otherwise, the two values are not disturbed. Next, the second and third items in the array are compared, and an exchange is made if necessary. This process continues until the end of the array is reached.

   If any exchanges are made during a given pass through the array, the entire array must be reexamined. If no exchanges are made during a pass through the array, the process ends. The resulting array contents are in ascending order.

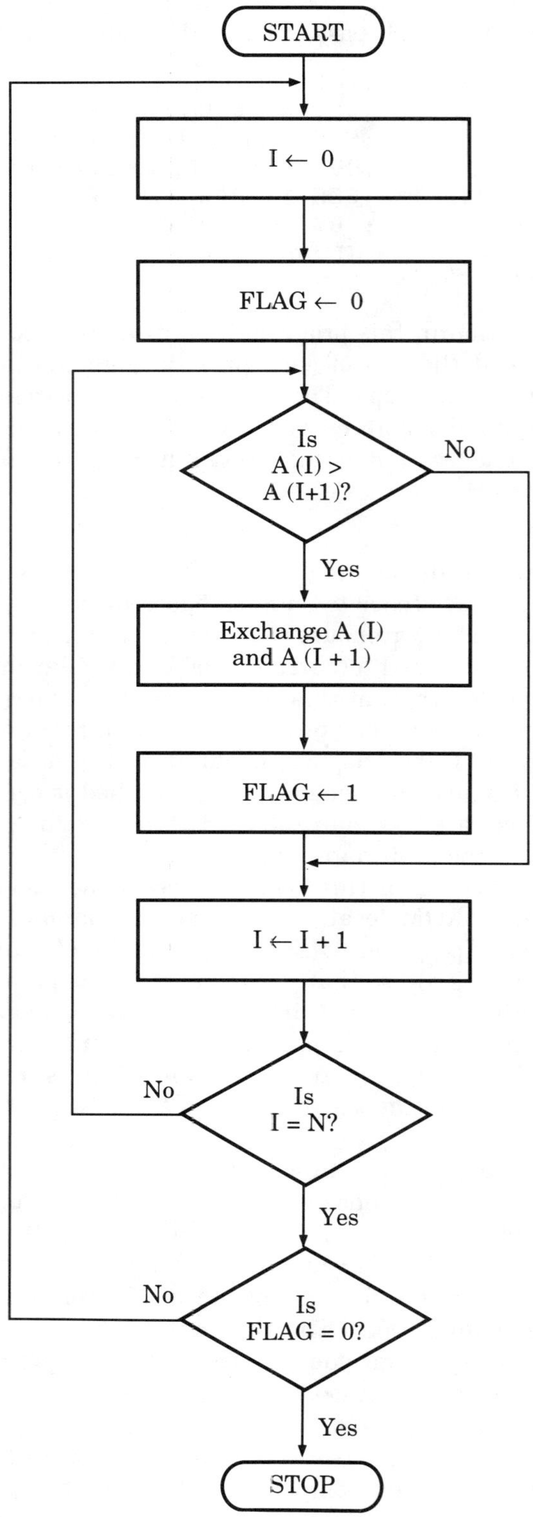

FIGURE 4.2
Flowchart for Exchange Sort of N Items in Array A(I)

The exchange sort algorithm described here is fairly slow. However, for the sake of simplicity, program refinements that could make the program run faster are not included in this algorithm. Many other sorting techniques are available that have distinct advantages over the exchange sort. Still, the exchange sort is popular, owing to its simplicity, when small quantities of data are being sorted.

Study the exchange sort algorithm and try the sorting technique manually before you begin to write your program. Choose a value of N = 5 and write down memory and pointer values for each pass through the array. Use array pointers very carefully in coding this algorithm; otherwise you can expect unsatisfactory results.

Configure your program to sort the contents of RAM locations 2080H–209FH. Test your sort program by writing another program to copy the contents of the SDK-85 monitor ROM locations 0000H–001FH into RAM locations 2080H–209FH; execute your sort program to put these data values in the correct order.

Additional Activities

1. Write an 8085 program to copy the contents of ROM locations 0000H–001FH to RAM locations 2080H–209FH. Execute your program and check the results.
2. Write an 8085 program that will copy the contents of locations 2080H–208FH to locations 2088H–2097H. Notice that the source and destination arrays overlap each other, with the beginning of the destination array corresponding with the middle of the source array. Because of this overlap, use index pointers very carefully to avoid accidentally writing over data.
3. Write an 8085 program that will copy the contents of locations 2088H–2097H to locations 2080H–208FH. Note that the source and destination arrays overlap each other, with the beginning of the source array corresponding to the middle of the destination array.

Review Questions

1. Programming errors often prevent array-processing programs from working properly. The following program is supposed to clear bit 3 of each memory location between 2050H and 205FH, but several errors cause it to malfunction. Find and correct each error.

```
       LXI H,2050H    ;INITIALIZE POINTER TO ARRAY
MORE:  MVI B,0FH      ;INITIALIZE LOOP COUNTER
       MOV M,A        ;GET A BYTE FROM MEMORY
       ANI 08H        ;CLEAR BIT 3
       MOV A,M        ;SAVE THE RESULTS
       DCR B          ;DECREMENT LOOP COUNTER
       JZ MORE        ;REPEAT UNTIL ALL BYTES HAVE BEEN PROCESSED
       RST 1          ;QUIT
```

2. The following program manipulates the numbers in an array. What specific operation is performed on each array location? Which locations are affected?

```
       LXI H,3000H
MORE:  MVI A,00H
       SUB M
       MOV M,A
       INX H
       MVI A,40H
       CMP H
       JNZ MORE
       RST 1
```

EXPERIMENT 5

Parallel I/O Using the 8355

Objectives

Computers can monitor the outside world using input ports; they can control it using output ports. An 8085 microprocessor performs input/output (I/O) tasks using special I/O instructions and some external hardware. At the conclusion of this experiment, you will be able to

- Perform simple input and output data transfers using the IN and OUT instructions
- Use the I/O ports on the Intel 8355 integrated circuit
- Use a polling technique to complete data transfers

Reference Reading

Gaonkar, Ramesh S. *Microprocessor Architecture, Programming, and Applications with the 8085/8080A*. 2nd ed. Columbus, OH: Merrill, 1989. Sections 4.11, 4.12, 6.1, and 14.27, and Appendix F.

The MCS-80/85 Family User's Manual. Santa Clara, CA: Intel Corp., 1986. Pages 5–1 to 5–13 and 5–16.

Materials Needed

8085 single-board computer
Breadboard with logic switches and LED indicators

Discussion

8085 I/O Instructions

Data transfers between the 8085 and external hardware are performed using the following specialized data transfer instructions:

Instruction	*Description*
IN 8-bit port address	Transfers an 8-bit value into the accumulator from the input port specified.
OUT 8-bit port address	Transfers an 8-bit value from the accumulator to the output port specified.

The second byte of each instruction is the 8-bit port address. Valid port addresses range from 00H to FFH.

Polled I/O

In many I/O applications, the microcomputer must wait for the peripheral device to become "ready" before it can complete an I/O exchange. The peripheral can tell the microcomputer that it is ready for data exchange by activating a status signal. When the microcomputer discovers that this signal is active, it completes the I/O transfer. This I/O transfer technique is known as *polled I/O* (also known as status check I/O). Figure 5.1 illustrates this polled I/O concept.

The following program is an example of a polled I/O transfer. The program reads the status of the peripheral on bit 7 of port 00H. When bit 7 of the input port becomes a logic 1, the contents of register C are output to port 01H.

```
WAIT: IN 00H      ;READ THE INPUT PORT
      ANI 80H     ;MASK OFF ALL BITS EXCEPT BIT 7
      JZ WAIT     ;IF BIT 7 IS NOT ACTIVE (HIGH), JUMP BACK
      MOV A,C     ;GET DATA TO BE OUTPUT
      OUT 01H     ;SEND DATA TO OUTPUT PORT
```

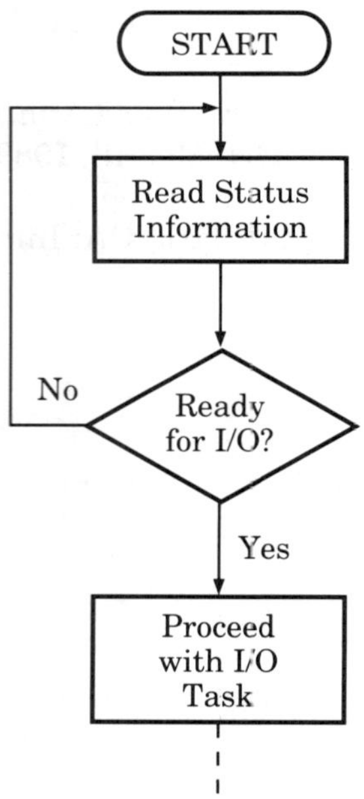

FIGURE 5.1
Flowchart for Polled I/O Technique

The 8355 I/O Device

The SDK-85 computer contains two devices that are useful for I/O interfacing. The 8355 contains the monitor program ROM and 16 I/O lines. The 8155 contains the system RAM, a 14-bit counter/timer function, and also 22 I/O lines. The 8355 is the subject of this experiment; the 8155 will be examined in Experiment 11.

The 8355 input/output section includes two 8-bit I/O ports, known as port A and port B. The user may program each of these 16 I/O lines as an input or an output. The data direction is programmed by writing to a data direction register (DDR) for each of the two ports. A logic 1 in a DDR bit configures the corresponding port line as an output, while a logic 0 configures the corresponding port line as an input. Figure 5.2 shows this relationship.

The 8355's two data ports and two data direction registers are accessed at the following I/O addresses in the SDK-85 system:

Address	*Selection*
00H	Port A
01H	Port B
02H	Port A data direction register
03H	Port B data direction register

The microprocessor can read the two data ports even when they are configured as output ports. The 8355 data direction registers, however, cannot be read. The RESET key on the SDK-85 resets the logic in the 8355. This action clears all bits in the control register and, in doing so, configures all port lines as inputs.

The following program illustrates a simple 8355 I/O application. Each bit of port A is configured as an input, and each bit of port B is configured as an output. The program continually reads the information on port A and writes it to port B.

```
PORTA EQU 00H       ;EQUATE SYMBOLIC NAMES TO 8355 ADDRESSES (SDK-85)
PORTB EQU 01H
DDRA  EQU 02H
DDRB  EQU 03H
      MVI A,00H     ;DEFINE PORT A BITS AS INPUTS
      OUT DDRA
      MVI A,FFH     ;DEFINE PORT B BITS AS OUTPUTS
      OUT DDRB
LOOP: IN PORTA      ;GET DATA FROM PORT A
      OUT PORTB     ;SEND DATA TO PORT B
      JMP LOOP      ;REPEAT FOREVER
```

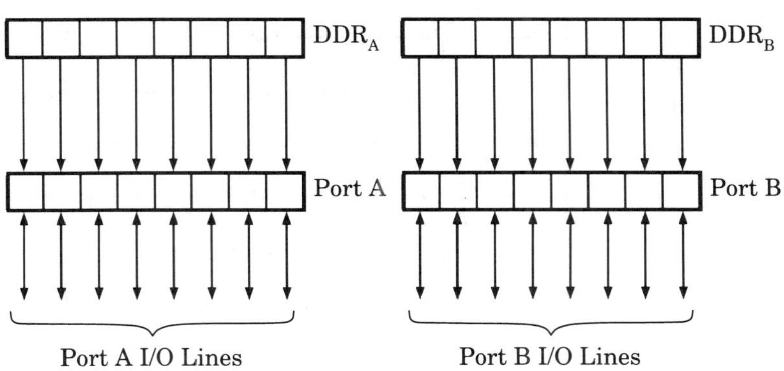

FIGURE 5.2
8355 I/O Port Structure

The 8355 port lines are connected to connector J3 on the SDK-85, as described in Appendix E.

Procedure

These exercises assume that a breadboard system is available with eight logic switches and eight LED indicators. If these input and output capabilities are not available, you can wire eight logic switches and eight LED indicators as shown in Figure 5.3.

1. Connect the 8355 port A lines to eight logic switches on the breadboard. Connect the eight port B lines to eight LED indicators. Connect the GROUND pin on the J3 connector of the SDK-85 to a ground point on the breadboard.

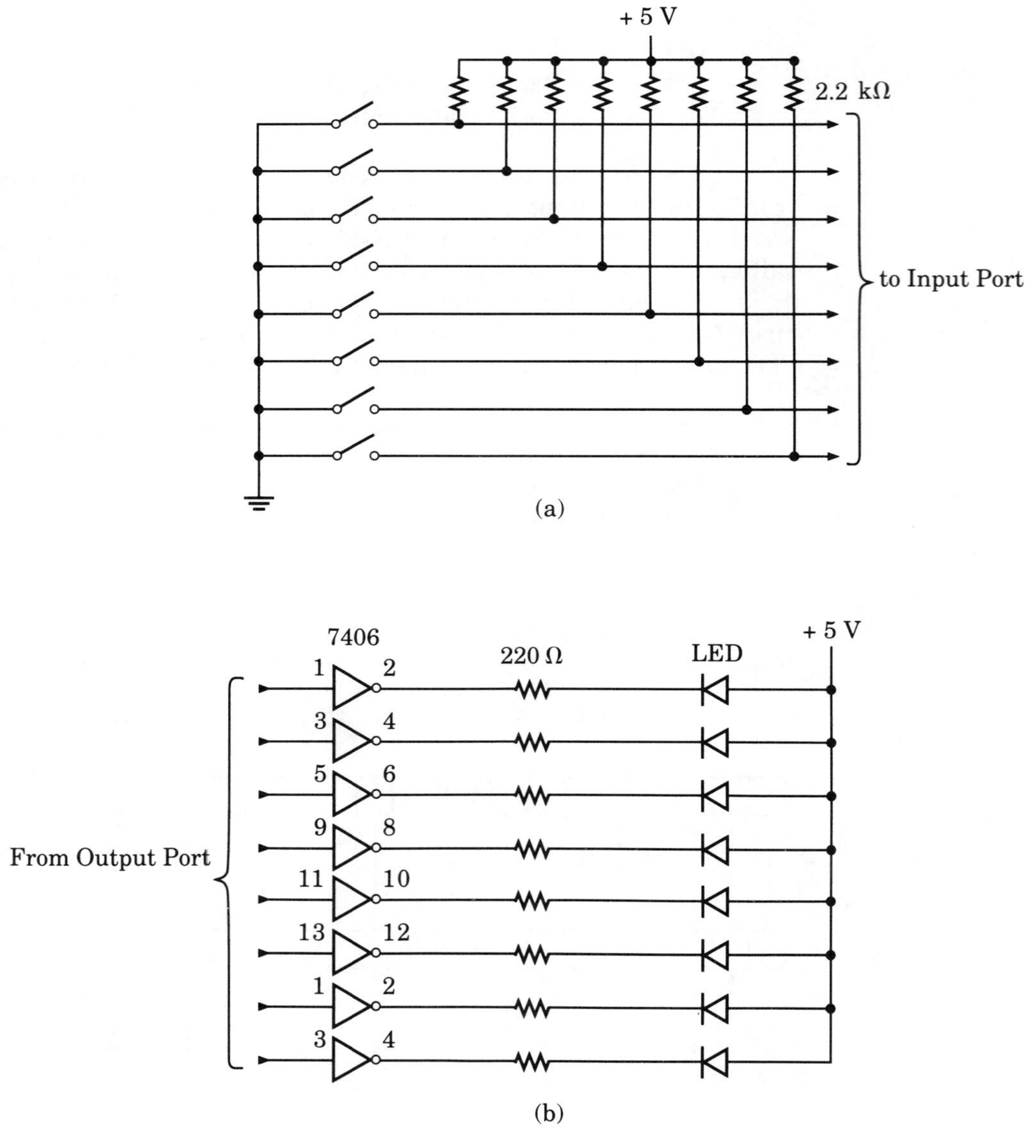

FIGURE 5.3
(a) Logic Switches, (b) LED Indicators

***WARNING*: Power must be *off* on both the breadboard and the SDK-85 before making these connections. Check the wiring carefully before turning on either system. If a port output line is shorted to +5 V, GND, or an adjacent pin, even momentarily, that port output *will* be destroyed!**

2. Assemble the test program, discussed previously, that reads the switches on port A and sends this information to the corresponding LED indicators on port B. Execute the program. Each LED indicator should light as the corresponding logic switch is placed in the logic 1 position. Correct all wiring errors before proceeding.
3. A microcomputer controls the safety interlock on an automated machine tool. Each authorized user of the machine tool has a key that activates the tool. A specific sequence must occur to turn on the machine: First, the key switch must be activated. Next, two switch buttons on the control console must be pressed simultaneously. Finally, a foot-activated switch must be pressed.

   Write the 8085 program to control the safety interlock system. Use the switch connected to the 8355 PA-7 input as the key switch, the PA-4 and PA-1 switches as the two switch buttons, and the PA-6 input as the foot-activated switch. Use all eight LEDs (PB-0 through PB-7) to simulate the machine tool motor; all eight LEDs should be off to represent the motor in the off condition, and they all should be on to simulate the motor in the on state.
4. A microcomputer is used to count the number of people entering a movie theater. A pulse is produced as each person passes through the turnstile at the entrance of the theater. A microcomputer counts these pulses and displays the result in the manager's office. Your task is to write the 8085 program to count these "people pulses."

   Connect a logic switch to the 8355 PA-0 input port to simulate the turnstile signal. Write a program to count these pulses and display the count in hexadecimal sequence on the address field of the SDK-85 display.

   NOTE: If your logic switches are not "debounced" electrically, you may see several counts whenever you change the switch setting. This is due to the mechanical nature of the switch contacts. Closing or opening the switch contact does not happen instantaneously, and the contact may bounce several times before coming to rest. If you desire, you can debounce a switch using the simple logic circuit shown in Figure 5.4. Another alternative will be explored in Experiment 13 when you will learn how to debounce a switch using software.

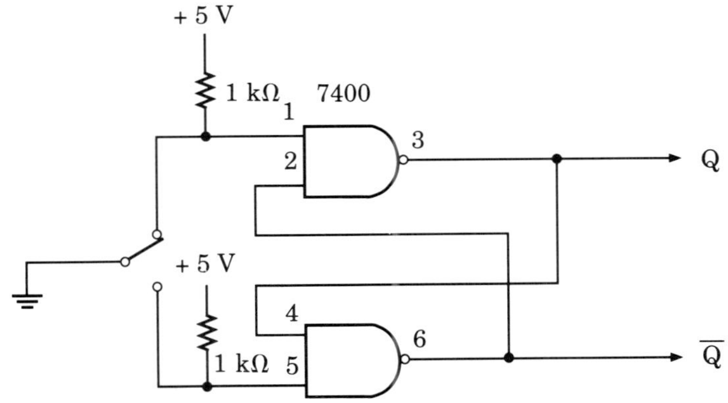

FIGURE 5.4
Debounced Switch Circuit

Additional Activities

1. Simulate a set/reset flip-flop using the microcomputer. Connect the 8355 bit PA-0 to a logic switch to simulate the SET input of the flip-flop. Connect PA-7 to a logic switch to simulate the RESET input. Connect PB-0 to an LED indicator to serve as the Q output. Write an 8085 program that will turn on the LED indicator whenever PA-0 (SET) receives a logic 1, and will turn off the LED whenever PA-7 (RESET) receives a logic 1.
2. Design an 8085 program that will output the contents of the SDK-85 monitor ROM (locations 0000H–07FFH) to an 8355 output port, one byte at a time, under the control of a logic switch. Connect the logic switch to 8355 input PA-0 and eight LED indicators to 8355 outputs PB-0 through PB-7. The program should show the next ROM byte on the LED display whenever the logic switch output goes from low to high. Use a debounced logic switch; otherwise your program will appear to skip memory locations occasionally.
3. Simulate an up/down counter integrated circuit using the SDK-85. Design your program to send a 16-bit count to the address field of the display. The counter should count up when PA-0 detects a pulse, and should count down when PA-7 detects one. A logic 1 on PA-1 should clear the count. Produce the up and down count pulses with debounced logic switches.

Review Questions

1. How many I/O locations are accessible by the 8085?
2. In the following program segment, which 8355 bits are configured as inputs? Which bits are configured as outputs?

```
MVI A,0FH
OUT DDRA
MVI A,7FH
OUT DDRB
```

3. What condition must be met in the following program to reach the MOV A,B instruction?

```
LOOP:   IN PORTA
        ANI 55H
        JNZ LOOP
        MOV A,B
```

EXPERIMENT 6

Bit Manipulation

Objectives

Bit manipulation techniques are used in a variety of microprocessor applications. Bit manipulation tasks include setting, resetting, and complementing individual bits of information and also shifting and rotating groups of bits. After completing this experiment, you will be able to

- Use the 8085 logical instructions to set, clear, or complement individual bits
- Use the 8085 rotate instructions to manipulate groups of bits
- Multiply two binary values using a shift-and-add technique

Reference Reading

Gaonkar, Ramesh S. *Microprocessor Architecture, Programming, and Applications with the 8085/8080A*. 2nd ed. Columbus, OH: Merrill, 1989. Chapter 5, Sections 6.3, 7.4, and 10.8, and Appendix F.

The MCS-80/85 Family User's Manual. Santa Clara CA: Intel Corp., 1986. Pages 5–1 to 5–13.

Materials Needed

8085 single-board computer
Breadboard with logic switches and LED indicators

Discussion

8085 Bit Manipulation Instructions

The 8085 logical instructions can set, reset, or complement individual data bits. Here is a summary of some of the logical instructions that can be used for bit manipulation:

Instruction	*Description*
ANA r	AND contents of register r with accumulator.
ANA M	AND contents of memory with accumulator.
ANI 8-bit data	AND immediate data with accumulator.
ORA r	OR contents of register r with accumulator.
ORA M	OR contents of memory with accumulator.
ORI 8-bit data	OR immediate data with accumulator.
XRA r	Exclusive-OR contents of register r with accumulator.
XRA M	Exclusive-OR contents of memory with accumulator.
XRI 8-bit data	Exclusive-OR immediate data with accumulator.
CMA	Complement accumulator contents.
CMC	Complement carry.
STC	Set carry.

Here are several examples that demonstrate various bit manipulation techniques. The logical instruction operands are given in binary form to show clearly which bits are being manipulated.

1. Clear bit 3 of register B:

```
MOV A,B         ;RETRIEVE REGISTER B CONTENTS
ANI 11110111B   ;CLEAR BIT 3
MOV B,A         ;SEND RESULT BACK TO B
```

2. Set bits 6 and 7 of memory location 2050H:

```
LDA 2050H       ;RETRIEVE MEMORY CONTENTS
ORI 11000000B   ;SET BITS 6 AND 7
STA 2050H       ;SEND RESULT BACK TO MEMORY
```

3. Complement upper four bits of register D:

```
MOV A,D         ;RETRIEVE REGISTER B CONTENTS
XRI 11110000B   ;COMPLEMENT UPPER 4 BITS, DO NOT CHANGE OTHERS
MOV D,A         ;SEND RESULT BACK TO D
```

The 8085 rotate instructions are easy to understand if described graphically (see Figure 6.1). Notice how each of these instructions manipulates the accumulator and the CY flag during the rotation process.

The rotate instructions are often used to test the status of an individual bit. This is done by rotating the bit into the CY flag, then using the JC or JNC instruction to jump, based on the CY flag value. For example, the following program jumps to the label ONE if bit 3 of register B is set. If bit 3 is zero, the program continues at label ZERO.

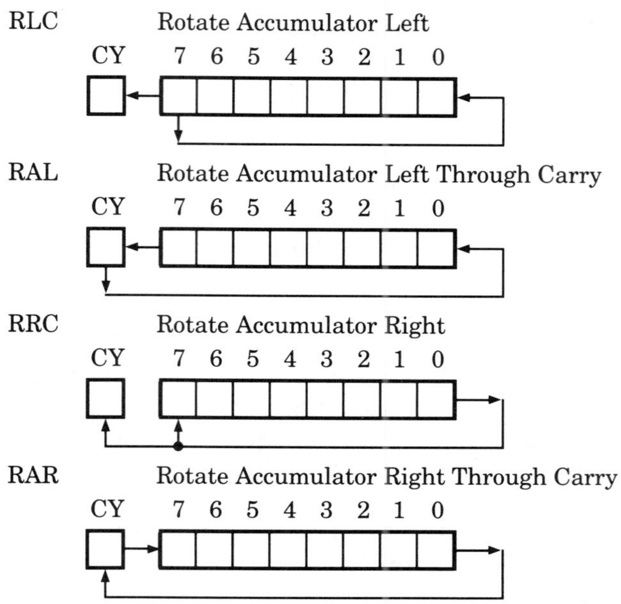

FIGURE 6.1
8085 Rotate Instructions

```
        MOV A,B     ;GET VALUE TO BE TESTED
        RAR         ;SHIFT BIT 0 INTO CARRY
        RAR         ;SHIFT BIT 1 INTO CARRY
        RAR         ;SHIFT BIT 2 INTO CARRY
        RAR         ;SHIFT BIT 3 INTO CARRY
        JC ONE      ;JUMP TO "ONE" IF BIT 3 WAS ONE
ZERO:   ...         ;ELSE, CONTINUE HERE
        ...
ONE:    ...
```

Rotate instructions are also used to perform binary multiplication and division. A binary value is multiplied by 2 by shifting the bits to the left by one bit position. Similarly, a number is divided by 2 by shifting it right. Multibyte shifts are performed by using a series of RAL or RAR instructions, provided that the carry bit is properly shifted from one byte to the next.

Procedure

1. Write an 8085 program that will manipulate the bits in the accumulator as follows: If bit 7 is a logic 1, complement the remaining seven bits. If bit 7 is low, clear bits 0 and 1, set bit 2, and complement bits 3–6. Test your program for each of these values: 80H, 00H, 55H, and AAH.
2. An audio level meter is being designed to monitor ambient noise in a manufacturing facility. The output section of this instrument is to convert a 3-bit binary code corresponding to sound level into codes that can drive a bar graph display. The bar graph display consists of eight lamp circuits that turn on when logic 1s are sent to them. The desired light pattern looks like this:

Binary Input Code	*Bar Graph Display Pattern*
0 0 0	0 0 0 0 0 0 0 1
0 0 1	0 0 0 0 0 0 1 1
0 1 0	0 0 0 0 0 1 1 1
0 1 1	0 0 0 0 1 1 1 1
1 0 0	0 0 0 1 1 1 1 1
1 0 1	0 0 1 1 1 1 1 1
1 1 0	0 1 1 1 1 1 1 1
1 1 1	1 1 1 1 1 1 1 1

Your assignment is to write an 8085 program that will read the 3-bit sound level code and generate the appropriate bar code pattern. Use three breadboard switches to produce the input code and eight LEDs to make the bar graph display. HINT: Use a rotate instruction to shift a logic 1 through the display.

3. A microcomputer monitors the power consumed by the heating element in an electric furnace. Two transducers detect the current flowing through the heater and the voltage developed across it; the output signals from these transducers are converted into two 8-bit binary values. After the microcomputer reads the transducer outputs, it multiplies these current and voltage quantities to produce and display a value for the power consumed.

   Your assignment is to develop software to perform the power measurement. First, your program should input the two 8-bit quantities from the 8355 input ports. Next, the program should compute the power (multiply the two 8-bit readings) using the shift-and-add multiplication logic described in Figure 6.2. Finally, output the product to the address field of the SDK-85 display. This input/compute/display process should continue in an endless loop.

   Study this multiplication algorithm carefully. Work through the process manually with some test values before you begin writing the program.

   NOTE: You will need 16 input signals; if you do not have that many logic switches on your breadboard, produce the logic 1s and 0s by connecting port inputs to +5 V and ground, respectively.

Additional Activities

1. Write an 8085 program that will count the number of bytes in the entire monitor ROM (locations 0000H–07FFH in the SDK-85) that have even parity. Use the rotate instructions to count the number of logic 1s in each byte; do *not* use the JPO or JPE conditional jump instructions. Display the total number in the address field of the SDK-85 display.
2. Write an 8085 program that will input an 8-bit quantity through an 8355 input port, then add the upper four bits of the 8-bit value to the lower four bits. The data field LEDs on the SDK-85 should display the sum.

Review Questions

1. The 8085 instruction set does not include a Clear Accumulator instruction. Which single-byte logical instruction can perform this task?
2. The 8085 instruction set does not include a Clear Carry instruction. Which single-byte logical instruction can clear the carry without modifying the contents of the accumulator?

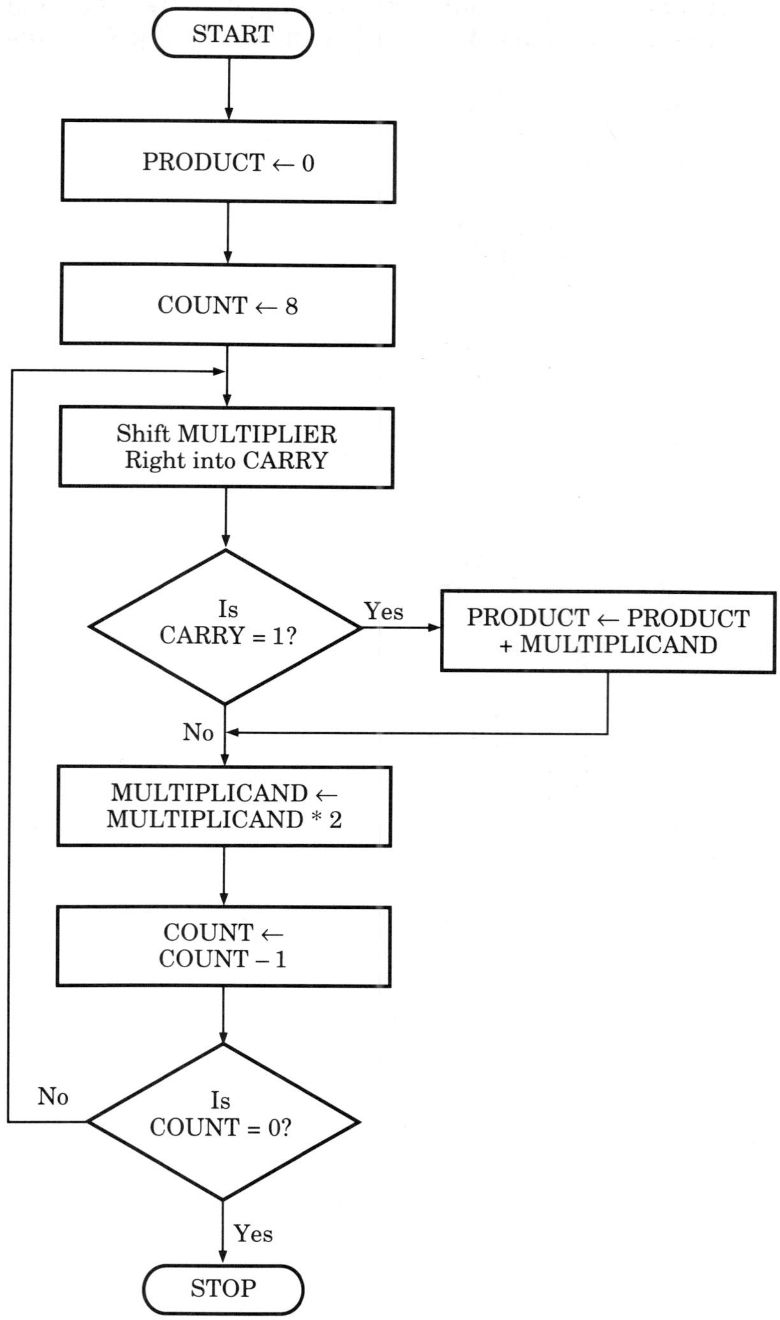

FIGURE 6.2
Flowchart for Shift-and-Add Multiplication

3. What value will remain in the accumulator after executing each of the following program segments? What will be the status of the CY and Z flags?

a.
```
MVI A,0FH
MVI B,55H
XRA B
```

b.
```
MVI A,AAH
ANI 0FH
ORI 80H
```

c.
```
MVI A,96H
XRI FFH
```

d.
```
STC
MVI A,55H
RAL
```

e.
```
MVI B,12H
MVI C,34H
MOV A,C
ORA A
RLC
MOV C,A
MOV A,B
RAL
MOV B,A
```

EXPERIMENT 7

Programmed Time Delays

Objectives

The microprocessor is frequently used in industrial environments to precisely measure and control time intervals between events. Hardware methods for time interval generation using the 8253 interval timer circuit will be examined in future laboratory experiments. Software delay loops are often used to minimize hardware costs in situations not requiring a great deal of flexibility. After completing this experiment, you will be able to

- Compute the time required to execute an 8085 assembly language program
- Design nested delay loops to generate a precise delay time
- Generate a repetitive digital signal having a precise frequency

Reference Reading

Gaonkar, Ramesh S. *Microprocessor Architecture, Programming, and Applications with the 8085/8080A.* 2nd ed. Columbus, OH: Merrill, 1989. Sections 3.1 and 3.2, and Chapter 8.

The MCS-80/85 Family User's Manual. Santa Clara, CA: Intel Corp., 1986. Pages 2–7 to 2–13 and 5–19.

8085 Instruction Set Summary, Appendix B.

Materials Needed

8085 single-board computer
Breadboard with logic switches and LED indicators
Stopwatch or digital wristwatch
Oscilloscope
Frequency counter

Discussion

Each 8085 program instruction requires a specific amount of execution time. In most applications, the programmer will attempt to minimize this execution time by writing the program in an efficient manner. There are many situations, however, in which it is desirable to generate a time delay. This delay time can serve as a time base to generate periodic waveforms or to sequence industrial processes.

The execution time required by each 8085 instruction is a function of the number of T-states in its instruction cycle (see Appendix B). Each T-state is equal to one period of the 8085 system clock. For example, if an 8085 microprocessor has a clock frequency of 3.125 MHz, then each T-state equals 320 ns. Assuming this clock frequency, the instruction DCR D, which consumes four T-states, would be executed in

$$(4 \text{ T-states})(320 \text{ ns/T-state}) = 1.28\ \mu s$$

The time delay generated by a program is compounded by nesting loops within other loops. The flowchart in Figure 7.1 illustrates the multiplying effect that takes place when loops are nested. Program 1 uses this logic with 8-bit loop counters to create a substantial time delay. Study the program analysis, which demonstrates the time-delay computation.

Program 1

```
Object Code   Source Code               T-States × Repetitions

              L3       EQU  00H
              L2       EQU  00H
              L1       EQU  00H

06 00                  MVI  B,L3        7 × 1
0E 00         LOOP3:   MVI  C,L2        7 × L3
16 00         LOOP2:   MVI  D,L1        7 × L2 × L3
15            LOOP1:   DCR  D           4 × L1 × L2 × L3
20 FD                  JNZ  LOOP1       ((10 × L1) - 3) × L2 × L3
0D                     DCR  C           4 × L2 × L3
20 F8                  JNZ  LOOP2       ((10 × L2) - 3) × L3
05                     DCR  B           4 × L3
20 F3                  JNZ  LOOP3       (10 × L3)- 3
CF                     RST  1           12 × 1

Total States = 7 + 7(L3) + 7(L2)(L3) + 4(L1)(L2)(L3) + 10(L1)(L2)(L3)
               - 3(L2)(L3) + 4(L2)(L3) + 10(L2)(L3) - 3(L3) + 4(L3)
               + 10(L3) - 3 + 12
             = 16 + 18(L3) + 18(L2)(L3) + 14(L1)(L2)(L3) T-STATES
```

Notice that L3, L2, and L1 are single-byte repetition constants that control the number of loop repetitions made in loops 3, 2, and 1, respectively. A value of 00H will cause the instructions in the loop body to be executed 256 times, while a value of 01H causes the same code to be executed only once. For example, if L1 = L2 = L3 = 00H,

$$\begin{aligned}\text{Total states} &= 16 + 18(256) + 18(256)(256) + 14(256)(256)(256)\\ &= 236{,}065{,}296 \text{ T-states}\end{aligned}$$

Using an 8085 with a clock frequency of 3.072 MHz, the total time required by this program can be calculated:

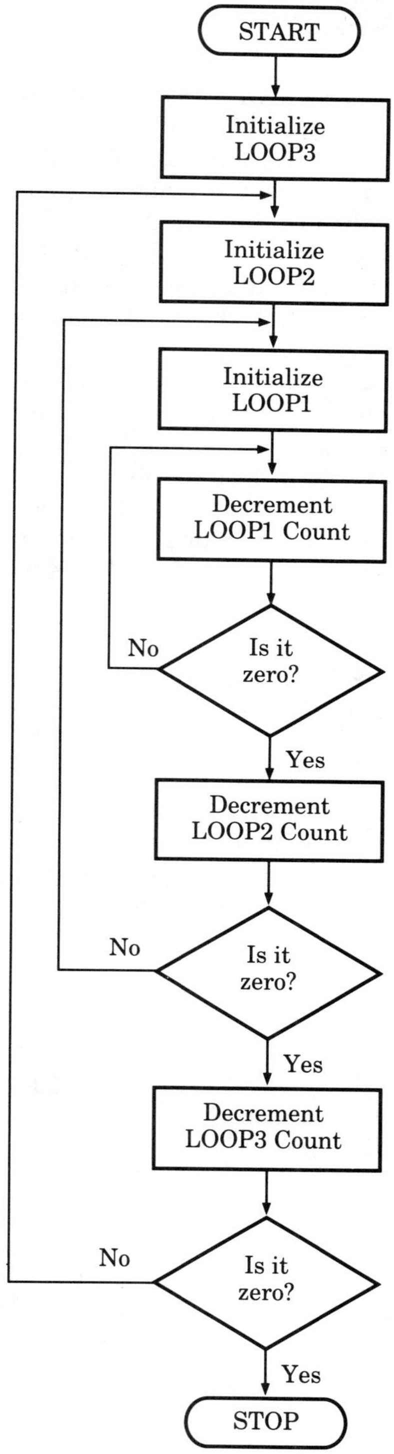

FIGURE 7.1
Flowchart for Time Delay Generation Using Nested Loops

$$\text{Total time} = \frac{236{,}065{,}296 \text{ T-states}}{3.072 \text{ MHz}} = 76.8 \text{ s}$$

The T-state equation for the JNZ LOOP3 instruction shows that this instruction consumes ten T-states when the jump test is met and the program "jumps back," but it consumes only seven T-states when the jump test is not met and the program proceeds with the next instruction in memory. During each pass through the loop, except for the last pass, the JNZ LOOP3 instruction requires ten T-states. The last time through the loop, the JNZ LOOP3 instruction requires only seven T-states, which is three less than the ten that were consumed on prior passes. Thus, the expression $(10 \times L3)-3$ is a simpler way of stating $(10 \times (L3-1))+7$.

Sometimes, very long delays (several minutes, hours, or even longer) are required. These long delays are obtained easily using 16-bit register pairs for loop counters instead of 8-bit registers. Another approach is to use additional levels of loop nests. When using register pairs for loop counters, notice that the INX rp and DCX rp instructions do *not* modify the Z flag. In other words, a JZ or JNZ instruction immediately following a DCX rp or INX rp instruction is not satisfactory. To force the Z flag to be influenced by DCX rp or INX rp so that the jump test can be made properly, you must follow these steps:

```
DCX H           ;DECREMENT HL
MOV A,H         ;GET H VALUE
ORA L           ;OR WITH L VALUE, IF H = L = 0, THE
                ; Z BIT WILL NOW BE SET
```

Program 2 illustrates the use of 16-bit register pairs as loop counters. Study the program to understand how the loop jump tests are made. The XTHL instructions are used as "padding" for the inner loop; they are included solely to increase the total time delay produced.

Program 2

```
        LXI H,0000H     ;INITIALIZE LOOP 3 COUNTER
LOOP3:  LXI D,0000H     ;INITIALIZE LOOP 2 COUNTER
LOOP2:  LXI B,0000H     ;INITIALIZE LOOP 1 COUNTER
LOOP1:  DCX B           ;DECREMENT LOOP 1 COUNTER
        XTHL            ;CONSUME SOME TIME HERE
        XTHL
        XTHL
        XTHL
        MOV A,B         ;TEST LOOP 1 COUNTER
        ORA C
        JNZ LOOP1       ;LOOP BACK IF NOT YET ZERO
        DCX D           ;ELSE, DECREMENT LOOP 2 COUNTER
        MOV A,D         ;TEST LOOP 2 COUNTER
        ORA E
        JNZ LOOP2       ;LOOP BACK IF NOT YET ZERO
        DCX H           ;ELSE, DECREMENT LOOP 3 COUNTER
        MOV A,H         ;TEST LOOP 3 COUNTER
        ORA L
        JNZ LOOP3       ;LOOP BACK IF NOT YET ZERO
        RST 1           ;ELSE, STOP
```

Procedure

1. Compute the delay time generated by program 2. Assume a system clock frequency of 3.072 MHz. For reasons that will then be obvious, do *not* try to execute this program.
2. A microcomputer controls the mixing system in a food processing plant. The system includes several solenoid valves that control the flow of ingredients into the mixer. When the operator of the system momentarily presses a particular switch on the mixer control panel, the corresponding valve must open for a predefined time period, then close.

   Your task is to write the program to control one solenoid valve. Your program should poll the switch until the switch output signal goes high. The 8085 should then turn on the valve for 15 s, turn it off, then resume its polling activity.

   Revise the loop constants in program 2 to produce the 15 s time delay. Simulate the mixing system with your logic breadboard. Connect bit PA 7 of the 8355 to a logic switch to simulate the switch on the control panel. Connect bit PB-7 of the 8355 to an LED indicator light to simulate the solenoid valve. Execute the program and time the 15 s delay with a digital wristwatch or stopwatch.
3. A *baud-rate generator* is a circuit used to generate signals in data communications applications. These precision-frequency signals are used to control the data exchange rate between two digital systems. Although a digital counter circuit is often used as a baud-rate generator, a microcomputer can also perform this task using timing loop techniques. The software approach is more flexible because the frequency is programmable; the frequency can be changed without modifying the system hardware.

   Write an 8085 program that will produce eight of the standard data communication frequencies: 9600 Hz, 4800 Hz, 2400 Hz, 1200 Hz, 600 Hz, 300 Hz, 150 Hz, and 75 Hz. Do this by creating an 8-bit binary count sequence on port B of the 8355. (The count should increment 19200 times per second with the frequency on PB-0 equal to 9600 Hz, the frequency on PB-1 equal to 4800 Hz, etc.) Using a frequency counter, measure the signal frequency on each 8355 port B line, and use an oscilloscope to observe the duty cycle and timing relationships of the signals.

Additional Activities

1. Write a BASIC program that will allow the user to input the desired delay time and then will compute optimum loop constant values for program 2. The program should output the delay constant values for loops 1–3 and also the exact delay time produced using these values.
2. Write an 8085 assembly language program that will generate audio frequencies on the output port of the 8355. Use this output signal to drive an audio amplifier and speaker system to "play" a song. Include provisions for different note durations and pitches. (See Experiment 11 for a list of musical note frequencies.)

Review Questions

1. Program timing calculations are dependent on the speed of the 8085's system clock. How will the results of program 1 change if an 8085AH-1 microprocessor is used with a clock frequency of 6.0 MHz?
2. The following delay program uses register pair HL to control the time-delay length. Explain why the program as written does not perform properly. Correct the program so that it functions as required.

```
        LXI H, 5000H    ;INITIALIZE LOOP COUNTER
LOOP:   DCX H           ;DECREMENT LOOP COUNTER
        JNZ LOOP        ;LOOP UNTIL IT REACHES ZERO
        RST 1           ;THEN QUIT
```

3. Explain the sequence of events that occurs as the four XTHL instructions in program 2 are executed. How are specific registers modified as a result of these four instructions? Remove the four XTHL instructions and calculate the delay time generated by the revised program.

EXPERIMENT 8

Subroutines and the Stack

Objectives

Subroutines provide an efficient means of repeating a series of instructions in a program. Subroutines are linked with the main program through the use of the stack, a special memory area that is used to "remember" where to return after a subroutine is executed. The stack is also used for temporary data storage. At the conclusion of this laboratory experiment, you will be able to

- Understand the role of the stack pointer in controlling stack accesses
- Use the stack to link a subroutine to its calling program
- Use the stack for temporary data storage
- Perform input and output operations using built-in subroutines on the single-board computer

Reference Reading

Gaonkar, Ramesh S. *Microprocessor Architecture, Programming, and Applications with the 8085/8080A*. 2nd ed. Columbus, OH: Merrill, 1989. Chapter 9, Section 10.7, and Appendix F.

The MCS-80/85 Family User's Manual. Santa Clara, CA: Intel Corp., 1986. Pages 5–1 to 5–22.

Materials Needed

8085 single-board computer

Discussion

8085 subroutines are called from user programs to perform a variety of tasks. Before subroutines can be used, however, an address linkage from the subroutine back to the calling program must be established. This linkage is made using a special area in RAM known as the *stack*. When a subroutine is called, the stack receives the address to which the program is to return after the subroutine has finished.

The 8085 uses contiguous RAM locations for its stack. The 16-bit *stack pointer* register contains the address of the *last* stack location used. It is important to note that the stack pointer must be initialized *before* any stack operations can take place. In the SDK-85, available user RAM extends from 2000H through 20C1H. The stack pointer therefore should be initialized to 20C2H, one location beyond the end of the stack area in RAM; do this using the LXI SP,20C2H instruction.

8085 Stack Control and Subroutine Instructions
Here are some of the 8085 instructions used in stack and subroutine applications:

Instruction	*Description*
LXI SP,16-bit data	Load stack pointer with 16-bit value.
CALL 16-bit address	Call subroutine at address specified.
CC 16-bit address	Call subroutine if CY = 1.
CNC 16-bit address	Call subroutine if CY = 0.
CZ 16-bit address	Call subroutine if Z = 1.
CNZ 16-bit address	Call subroutine if Z = 0.
RET	Return to calling program.
RC	Return if CY = 1.
RNC	Return if CY = 0.
RZ	Return if Z = 1.
RNZ	Return if Z = 0.
PUSH rp	Push register pair onto stack.
POP rp	Pop register pair from stack.
XTHL	Exchange top of stack with HL contents.
SPHL	Move HL contents to stack pointer.
DAD SP	Add stack pointer contents to HL.

Instructions in the CALL and RETURN instruction group automatically use the stack to create the linkage between a main program and a subroutine. If a subroutine modifies the contents of certain registers, and if you must use these values later in the program, then place the contents of the registers in a safe place *before* calling the subroutine. Either copy the contents of the registers to memory using data transfer instructions, or place the values temporarily on the stack. Store data on the stack using the PUSH instructions; later, retrieve the data using corresponding POP instructions. For example, the following program segment saves H and L on the stack, executes the subroutine, then restores H and L to their original values:

```
LXI SP, 20C2H        ;INITIALIZE STACK POINTER
PUSH H               ;SAVE HL ON STACK
CALL SUB1            ;CALL SUBROUTINE SUB1
POP H                ;RESTORE HL TO ORIGINAL VALUE
```

When saving several register pairs on the stack, the order of pushing and popping is very important. Consider the following example, which demonstrates the Last-In-First-Out nature of the stack:

```
PUSH H          ;SAVE HL
PUSH D          ;SAVE DE
CALL SUB1       ;CALL SUBROUTINE SUB1
POP D           ;RESTORE DE
POP H           ;RESTORE HL
```

If the registers are restored in the wrong sequence, problems may arise:

```
PUSH H          ;SAVE HL
PUSH D          ;SAVE DE
CALL SUB1
POP H           ;RESTORE HL TO OLD DE VALUE
POP D           ;RESTORE DE TO OLD HL VALUE
```

In this program, the contents of register pairs D and H are exchanged, which may not be the intended result.

The instruction PUSH PSW is used to place the processor status word, or PSW, on the stack. The PSW consists of the accumulator in the most significant byte and the flag register in the least significant byte. This instruction provides a useful way to access the contents of the flag register. For example, the program segment

```
PUSH PSW
POP H
```

places the flag register contents into register H and moves the accumulator contents to register L.

The DAD SP instruction is overlooked by many 8085 programmers. It provides the only way to transfer the stack pointer contents to another register for examination. The following program segment demonstrates this application:

```
LXI H,0000H     ;CLEAR HL
DAD SP          ;ADD STACK POINTER CONTENTS TO HL
```

Register pair HL now contains a copy of the stack pointer contents.

Subroutine Documentation

General program documentation is important when programming in assembly language; it is particularly important to document subroutines clearly to describe all parameter-passing details. Each subroutine should include

- A description of the subroutine
- Input and output parameters passed
- Registers modified
- Names of other subroutines called

Here is a sample subroutine, documented to include appropriate details:

```
;*****************************************************
;***** SUBROUTINE NAME: DEMO                     *****
;***** DESCRIPTION: PRODUCES A TIME DELAY        *****
;***** INPUTS: REGISTER B IS DELAY LOOP CONSTANT *****
;***** OUTPUTS: NONE                             *****
;***** CALLS: NOTHING                            *****
;***** REGISTERS MODIFIED: B AND FLAGS           *****
;*****************************************************
DEMO:   DCR B       ;DECREMENT LOOP COUNTER
        JNZ DEMO    ;LOOP UNTIL DONE
        RET
```

Monitor Subroutines

The monitor ROM in most single-board microcomputers contains several subroutines that can be used to simplify information processing. The UPDAD and UPDDT subroutines, introduced in Experiment 3, are used to display information on the LED digits. In addition to those two subroutines, here are two additional ones available in the SDK-85 monitor ROM. If you are using a different single-board computer, your instructor can furnish descriptions of similar subroutines that you can use.

Subroutine Name: RDKBD
Calling Address: 02E7H
Description: Waits until key is pressed, then returns the key code. For RDKBD to work properly, first unmask the RST 5.5 interrupt as follows:

```
MVI A,08H
SIM
```

Inputs: None.
Outputs: Accumulator returns key code:

Key Pressed	*Value Returned*	*Key Pressed*	*Value Returned*
0	00H	B	0BH
1	01H	C	0CH
2	02H	D	0DH
3	03H	E	0EH
4	04H	F	0FH
5	05H	EXEC	10H
6	06H	NEXT	11H
7	07H	GO	12H
8	08H	SUBST MEM	13H
9	09H	EXAM REG	14H
A	0AH	SINGLE STEP	15H

Registers Modified: A, H, L, and flags.

Subroutine Name: OUTPT
Subroutine Calling Address: 02B7H
Description: Outputs characters to display.
Inputs: Accumulator selects field: (A) = 00 selects address field, (A) = 01 selects data field. Register B controls decimal point (DP) at right edge of field: (B) = 01 turns on DP, (B) = 00 turns off DP. HL contains starting address of character array to be displayed.
Outputs: Characters on selected display digits:

Character Displayed	*Hexadecimal Value Pointed to by HL*	*Character Displayed*	*Hexadecimal Value Pointed to by HL*
0	00	b	0B
1	01	C	0C
2	02	d	0D
3	03	E	0E
4	04	F	0F
5	05	H	10
6	06	L	11
7	07	P	12
8	08	I	13
9	09	r	14
A	0A	S	05
		Blank	15

Registers Modified: A, B, C, D, E, H, L, and flags.

Here is a sample program that reads the SDK-85 keyboard until a key is pressed, then displays the corresponding key code on the data field of the display:

```
RDKBD   EQU 02E7H      ;DEFINE ADDRESSES FOR SDK-85 SUBROUTINES
UPDDT   EQU 036EH
        LXI SP,20C2H   ;INITIALIZE SP
        MVI A,08H      ;UNMASK KEYBOARD INTERRUPT
        SIM
LOOP:   CALL RDKBD     ;READ CHARACTER FROM KEYBOARD
        MVI B,00       ;TURN OFF DOT
        CALL UPDDT     ;DISPLAY THE CHARACTER
        JMP LOOP       ;DO IT AGAIN!
```

This program displays the message PASS on the address field of the display:

```
OUTPT   EQU 02B7H              ;DEFINE ADDRESS OF SDK-85 SUBROUTINE
        LXI SP,20C2H           ;INITIALIZE SP
        MVI A,00               ;USE ADDRESS FIELD
        MVI B,00               ;TURN OFF DOT
        LXI H,DATA             ;POINT TO BEGINNING OF CHARACTER ARRAY
        CALL OUTPT             ;SEND 4 CHARACTERS TO DISPLAY
        JMP $                  ;STAY HERE FOREVER
DATA:   DB 12H,0AH,05H,05H     ;DATA BYTES TO BE DISPLAYED
```

Procedure

1. The following program manipulates stack data. Study the program and predict what will happen to memory locations 2050H–205FH.

```
        ORG 2000H
        LXI SP,205FH ;INITIALIZE STACK POINTER
        XRA A        ;CLEAR ACCUMULATOR
        LXI H,2050H  ;POINT TO START OF ARRAY
        MVI B,10H    ;LOOP COUNTER
LOOP:   MOV M,A      ;CLEAR A LOCATION
        INX H
        DCR B
        JNZ LOOP     ;REPEAT UNTIL DONE
        LXI H,1234H
        LXI D,5678H
        CALL SUB1
        LXI SP,20C2H ;PUT SP HERE BEFORE QUITTING SO THE
                     ; MONITOR PROGRAM WILL NOT BOTHER IT
        RST 1        ;QUIT

SUB1:   PUSH H       ;SUBROUTINE STARTS HERE
        PUSH D
        LXI H,0000H  ;DO THIS TO CAPTURE SP VALUE
        DAD SP
        SHLD 2050H   ;SAVE IT IN MEMORY
        POP D
        POP H
        RET
```

Assemble and execute the program. Examine memory locations 2050H–205FH to see if those values were manipulated as you predicted. Observe the contents of DE and HL. NOTE: Locations 2050H–205FH were cleared before doing any stack operations. The program did this only to show you more clearly how the stack operations work; normally, the stack area is not cleared before use.

2. Write an 8085 subroutine to generate a precise time delay, where the delay time parameter is passed to the subroutine in register B. Use this calling program to test your subroutine:

```
LXI SP,20C2H        ;INITIALIZE SP
MVI B,XXH           ;XXH IS DELAY IN SECONDS (HEX)
CALL DELAY
RST 1               ;STOP AND DISPLAY MONITOR PROMPT
```

Test your subroutine by producing delay times of 1, 10, 30, and 60 s. Verify the results using a stopwatch or digital wristwatch.

3. Write a program that will wait for someone to press the 0 key on the keyboard, then display the countdown sequence 09, 08, . . . , 01, 00. The count should decrement once per second. When the count reaches 00, the display should flash the word HELP on and off at a 2 Hz rate. For this program, modify the subroutine that you designed in step 2 so that it produces a delay interval in increments of 0.1 s.

Additional Activities

1. Write an 8085 subroutine to fill an array with a specified character. Pass the starting address of the array to the subroutine in register pair HL. Pass the array length (number of bytes) in register pair DE, and pass the fill character in register B. Test the program carefully, or it may inadvertently write over itself!
2. Write an 8085 program that will display one of several messages, depending on which key is pressed. The display should show HELP if the 0 key is pressed. The 5 key should cause PASS to appear, and the F key should produce the message FAIL. The program should ignore any other keys that are pressed.

Review Questions

Each of the following program segments uses the stack. For each program segment, specify the resulting contents of any affected registers. Draw a memory map showing the stack locations used and their final contents.

1.
```
LXI SP,6000H
LXI H,1234H
PUSH H
```

2.
```
LXI SP,2050H
LXI H,1234H
SPHL
PUSH H
```

3.
```
LXI SP,3040H
LXI D,1234H
PUSH D
LXI H,5678H
XTHL
```

4.
```
ORG 2000H
LXI SP,3000H
CALL SUB1
```

EXPERIMENT 9

BCD Arithmetic

Objectives

Calculations involving binary coded decimal (BCD) values are simple for human beings, but not for microcomputers; the 8085 microprocessor must use special techniques to add or subtract BCD quantities. After completing this experiment, you will be able to

- Use the Decimal Adjust Accumulator (DAA) instruction
- Add multidigit BCD quantities
- Subtract multidigit BCD quantities using 10's complement arithmetic
- "Pack" BCD digits into memory

Reference Reading

Gaonkar, Ramesh S. *Microprocessor Architecture, Programming, and Applications with the 8085/8080A*. 2nd ed. Columbus, OH: Merrill, 1989. Sections 10.1–10.6.

The MCS-80/85 Family User's Manual. Santa Clara, CA: Intel Corp., 1986. Pages 5–6 to 5–9.

Materials Needed

8085 single-board computer

Discussion

BCD Addition

Although some microprocessors can directly add or subtract BCD quantities, the 8085 cannot. However, the 8085 can perform BCD arithmetic with the help of the DAA instruction. Following the addition of two 2-digit BCD quantities, the DAA instruction checks the Auxiliary Carry (AC) and CY flags. The value 6 is added to the accumulator if the least significant four bits of the accumulator are greater than 9 or if the AC flag is set. Next, 6 is added to the upper four bits of the accumulator if those bits are greater than 9 or if the CY flag is set.

For example, here is how the DAA instruction adds the 4-digit BCD contents of register pairs DE and HL. The BCD sum is stored in register pair BC.

```
MOV A,E     ;GET 2 LS DIGITS FROM DE
ADD L       ;ADD WITH 2 LS DIGITS OF HL
DAA         ;DECIMAL ADJUST THE 2 LS SUM DIGITS
MOV C,A     ;SAVE LS 2 DIGITS OF SUM
MOV A,D     ;GET 2 MS DIGITS FROM DE
ADC H       ;ADD WITH CY THE 2 MS DIGITS OF HL
DAA         ;DECIMAL ADJUST THE 2 MS SUM DIGITS
MOV B,A     ;SAVE MS 2 DIGITS OF SUM
RST 1       ;QUIT
```

BCD Subtraction

The DAA instruction *does not* correct the results of a BCD subtraction. BCD subtraction must be done using 10's complement arithmetic. In 10's complement arithmetic, the 10's complement of the subtrahend (number being subtracted) must be *added* to the minuend (the number being subtracted from).

The 10's complement technique is similar to the 2's complement method used for binary subtraction. To find the 10's complement of a 4-digit BCD number, subtract the number from 9999, then add 1. For example, to subtract the BCD number 2495 from the BCD number 8127,

- Subtract subtrahend (2495) from 9999:
```
  9999
- 2495
  7504
```
- Add 1 to produce the 10's complement:
```
  7504
+ 0001
  7505
```
- Add the 10's complement value 7505 to the minuend (8127):
```
  8127
+ 7505
 15632
```

The result (5632) is the correct difference. Notice that the carry bit is 1, indicating that the answer is a positive number. A carry bit of 0 indicates that the result is negative and the 10's complement of the actual magnitude.

Here is an 8085 program that demonstrates the 10's complement BCD subtraction method. The program subtracts the contents of register pair HL from register pair DE and places the difference in register pair BC.

```
MVI A,99H    ;SUBTRACT MINUEND FROM 9999
SUB L        ;LS BYTE FIRST,
MOV L,A
MVI A,99H    ;THEN MS BYTE
SUB H
MOV H,A
MOV A,L      ;NOW ADD 1 TO GET 10'S COMPLEMENT
ADI 01H
DAA
MOV L,A      ;SAVE LS BYTE
MOV A,H      ;PROPAGATE CARRY (IF ANY) TO MS BYTE
ACI 00H
DAA
MOV H,A      ;SAVE MS BYTE
MOV A,L      ;NOW ADD 10'S COMPLEMENT OF
ADD E        ; SUBTRAHEND TO MINUEND (LS BYTES)
DAA
MOV C,A      ;SAVE LS BYTE
MOV A,H      ;NOW ADD MS BYTES
ADC D
DAA
MOV B,A      ;SAVE MS BYTE
RST 1        ;QUIT
```

As you can see, multibyte subtraction in BCD is far more complicated than in binary!

Procedure

1. A BCD electronic counter counts the pizzas manufactured in a food processing plant. At the end of each day, a microcomputer reads the counter, then computes and displays the total number of pizzas made for the month. Your assignment is to write an 8085 program to add the 6-digit BCD counter value to the 8-digit monthly total.

   Assume that the 6-digit counter value is stored in locations 2080H–2082H, with location 2080H containing the least significant byte. The 8-digit total is in locations 2090H–2093H, with location 2090H containing the least significant byte. Test your program for these three cases:

   a. COUNT = 943723 TOTAL = 23790189
   b. COUNT = 123456 TOTAL = 99982734
   c. COUNT = 479381 TOTAL = 00023471

2. Write a program that will turn your microcomputer into a "BCD subtracting machine." Design the program to read four minuend digits, the Subtract key, and then four subtrahend digits from the keyboard. When the Equals key is pressed, the difference should appear. Since the SDK-85 does not have − or = keys, use the F and E keys instead. For example, the program should perform the operation 8497-4932 as follows:

Display	*Key Pressed*	*Description*
0000	None	Initial display
0008	8	First digit of minuend
0084	4	Second digit of minuend
0849	9	Third digit of minuend
8497	7	Fourth digit of minuend
0000	F	Subtract key
0004	4	First digit of subtrahend
0049	9	Second digit of subtrahend
0493	3	Third digit of subtrahend
4932	2	Fourth digit of subtrahend
3565	E	Equals key

To do the subtraction operation, the individual BCD digits must be "packed" into memory, two digits per byte. You may wish to develop a general-purpose packing subroutine for this task; this packing process is frequently used when processing data inputs from a keyboard.

Additional Activities

1. Write an 8085 subroutine to 10's complement a multidigit BCD number stored in memory. The calling program must pass these parameters to the subroutine:

   Register B: Contains number of BCD bytes in the number.
   Register pair HL: Points to least significant byte of the number.

   The subroutine must not modify any registers. Test your program for these three cases:

   a. NUMBER: 47 LOCATION: 2080H
   b. NUMBER: 28193472 LOCATION: 2080H–2083H
   c. NUMBER: 1245 LOCATION: 2080H–2081H

2. Write an 8085 subroutine to subtract two multidigit BCD numbers stored in memory. The two numbers must be of equal length. The calling program must pass these parameters to the subroutine:

   Register B: Contains number of BCD bytes in each number.
   Register pair HL: Points to least significant byte of minuend.
   Register pair DE: Points to least significant byte of subtrahend.

   The difference is stored in the space formerly occupied by the subtrahend. The subroutine must not modify any registers. Test your program for these three cases:

   a. MINUEND: 8497 LOCATION: 2080H–2081H
      SUBTRAHEND: 4932 LOCATION: 2082H–2083H
   b. MINUEND: 48 LOCATION: 2080H
      SUBTRAHEND: 83 LOCATION: 2081H
   c. MINUEND: 47832133 LOCATION: 2080H–2083H
      SUBTRAHEND: 00003415 LOCATION: 2084H–2087H

3. Write an 8085 program to increment a 4-digit BCD count whenever the 1 key is pressed on the keyboard. The program should decrement the count whenever the 0 key is pressed. Display the count in the address field of the display.

Review Questions

1. Study this program, then answer the questions that follow:

```
MVI A,64H
ADI 27H
DAA
```

   a. What does the accumulator contain immediately after the ADI instruction is executed? What do the CY and AC flags contain?
   b. What does the accumulator contain after the DAA instruction is executed? What do the CY and AC flags contain?
2. Find the 10's complement of the BCD number 461093.
3. Manually subtract these numbers using the 10's complement addition method:

$$\begin{array}{r} 7815 \\ -\ \underline{2942} \end{array}$$

EXPERIMENT 10

Lookup Tables

Objectives

Microcomputers use lookup tables to convert digital codes from one form to another and to determine quickly the value of a mathematical function. Lookup tables are often used when the alternative methods are very complex or time-consuming. After completing this experiment, you will be able to use lookup tables to

- Convert a binary number into 7-segment display codes
- Compute the value of a mathematical function
- Convert a value from one unit of measure to another

Reference Reading

Gaonkar, Ramesh S. *Microprocessor Architecture, Programming, and Applications with the 8085/8080A*. 2nd ed. Columbus, OH: Merrill, 1989. Section 10.3.

Materials Needed

8085 single-board computer
Breadboard with logic switches
Two 7406 hex inverters (open collector)
MAN72A common-anode 7-segment LED display
Eight 220 Ω resistors

Discussion

Lookup Tables

Lookup tables are often used to compute the value of a mathematical function such as the logarithm of a number. Determining the value of a function with a lookup table is usually faster than computing the function mathematically. An added advantage of the lookup table approach is that the values in the table can be revised or adjusted easily to accommodate different mathematical functions; no new software calculations are needed.

Lookup tables are ideal for code conversion applications. They are used to convert binary code into ASCII, Gray code into binary, and BCD code into 7-segment display code. They are also used to convert ASCII values into the character patterns displayed on video terminals and printed on dot-matrix printers.

A common application of lookup tables is the conversion from one unit of measure to another. For example, to convert inches into centimeters, we could construct the following conversion table:

Inches	*Centimeters*
0	0.00
1	2.54
2	5.08
3	7.62
4	10.16
5	12.70
6	15.24

To convert 5 in. into centimeters, we simply "look up" the value in the centimeters column corresponding to the value 5 in the inches column. The microprocessor can use indexing techniques to do the same job, as the following program segment demonstrates. This program converts the number of inches in register B into a 4-digit BCD centimeter value in register pair HL. (Register H contains the integer portion and register L contains the fractional portion of the result.)

```
        LXI D,TABLE ;PUT ADDRESS OF FIRST TABLE LOCATION INTO DE
        MOV A,B     ;PUT ''INCH'' NUMBER INTO ACCUMULATOR
        ADD A       ;DOUBLE IT
        ADD E       ;NOW ''BUILD'' THE ADDRESS OF THE TABLE ENTRY
        MOV E,A     ; LS ADDRESS BYTE FIRST
        MOV A,D     ; THEN MS ADDRESS BYTE
        ACI 00H
        MOV D,A
        LDAX D      ;READ FRACTION BYTE
        MOV L,A     ;SAVE IT
        INX D       ;POINT TO INTEGER BYTE
        LDAX D      ;READ INTEGER BYTE
        MOV H,A     ;SAVE IT
        RST 1
TABLE:  DB 00H,00H,54H,02H,08H,05H,62H,07H
        DB 16H,10H,70H,12H,24H,15H
```

Study this sample program carefully; pay particular attention to the index pointer used to locate items in the table. Similar techniques can locate items in tables containing thousands of entries.

Procedure

1. A microcomputer is used to sense and display the oil pressure in an automobile engine. The indicator is a single 7-segment LED display digit, driven by an 8355 I/O device. The 8355 also reads a 4-bit code produced by a pressure transducer module; the microprocessor uses this 4-bit code to determine the relative oil pressure, with low- and high-pressure conditions indicated as follows:

Binary Input	*Displayed Character*
0000	L
0001	L
0010	L
0011	0
0100	1
0101	2
0110	3
0111	4
1000	5
1001	6
1010	7
1011	8
1100	9
1101	H
1110	H
1111	H

Your assignment is to control the oil pressure indicator. First, connect the LED display as shown in Figure 10.1. Test each segment using breadboard switches before connecting it to your single-board computer. Notice that the digit is a common-anode device, which means that an input to an inverter must be 1 to turn on the corresponding LED segment. After testing the LED display circuit, connect it to port B of the 8355. Connect four logic switches to lines PA-0 through PA-3 on the 8355 to represent the 4-bit pressure code.

Write an 8085 program to control the display pattern, with the display code for each input condition stored in a lookup table. Your program should continually read the four input bits and update the display. Test your program for each input value.

2. A microcomputer interfaced to an industrial robot must compute various trigonometric functions while controlling each mechanical movement. Write an 8085 program to read from the keyboard a 2-digit BCD angle between 00 and 45 degrees, in 5-degree increments. Design the program to ignore invalid entries such as 32 or 50 degrees. The program should determine the sine of the angle using lookup table techniques. The displayed results should be accurate to six decimal places. (Assume that the decimal point is to the left of the six LED digits.)

Additional Activities

1. Write and test a program to determine Y from the equation

$$Y = X^4 * \sqrt{2}$$

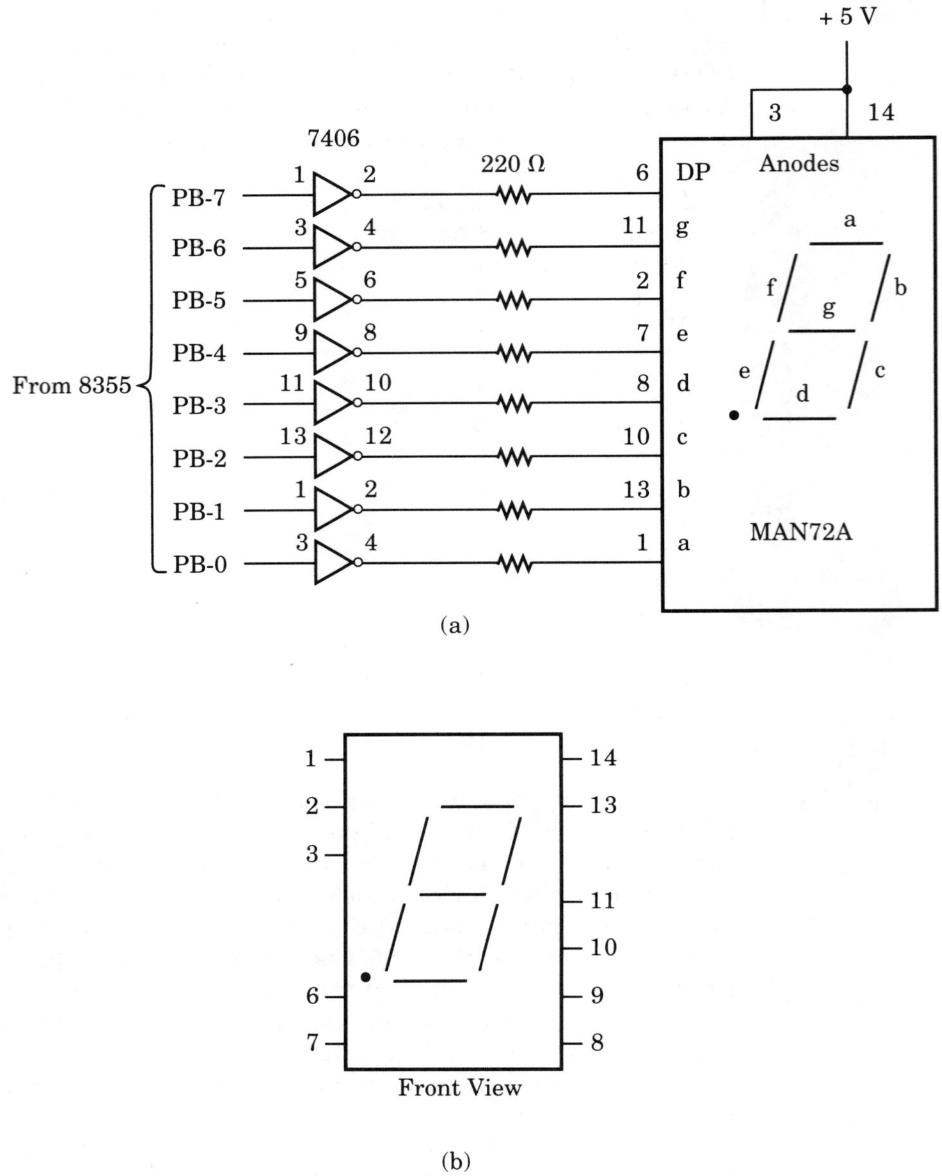

FIGURE 10.1
(a) LED Display Circuit, (b) MAN72A Pin Connections

for values of X between 0 and 9. Your program should input the single-digit number X from the keyboard; it should ignore invalid input numbers (keys other than 0–9.) Next, the program should retrieve the function's value from a lookup table, then output the integer portion of the result to the address field and the fractional portion to the data field of the display.

2. Enhance your sine lookup program to allow it to determine the sine of any angle between 0 and 45 degrees, in 1-degree increments. Use a *linear interpolation* technique to determine the sine of angles between the 5-degree intervals in the table.

Review Questions

1. What are some advantages of the lookup-table approach for determining the value of a function? What are some disadvantages?
2. Consider the inches-to-centimeters program given earlier. Which requires more conversion time, 2 or 6 in.?
3. In the inches-to-centimeters program, why are the following instructions included? Are these instructions always necessary?

```
MOV A,D
ACI 00H
MOV D,A
```

EXPERIMENT 11

The 8155 Programmable I/O and Timer Device

Objectives

The 8155 is a programmable interface device that contains RAM, parallel I/O ports, and a 14-bit timer. This experiment explores some of the operating modes and applications of the 8155. After completing this experiment, you will be able to

- Use the 8155 for simple parallel input and output tasks
- Program the 8155 timer to generate precise output frequencies

Reference Reading

Gaonkar, Ramesh S. *Microprocessor Architecture, Programming, and Applications with the 8085/8080A*. 2nd ed. Columbus, OH: Merrill, 1989. Sections 14.1 and 14.21–14.26.

The MCS-80/85 Family User's Manual. Santa Clara, CA: Intel Corp., 1986. Pages 6–26 to 6–37.

Materials Needed

8085 single-board computer
8155 programmable I/O and timer device
Breadboard with logic switches and LED indicators
Frequency counter
PN2222 transistor
100 Ω resistor
2.2 kΩ resistor
8 Ω speaker

Discussion

The Intel 8155 contains 256 bytes of RAM, two 8-bit and one 6-bit I/O ports, and a 14-bit binary timer/counter. The 8-bit ports are referred to as port A and port B; the 6-bit port is known as port C. Unlike the 8355 device (see Experiment 5), the 8155 does not use data direction registers. All bits for a given port are configured in the same way; they are all inputs or are all outputs. Figure 11.1 shows the 8-bit control and status registers contained in the 8155.

SDK-85 Port Addresses

The SDK-85 microcomputer includes provisions for two 8155s. One 8155 (device A16) contains the system RAM. The timer in that device controls the single-step mode of the machine. The second 8155 (device A17) is part of the SDK-85 expansion circuitry and may be installed by the user to increase RAM and I/O capabilities. The SDK-85 addresses the two 8155s as follows:

Standard 8155 (device A16)

Port Number	*Function*
20H	Control register/status register
21H	Port A
22H	Port B
23H	Port C
24H	Timer register (LS byte)
25H	Timer register (MS byte)

Expansion 8155 (device A17)

Port Number	*Function*
28H	Control register/status register
29H	Port A
2AH	Port B
2BH	Port C
2CH	Timer register (LS byte)
2DH	Timer register (MS byte)

Notice that pressing RESET on the SDK-85 clears the logic in the 8155, including all bits in the control register. Thus, after resetting the computer, all port data lines become inputs.

8155 Parallel I/O Applications

The following sample program demonstrates the initialization of the control register and the use of ports A and B for a simple input/output task. In this example, the microprocessor reads eight inputs on port A, then sends these bits to port B.

```
CONTROL EQU 20H         ;8155 CONTROL REGISTER ADDRESS ON SDK-85
STATUS  EQU CONTROL     ;8155 STATUS REGISTER

PORTA   EQU 21H         ;8155 PORT A
PORTB   EQU 22H         ;8155 PORT B
PORTC   EQU 23H         ;8155 PORT C

I8155:  MVI A,0EH       ;8155 MODE SETTING: TIMER OFF, ALT 2
                        ;MODE (PORT C WILL BE OUTPUTS),
        OUT CONTROL     ;PORT A WILL BE INPUTS, PORT B WILL
                        ;BE CONFIGURED AS OUTPUTS
LOOP:   IN PORTA        ;INPUT DATA FROM PORT A
        OUT PORTB       ;OUTPUT THE DATA TO PORT B
        JMP LOOP        ;DO IT FOREVER
```

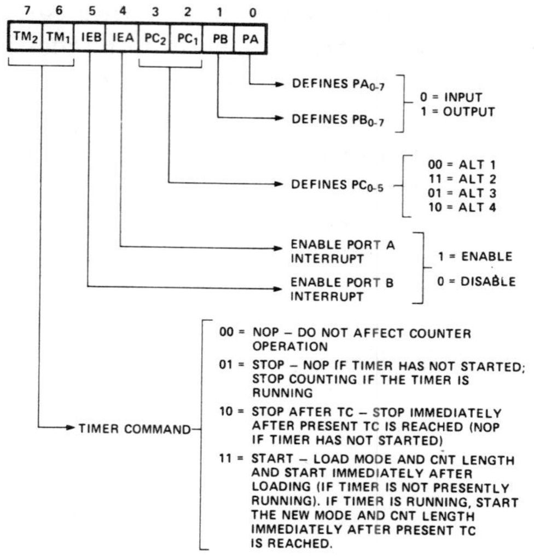

(a)

(b)

Pin	ALT 1	ALT 2	ALT 3	ALT 4
PC0	Input Port	Output Port	A INTR (Port A Interrupt)	A INTR (Port A Interrupt)
PC1	Input Port	Output Port	A BF (Port A Buffer Full)	A BF (Port A Buffer Full)
PC2	Input Port	Output Port	A $\overline{STB}$ (Port A Strobe)	A $\overline{STB}$ (Port A Strobe)
PC3	Input Port	Output Port	Output Port	B INTR (Port B Interrupt)
PC4	Input Port	Output Port	Output Port	B BF (Port B Buffer Full)
PC5	Input Port	Output Port	Output Port	B $\overline{STB}$ (Port B Strobe)

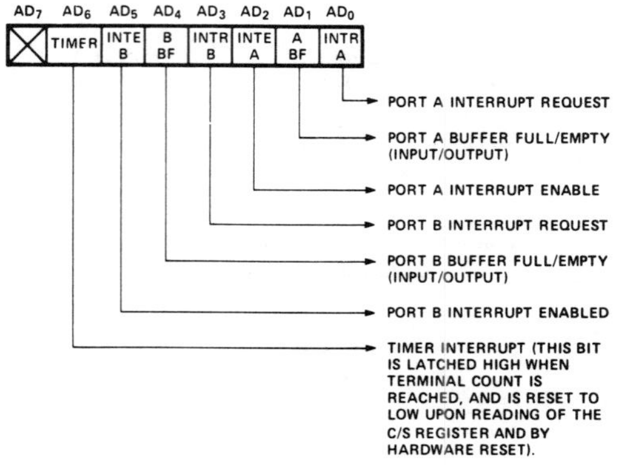

(c)

FIGURE 11.1
8155: (a) Control Register, (b) Port C Alternatives, (c) Status Register
SOURCE: Reprinted by permission of Intel Corporation, copyright 1985.

8155 Timer Applications

Timing loops were used in Experiment 7 to generate square waves of a specified frequency. The timing loop approach is easy to implement, but it has one serious disadvantage: The microprocessor cannot perform other useful tasks while it is busy in a timing loop. The 8155 timer, however, operates without constant supervision by the microprocessor. The microprocessor can perform other tasks while the 8155 timer continues to generate signals.

The 8155 timer function can generate single pulses, repetitive streams of pulses, or square waves. The two 8-bit timer registers consist of a 14-bit counter plus a 2-bit code used to determine the timer mode (see Figure 11.2).

The following program segment initializes an 8155 timer to generate a 1 kHz square wave, provided a 3.072 MHz signal is connected to the TIMER IN pin on the 8155:

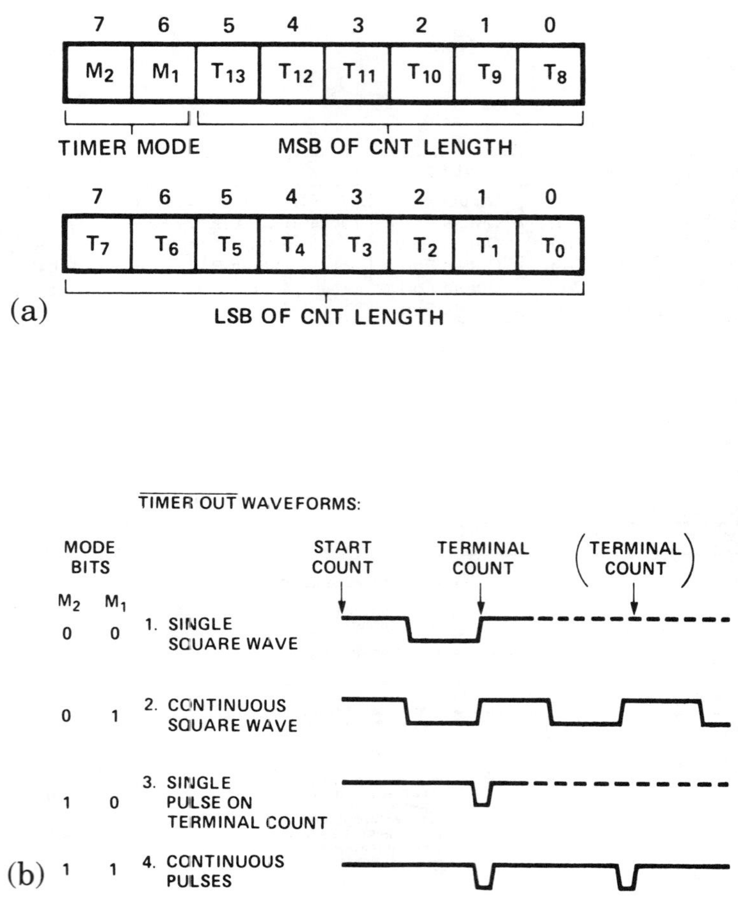

FIGURE 11.2
8155: (a) Timer Registers, (b) Timer Output Waveforms
SOURCE: Reprinted by permission of Intel Corporation, copyright 1985.

```
CONTROL EQU 28H         ;EXPANSION 8155 CONTROL REGISTER ON SDK-85
TIMLO   EQU 2CH         ;LS HALF OF TIMER REGISTER
TIMHI   EQU 2DH         ;MS HALF OF TIMER REGISTER
        MVI A,00H       ;LS BYTE OF 14-BIT COUNT
        OUT TIMLO
        MVI A,01001100B ;MODE 01 AND MS PORTION OF 14-BIT COUNT
        OUT TIMHI
        MVI A,11000000B ;START TIMER, PORTS A,B, AND C ARE INPUTS
        OUT CONTROL
```

The 14-bit count in this example is chosen by dividing the frequency on the TIMER IN pin of the 8155 by the desired output frequency. In this example,

$$\text{COUNT} = \frac{3.072 \text{ MHz}}{1.0 \text{ kHz}} = 3072_{10} = \text{C00}_{16}$$

Mode 01 places the 8155 in the square wave mode. The TIMER OUT pin of the 8155 now produces a 1.0 kHz square wave. Note: The minimum count value acceptable to the 8155 is 2_{10}.

Procedure

The single-step mode on the SDK-85 uses the timer inside of the standard 8155. Use an 8155 device inserted into the expansion socket (A17) for the following exercises; this will eliminate undesirable interaction with the single-step mode when debugging your 8155 timer-related programs. Connect a jumper from point 17 to point 18 to connect the 3.072 MHz system clock signal to the timer input on the expansion 8155. The output signal from the expansion 8155 is available on connector J5, pin 23.

1. Generate an alternating "high-low" tone effect similar to the siren sound produced by emergency vehicles. The two tones should alternate between 1000 and 500 Hz at a 1 Hz rate. Generate the tone signals with the 8155 timer and alternate them, using delay loops to control the tone durations. Use the circuit shown in Figure 11.3 to produce the tone on a small speaker.

   NOTE: The 8155 must receive a new START command each time the count value in the timer is redefined.
2. Programmable timers are often used to generate precise frequencies used in serial data communications systems. The 8155 can easily generate these

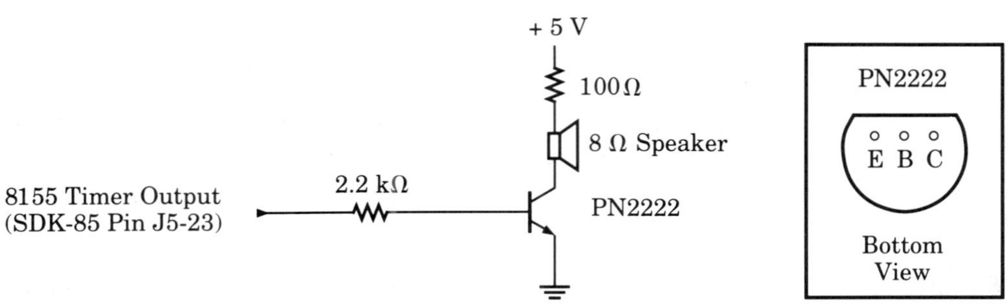

FIGURE 11.3
Audio Output Circuit

frequencies, known as *baud rates*. Write an 8085 program that will use the 8155 as a programmable baud-rate generator. The program should first determine the desired frequency by reading a 3-bit code read from port A of the 8155. The TIMER OUTPUT pin then should respond by producing the desired frequency. This frequency selection should be indicated on the display of the single-board computer.

The following list describes the required input and output conditions:

Port A Input Bits	*Timer Out Baud Rate*
0 0 0	Timer is off
0 0 1	300 baud
0 1 0	600 baud
0 1 1	1200 baud
1 0 0	2400 baud
1 0 1	4800 baud
1 1 0	9600 baud
1 1 1	19200 baud

Additional Activities

1. Design a simple musical instrument using the 8155. Connect eight logic switches to port A on the 8155 to serve as the "keyboard" for the instrument. Connect the audio output circuit (see Figure 11.2) to the timer output of the 8155. Program your microcomputer to produce a specific tone on the speaker whenever a single logic switch is high. The following list shows the notes and corresponding frequencies that should be created when a given logic switch is activated.

Switch	*Note*	*Frequency*
PA-7	C	523.3 Hz
PA-6	D	587.3 Hz
PA-5	E	659.3 Hz
PA-4	F	698.5 Hz
PA-3	G	784.0 Hz
PA-2	A	880.0 Hz
PA-1	B	987.8 Hz
PA-0	C	1046.5 Hz

2. Expand the musical instrument to include higher and lower octaves. You may wish to include all half-steps in the musical scale, including sharps and flats. The frequency of each half-step tone is $2^{1/12}$ times the frequency of the preceding one. For example, the frequency of the note C is 523.3 Hz, the frequency of C sharp is $523.3 \times 2^{1/12} = 554.4$ Hz. Connect additional I/O ports and logic switches as needed to expand the keyboard.

Review Questions

1. An 8155 timer input is connected to a 3.072 MHz signal. The upper byte of the timer register contains 01101101_2 and the lower byte contains 11001101_2.

   a. The timer is operating in which mode?
   b. What is the timer output frequency?

2. What *maximum* frequency can the 8155 timer produce if the timer input signal is 3.072 MHz?
3. What *minimum* frequency can the 8155 timer produce if the timer input signal is 3.072 MHz?

EXPERIMENT 12

Software-Controlled Display Multiplexing

Objectives

Multidigit LED displays are used in many applications. These displays are usually multiplexed to reduce power consumption and circuit complexity. After completing this experiment, you will be able to

- Multiplex a multidigit LED display using software
- Predict the effects of varying the digit multiplex rate

Reference Reading

Gaonkar, Ramesh S. *Microprocessor Architecture, Programming, and Applications with the 8085/8080A*. 2nd ed. Columbus, OH: Merrill, 1989. Sections 4.2 and 17.1.

Materials Needed

8085 single-board computer
Breadboard with logic switches
Frequency counter
Two 7406 hex inverters (open collector)
Four MAN72A common-anode 7-segment LED displays
Four PN2907 transistors
Eight 100 Ω resistors
Four 3.3 kΩ resistors

Discussion

Multidigit LED displays can be constructed using the display driver hardware concept introduced in Experiment 10. For example, to build a 10-digit LED display, we could connect ten 8-bit output ports to ten sets of segment driver buffers and current limit resistors. Unfortunately, this approach would be quite costly; it would require 80 segment drivers, 80 resistors, and five 8355 I/O chips. Not only would this circuit be expensive, but it would consume a considerable amount of current. If each segment in each digit were on, and assuming 10 mA of current per segment, the power supply would have to supply 800 mA of current just for the LEDs! Multiplexing the ten digits would greatly improve the efficiency of this circuit.

In a multiplexed display, the corresponding segments of each digit are wired in parallel. Each digit is selected independently, one after the other, to create the illusion that all digits are on steadily. The following steps describe the multiplexing procedure:

- Output segment bits for first digit.
- Turn on first digit.
- Turn off first digit.
- Output segment bits for second digit.
- Turn on second digit.

  .
  .
  .

This process continues for each digit in the display, then starts over again with the first digit. If the multiplex rate is fast enough, each digit in the display appears to be on constantly.

LED displays can be multiplexed using standard logic components, such as counters and shift registers. Display controller devices, such as the Intel 8279, can multiplex display systems containing 16 or more digits. In many small applications, however, hardware costs can be minimized using software to control the multiplexing process.

Figure 12.1 shows a 4-digit display circuit that can be interfaced to the output ports of a microcomputer.

The segments of the four common-anode LED digits in Figure 12.1 are controlled by the 7406 open-collector inverters. The digits are selected by the four PNP digit select transistors. An individual segment in a digit is on when the input to the corresponding 7406 inverter is high and the digit select line is low.

The flowchart in Figure 12.2 shows how the microcomputer can control the display multiplexing. The array SEGCODE contains the segment patterns for each of the display digits. The array DIGCODE contains patterns that select one of the N digits in the display. Notice that one digit is turned off before the segment data for the next digit is output. This step, known as *interdigit blanking,* prevents the segment code for one digit from appearing briefly on the next digit and blurring the display.

Procedure

1. Construct the circuit shown in Figure 12.1, but do not connect it to your microcomputer at this time. First, test the circuit by applying signals from breadboard logic switches to the segment lines and digit select lines. Be sure that each segment of each digit responds properly before proceeding.
2. Connect the display circuit to your microcomputer's 8355 I/O ports as shown.

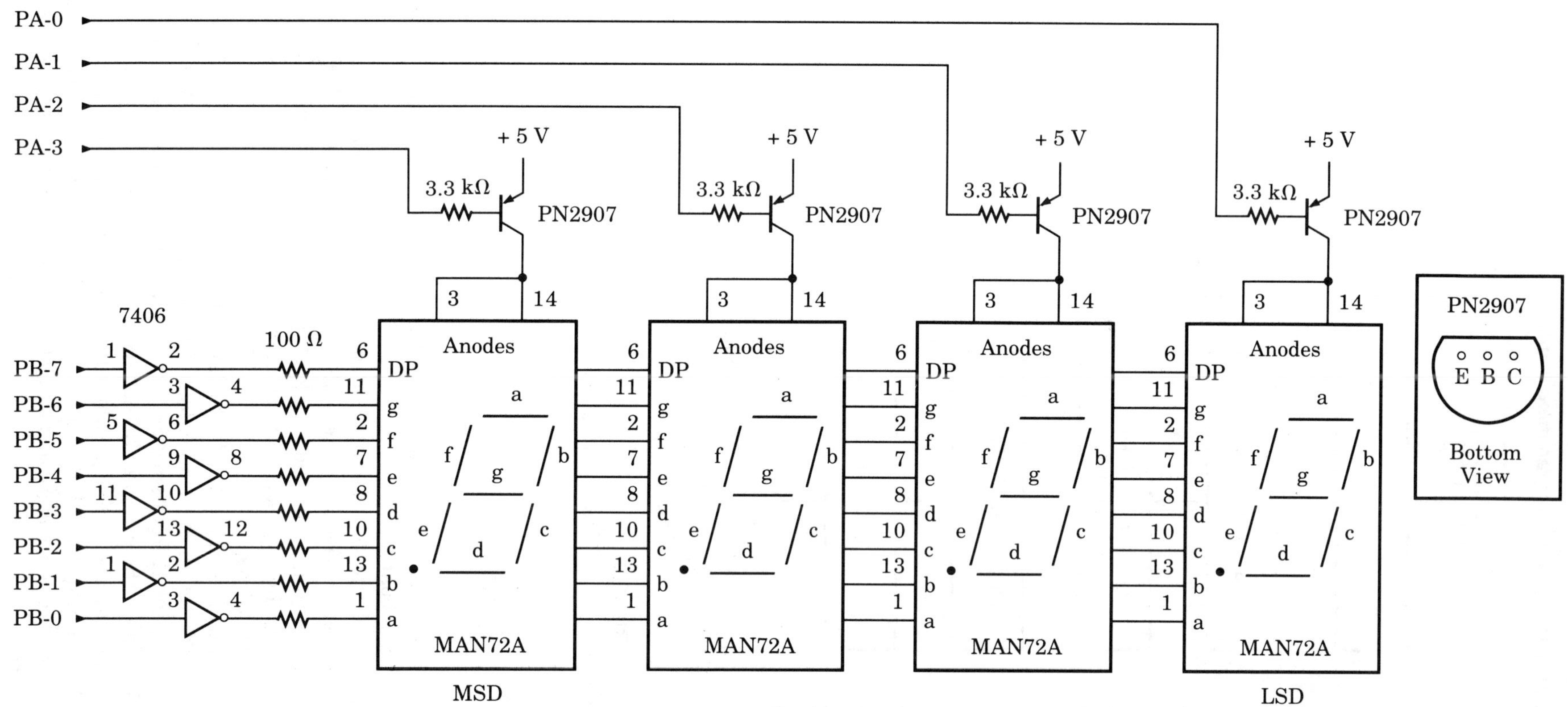

FIGURE 12.1
Four-Digit Multiplexed Display

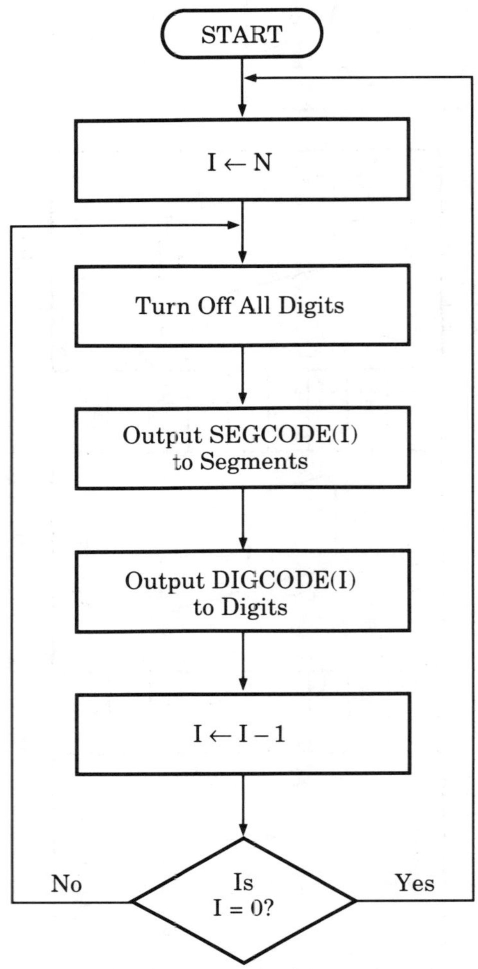

FIGURE 12.2
Flowchart for N-Digit Display Multiplexing

Remember to connect a ground wire between your microcomputer and the breadboard.

3. Write a program to implement the logic shown in Figure 12.2. Store the segment codes for the characters 1234 in the array SEGCODE. Test your program by executing it in the single-step mode to see if the segments and digits are controlled properly. After correcting all program errors, run the program at normal speed.
4. Calculate the rate at which the display is multiplexed. Also, calculate the duty cycle for an individual digit. Verify your multiplex rate calculation by measuring the signal frequency on a digit select line using a frequency counter.
5. Modify the program to include a time delay to reduce the scan rate. The program should call a delay subroutine immediately after it turns on the next digit. Increase the delay time until you find the slowest possible multiplex rate that produces a steady display. Measure this multiplex frequency with a frequency counter.

Additional Activities

1. A 4-digit LED display on the control panel of an 8085-controlled milling machine indicates the depth of cut in ten-thousandths of an inch. The depth of cut value is stored in BCD form in register pair DE of the 8085. Write a program to display the depth of cut on your 4-digit display circuit.
2. The program logic described in Figure 12.2 keeps the microcomputer occupied constantly; the microcomputer can perform no other useful tasks while stuck in the multiplexing loop. However, in most applications, the microprocessor must do other work while multiplexing the display digits. One solution to this problem is to update individual display digits periodically as the other tasks are being performed.

   To demonstrate this concept, write a subroutine called NEXTDIGI that will turn off all digits, point to the next digit, display it, then return to the calling program. Test your program using this main program:

```
      LXI SP,20C2H    ;STACK POINTER INITIALIZATION (SDK-85)
LOOP: CALL NEXTDIGI   ;UPDATE THE NEXT DIGIT
      JMP LOOP        ;REPEAT FOREVER
```

   In this program, the loop contains only the subroutine; in more realistic applications, the loop would include other data processing and control tasks as well.

Review Questions

1. What will the circuit shown in Figure 12.1 display if the segment code is 11100111B and the digit select code is 1101B?
2. What will the circuit shown in Figure 12.1 display if the segment code is 01100110B and the digit select code is 0000B?
3. What would happen if the segment data output and digit select steps in the flowchart (Figure 12.1) were exchanged?

EXPERIMENT 13

Software-Controlled Keyboard Scanning

Objectives

Computer keyboards are typically wired as rows and columns of individual key switches. This switch matrix is scanned using either hardware or software methods to determine if a key is pressed, and if so, which one. After completing this experiment, you will be able to

- Debounce a key switch using software
- Scan a matrix keyboard using software

Reference Reading

Gaonkar, Ramesh S. *Microprocessor Architecture, Programming, and Applications with the 8085/8080A*. 2nd ed. Columbus, OH: Merrill, 1989. Sections 4.3, 15.21 to 15.23, and 17.2.

Materials Needed

8085 single-board computer
Breadboard
16-key keyboard (4 × 4 matrix)
Four 1N914 diodes
Four 5.6 kΩ resistors

Discussion

Most calculator and computer keyboards consist of a number of individual switches arranged as a matrix of rows and columns. The switches are connected in a matrix configuration so that fewer signal wires and I/O port lines are needed to monitor them. A 16-key computer keyboard, for example, is organized as a 4-row by 4-column matrix, as shown in Figure 13.1.

In this circuit, the rows are connected to an output port, while the columns are connected to an input port. The controlling program detects a closed key switch by sending logic 0s out on the row lines, then watching the column lines. A closed switch is indicated when a column line goes low, since the pull-up resistors keep all column lines high at other times. The software can then determine exactly which key switch is closed by grounding one row at a time as it monitors each column.

The diodes in the circuit prevent damage to the output port (row lines) that might occur if two switches on the same column are closed at the same time. Without the diodes, the two closed switches would short together the two output port lines.

Figure 13.2 describes one technique for scanning a matrix keyboard. In the first part of the process, the program sends logic 0s to all rows, then waits for a column to go low. After a column goes low, the program delays before proceeding, giving the switch time to stop bouncing. Typically, the switch debounce delay time is 10–20 ms.

In the remaining steps in the procedure, the row pointer RPOINT and the column pointer CPOINT point to each row, one column at a time, until the position

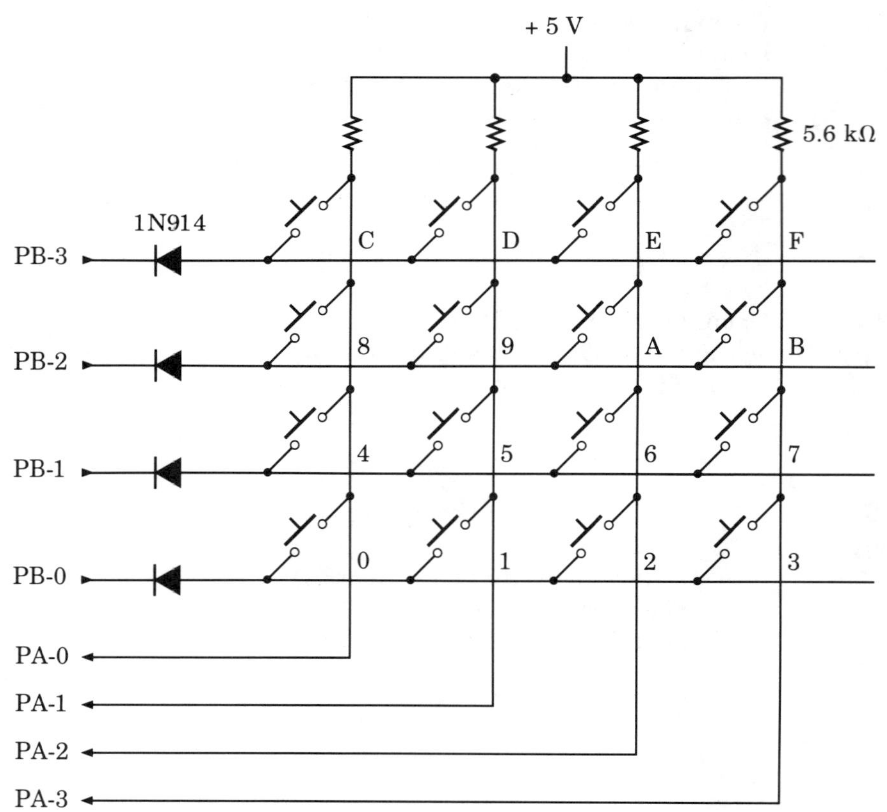

FIGURE 13.1
Matrix Keyboard Connections

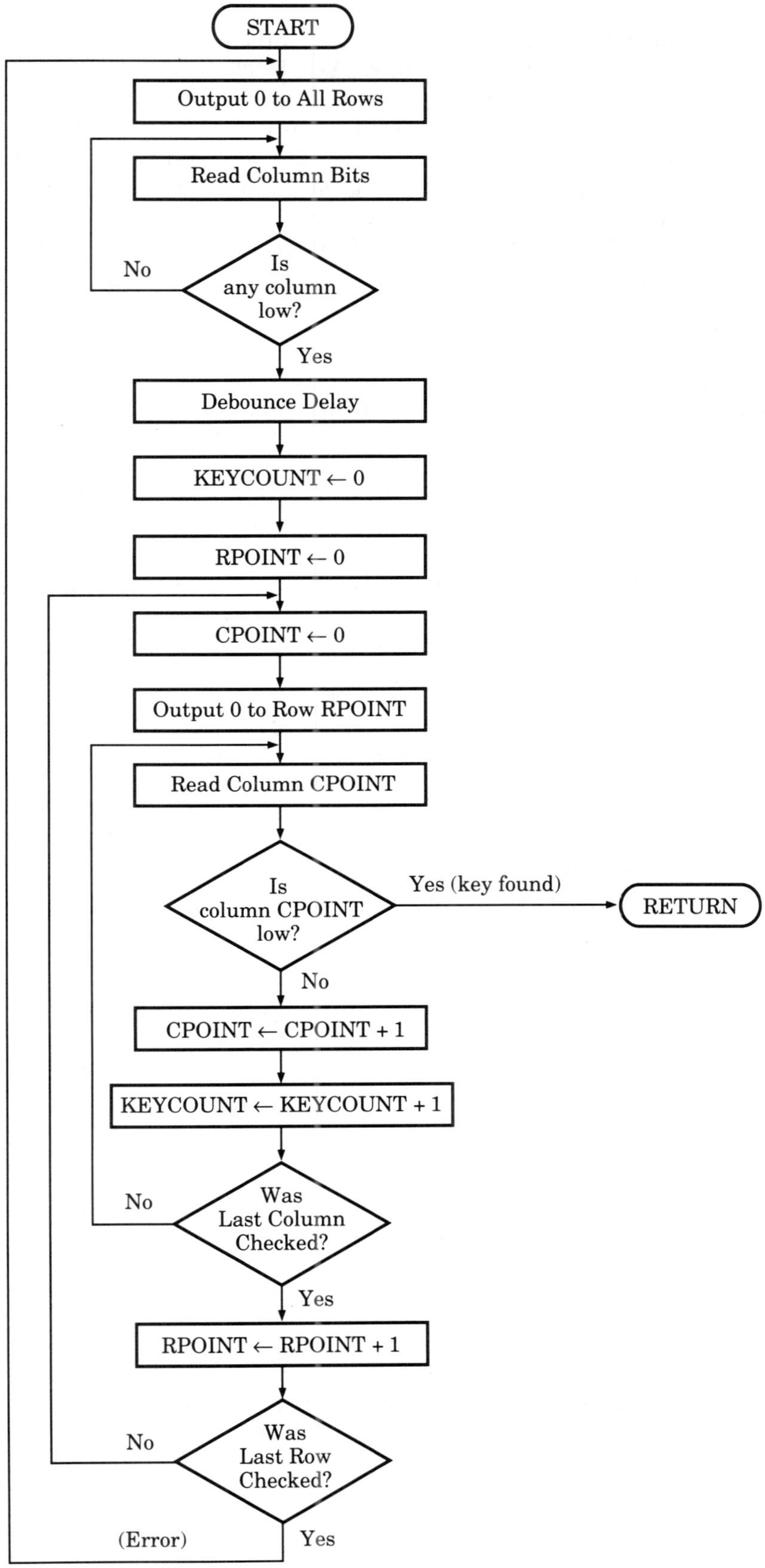

FIGURE 13.2
Flowchart for Keyboard Scan Subroutine

of the closed key switch is determined. The relative position of the key switch is returned as the variable KEYCOUNT.

The subroutine described in Figure 13.2 returns to the calling program as soon as a key is located. In many applications, the computer can detect a key closure, perform the indicated function, and begin to look for the next key closure before the first key switch is released. To prevent unintentional multiple readings of the first key closure, the program must wait until one key is released before searching for the next key. The flowchart in Figure 13.3 describes a subroutine that waits until all keys are released before returning to the calling program.

Procedure

1. Connect the matrix keyboard circuit shown in Figure 13.1 to the 8355 I/O device on your microcomputer. Connect the keyboard row lines to port B and the column lines to port A.
2. Write a subroutine called KEYGET to implement the logic shown in Figure 13.2. Design the subroutine to return the key code 00H to 0FH in the accumulator. No other registers should be modified by the subroutine.
3. Test your KEYGET subroutine using this main program:

```
UPDDT  EQU 036EH    ;DISPLAY SUBROUTINE LOCATION
       LXI SP,20C2H ;STACK POINTER INITIALIZATION (SDK-85)
LOOP:  CALL KEYGET  ;GET A KEY CODE
       CALL UPDDT   ;DISPLAY IT
       JMP LOOP     ;REPEAT
```

4. Write a subroutine called RELEASE to implement the logic shown in Figure 13.3. This program must not modify any registers or flags. Assemble, enter, and execute the following main program to test the RELEASE subroutine and demonstrate its application:

```
UPDDT  EQU 036EH     ;DISPLAY SUBROUTINE LOCATIONS
UPDAD  EQU 0363H
       LXI SP,20C2H  ;STACK POINTER INITIALIZATION (SDK-85)
       LXI D,0000H   ;CLEAR KEY REPEAT COUNTER
LOOP:  CALL KEYGET   ;GET A KEY CODE
       PUSH D
       PUSH PSW
       CALL UPDAD    ;DISPLAY KEY REPEAT COUNTER
       POP PSW
       CALL UPDDT    ;DISPLAY KEY CODE
       CALL RELEASE  ;WAIT UNTIL KEY IS RELEASED
       POP D
       INX D
       JMP LOOP      ;REPEAT
```

This program increments and displays a 16-bit count (register pair DE) every time a key is released. To demonstrate what would happen without the release subroutine, replace the CALL RELEASE instruction with three NOP instructions, then run the program. Your program should increment the displayed count continually until the key is released.

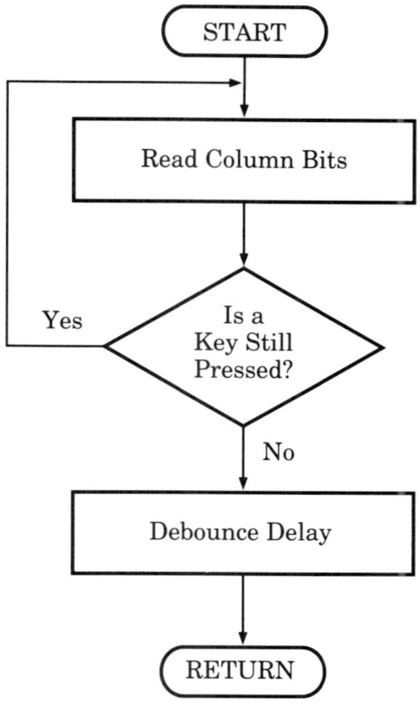

FIGURE 13.3
Flowchart for Key Release Subroutine

Additional Activities

1. Merge the display multiplexing software, developed in Experiment 12, with the keyboard scan subroutine. Design the resulting program so that keys pressed on the keyboard shift through the display digits from right to left. Your program should continue to refresh the display, even when a key is continually pressed.
2. An ASCII keyboard is to be interfaced to an automotive engine diagnostic system to allow the mechanic to enter engine parameters. Write a keyboard scan program to accommodate a 64-key unencoded ASCII keyboard organized as an 8 × 8 switch matrix. The program should return an ASCII character in the accumulator when a key is pressed. Include provisions for the SHIFT and CONTROL keys on the keyboard by connecting these two switches to two unused input port lines. Define the ASCII codes for uppercase characters, lowercase characters, and control codes using a lookup table.

Review Questions

1. What key code is returned by your KEYGET subroutine if keys 4 and 6 are pressed at the same time?
2. What key code is returned by your KEYGET subroutine if keys 2 and A are pressed at the same time?
3. What debounce delay length is needed to properly debounce a mechanical switch?
4. Can a debounce delay time be *too* long? Explain your answer.

EXPERIMENT 14

Programming Project—A Digital Alarm Clock

Objectives

Microprocessors control many modern consumer products, ranging from cameras to microwave ovens. The commercial success of these products largely depends on the quality of the interface between the product and its human operator. After completing this experiment, you will be able to

- Define the user-interface logic for a digital alarm clock
- Design software to control the time-setting, alarm-setting, and time-keeping modes of a digital clock
- Design software to scan a keyboard and multiplex an LED display simultaneously

Reference Reading

Gaonkar, Ramesh S. *Microprocessor Architecture, Programming, and Applications with the 8085/8080A*. 2nd ed. Columbus, OH: Merrill, 1989. Sections 17.1–17.3.

Materials Needed

8085 single-board computer, including expansion memory (2K × 8) and download connection to a personal computer
Breadboard
16-key keyboard (4 × 4 matrix)
Two 7406 hex inverters (open collector)
Four MAN72A common-anode 7-segment LED displays
Four PN2907 transistors
PN2222 transistor
Four 1N914 diodes

Nine 100 Ω resistors
2.2 kΩ resistor
Four 3.3 kΩ resistors
Four 5.6 kΩ resistors
8Ω speaker

Discussion

In this experiment, you will develop the software to control a digital alarm clock. Although most commercially available digital clocks are designed around dedicated clock chips, you will implement the functions of the clock using an 8085-based microcomputer. The software to control a digital alarm clock is similar in complexity to the control logic in many "high-tech" consumer products. By systematically developing the control program for the digital clock, you will gain valuable experience in each important step in the product design and development process.

Before writing control software for the digital alarm clock, you must carefully define all inputs, outputs, and other user-interface details. This step is very important to the commercial success of any consumer product. For example, very few consumers would purchase a digital clock that displayed the time of day in hexadecimal. Similarly, a clock that required the user to press the Time Set button 60 times to advance the minutes digits to the next hour would not sell very well either.

The design process normally begins with a general definition of the system features. For example, here are the minimum features that your digital clock must have:

- Display of hours, minutes, and seconds in 12-hour format
- A.M./P.M. indicator
- Audible alarm
- Time-setting provisions
- Alarm-setting provisions

Next, these general features must be described in sufficient detail so that the hardware and software can be designed. By describing the system carefully early on, you can minimize the time required to debug and (possibly) redesign hardware and software functions later.

Procedure

1. Figure 14.1 describes the digital clock hardware. Connect this circuit and check it carefully before continuing. Use the software you developed in Experiments 11, 12, and 13 to test the speaker, display, and keyboard circuits, respectively. Notice that the keyboard switches are not labelled in Figure 14.1; you will define each key in the next step.
2. Define *very carefully* each of the digital clock features:
    - *Keyboard layout.* What is the function of each key in the keyboard?
    - *Initial conditions.* What does the display show when the program begins? Is the clock in the time-setting mode, the alarm-setting mode, or the run mode?
    - *Time-setting mode.* How and when can the clock enter this mode? How are hours, minutes, and seconds set? How are A.M. and P.M. indicated? How can the clock exit this mode and enter the run mode?

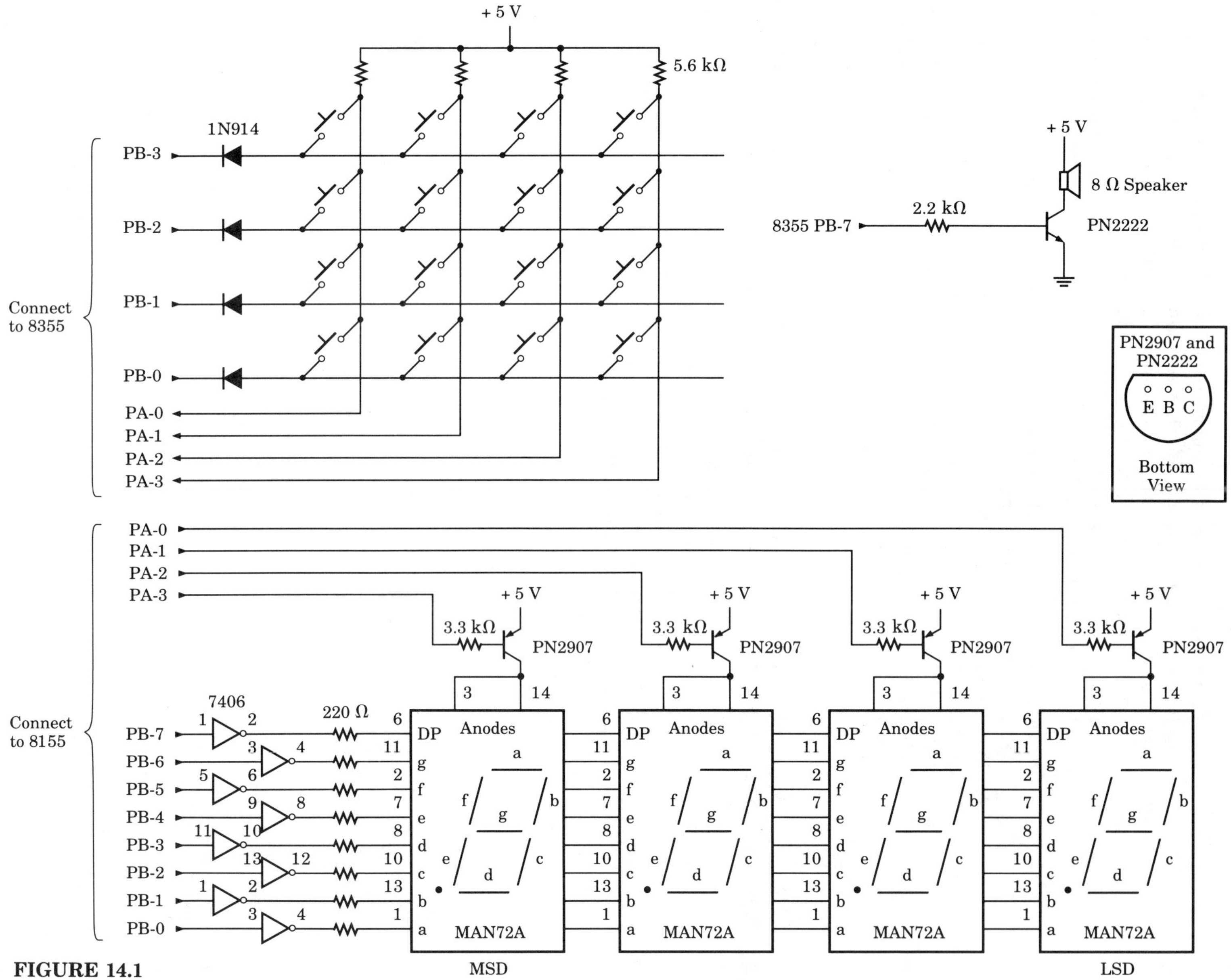

FIGURE 14.1
Digital Clock Hardware

- *Alarm-setting mode.* How and when can the clock enter this mode? How are hours, minutes, and seconds changed? How is the alarm feature enabled?
- *Audible alarm.* How is the alarm turned off? What tone frequency does the speaker produce? Is the tone steady or pulsating?
- *Run mode.* What serves as the time base for the clock: delay loops, an 8155 timer circuit, the 60 Hz power line, or an external oscillator?

3. Write a detailed flowchart to describe the clock-operating modes. Break the overall logic into small modules that can be coded and debugged easily.
4. Write the 8085 software to control the digital clock. Document your program thoroughly to reduce your program-debugging time. Cross-assemble your program and download it to your single-board microcomputer for debugging. Systematically debug individual program modules until the entire system works as required.

Additional Activities

Many additional features can be added to the basic digital clock. Here are some suggested features you may wish to add to the basic system:

- Day/date/year calendar display option
- Solid-state relay control of electric appliances
- Selectable 12-hour and 24-hour display format
- Audible beep on the hour
- Musical chimes or tune played when alarm time is reached
- Snooze feature

EXPERIMENT 15

Programming Project—A Four-Function Integer Calculator

Objectives

Modern electronic calculators contain logic circuitry that performs sophisticated mathematical computations. In this experiment, a simple calculator will be developed using an 8085-based microcomputer. After completing this experiment, you will be able to

- Design the user interface logic for a 4-function integer calculator
- Develop software to add, subtract, multiply, and divide integer BCD quantities

Reference Reading

Gaonkar, Ramesh S. *Microprocessor Architecture, Programming, and Applications with the 8085/8080A*. 2nd ed. Columbus, OH: Merrill, 1989. Sections 17.1–17.3.

Materials Needed

8085 single-board computer, including expansion memory (2K × 8) and download connection to a personal computer
Breadboard
16-key keyboard (4 × 4 matrix)
Two 7406 hex inverters (open collector)
Four MAN72A common-anode 7-segment LED displays
Four PN2907 transistors
Four 1N914 diodes

Eight 100 Ω resistors
Four 3.3 kΩ resistors
Four 5.6 kΩ resistors

Discussion

The "brain" in a commercially available electronic calculator is usually an LSI (large-scale integration) calculator chip. This device controls all mathematical, keyboard, and display features of the calculator. In this experiment, an 8085-based microcomputer will perform these computational and control tasks. The multiplexed display circuitry from Experiment 12 and the keyboard circuitry from Experiment 13 will provide output and input capabilities for a "homemade" calculator.

Procedure

1. Calculator Hardware

The 4-function calculator hardware is shown in Figure 15.1. Connect this circuit and check the wiring carefully before continuing. Use the display-multiplexing and keyboard-scanning software you developed in Experiments 12 and 13, respectively, to test the circuitry.

2. Calculator Specifications

Before beginning the software design phase of this project, study the specifications for the 4-function calculator:

- The four standard calculator functions are to be included: addition, subtraction, multiplication, and division.
- Four-digit integer arithmetic is to be performed on decimal quantities. No decimal fractions or floating-point computations are necessary.
- Simple one-operation calculations are to be supported. No chaining or cascading of algebraic computations is required. The following example shows a typical sequence of keystrokes and the resulting display:

Key Pressed	*Displayed Value*
3	0003
2	0032
*	0032
4	0004
=	0128
1	0001
9	0019
/	0019
7	0007
=	0002

- The display digits should shift in from the right until a maximum of four digits are entered. The digits should not continue to shift in after the fourth digit.
- The C key should clear the calculator to allow a new computation to begin. The clear function should be active at all times. The calculator should display the digits 0000 when cleared.

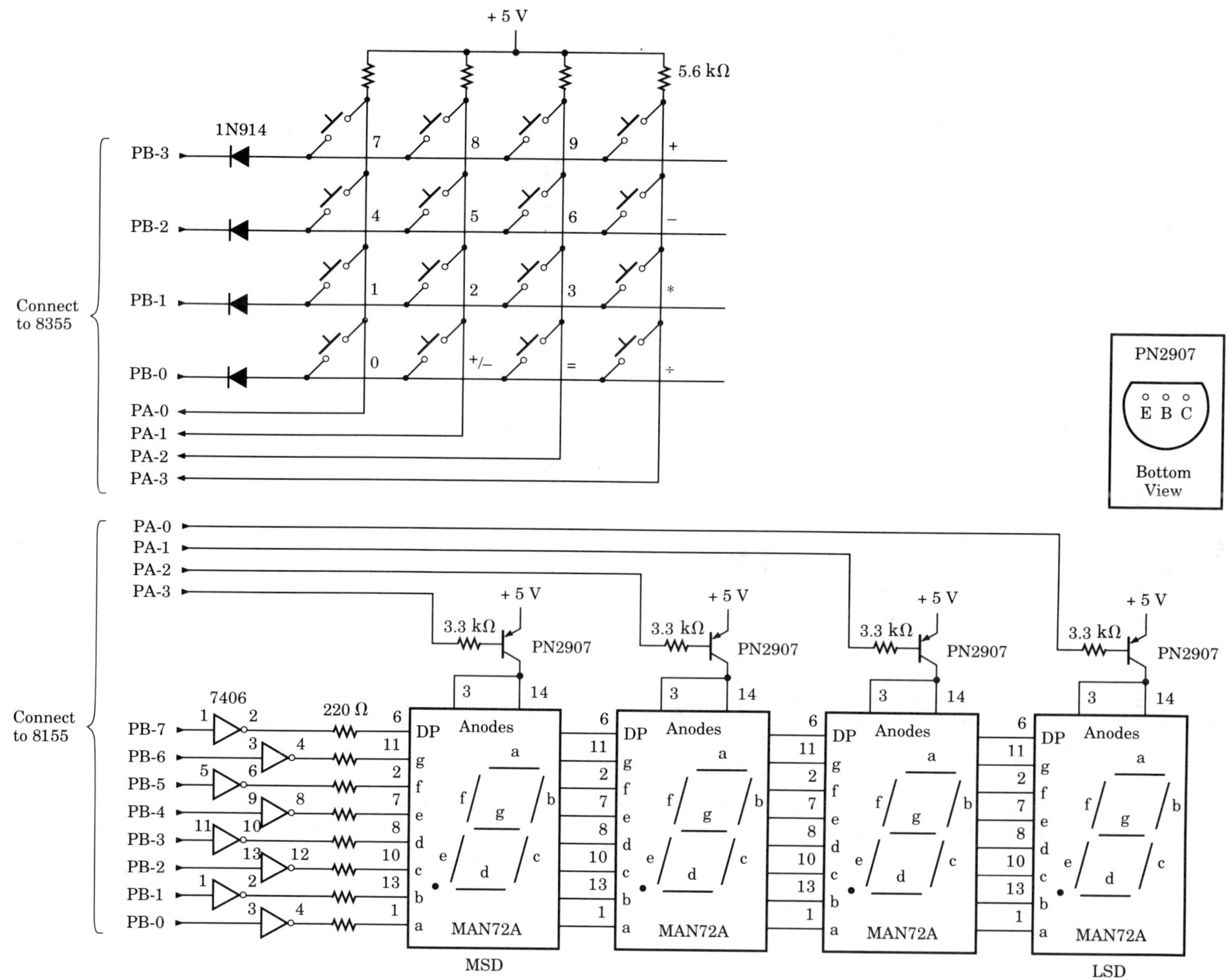

FIGURE 15.1
Four-Function Integer Calculator Hardware

- An overflow error message OFLO is to be displayed when the result of a computation is too large to fit in the 4-digit display.
- The error message Err0 is to be displayed to indicate that a division by zero has occurred.
- The sign of an operand may be changed by pressing the +/− key on the keyboard. The decimal point on the most significant display digit will be on to indicate a negative operand or to indicate that the results of a computation are negative.
- The calculator should ignore illegal keystroke sequences. For example, pushing = before both operands have been entered should cause no change in the display.
- The system must continue to multiplex the display while a key is depressed.

3. Calculator Software

You must use a very systematic approach if a large programming assignment such as this is to proceed smoothly. Here are a few suggestions that may assist you in your program design:

- Describe all necessary program logic in flowchart form before writing any program code.
- Carefully allocate the necessary storage locations for variables, lookup tables, display codes, etc.
- Write all program code in a modular fashion using subroutines, so that small program pieces can be tested and debugged individually.
- Strive for simplicity in your program design. Professional programmers use the slogan K.I.S.S.—Keep It Simple, Stupid—to describe this philosophy!

4. Program Debugging and Testing

Here are a few debugging and testing suggestions:

- Use the single-step and breakpoint modes of your single-board computer.
- Use the keyboard and display subroutines in the monitor program of your single-board computer as debugging tools. These subroutines are useful for input and output purposes while your calculator hardware interface is being debugged.
- Do not try to debug everything at once. Break the task into manageable pieces.
- Debug the addition function in the calculator first, then proceed to debug the subtraction, multiplication, and division logic.
- Test your software thoroughly using all possible sign and operation combinations. For example, divide a positive number by a negative number, a negative number by a negative number, etc.

Additional Activities

Many additional features can be added to this basic calculator. Here are some suggested features:

- Provisions for real-number operands and results
- Floating-point operations with scientific notation display
- Chaining of operations

- Trigonometric and logarithmic functions
- Operand store and recall
- Base conversion function (decimal to hexadecimal, etc.)

Complicated techniques are needed to implement many of these features. Refer to an algorithmic processes textbook for additional details.

PART TWO

8085 Microprocessor Peripheral Interfacing

EXPERIMENT 16

Logic Analyzer Applications

Objectives

The logic analyzer is a powerful tool than can diagnose hardware and software problems in microprocessor-based systems. After completing this experiment, you will be able to

- Trace the execution of a program with the logic analyzer
- Trace input and output machine cycles with the logic analyzer
- Use the delay and occurrence features of the logic analyzer to observe a specific pass through a program loop

Reference Reading

Gaonkar, Ramesh S. *Microprocessor Architecture, Programming, and Applications with the 8085/8080A*. 2nd ed. Columbus, OH: Merrill, 1989. Section 17.72.

Materials Needed

8085 single-board computer
Logic analyzer with user's manual

Discussion

Diagnosing hardware problems in complex digital circuits is very challenging, to say the least. Prototype microprocessor-based products often fail to operate properly when power is first applied to them. Existing computer systems may fail after many hours of satisfactory operation, with very few clues pointing to which hardware or software component actually failed.

Digital troubleshooting usually begins with a voltmeter, logic probe, and oscilloscope. In microprocessor-based systems, these tools alone are not enough; timing relationships that exist on system buses must be observed to analyze the system effectively. In an 8085-based microcomputer, for example, we must view the 8 data lines and 16 address lines simultaneously to determine whether machine code is being properly fetched from program memory. To view 24 separate signals concurrently, we could connect 12 dual-trace oscilloscopes to the circuit, but this approach would not be very practical. The logic analyzer, however, can monitor and display 24 signals and more with ease.

The basic logic analyzer is essentially a multiple-channel oscilloscope that is triggered by the occurrence of a specific digital signal pattern, known as the *trigger word*. After detecting this trigger word, the logic analyzer samples the input data and stores them in memory each time a clock signal transition occurs. The data are then displayed in one of several ways. Modern logic analyzers can display timing diagrams to represent information, but data are often more meaningful in tabular form. Most logic analyzers display data in binary, hexadecimal, or ASCII form; some systems even disassemble a machine language program as it executes and display the program instruction mnemonics.

The following activities will demonstrate the operation of a general-purpose logic analyzer. Each exercise focuses on a particular debugging technique. Consult the user's manual for your logic analyzer for specific operating instructions.

Procedure

Typical applications of a general-purpose logic analyzer are discussed in the following sections. This "generic" analyzer includes these input signals:

- 24 data input lines
- 1 clock input line
- 3 qualifier input lines

If your logic analyzer has only 16 data input lines, you can still perform the exercises by monitoring only the address bits, but not the data bits, of the microprocessor.

1. Connecting the Logic Analyzer to an 8085-based System

Turn off your microcomputer before connecting the logic analyzer. This precaution is recommended to prevent accidentally shorting signal lines (and possibly damaging components) while attaching the analyzer probes. Next, connect the logic analyzer input probes to your single-board computer as shown in Table 16.1. This table includes the connections needed to monitor program execution on an Intel SDK-85 microcomputer. If you are using a different type of microcomputer, your instructor will furnish the required connection details.

Turn on the SDK-85 power supply and enter the following test program. This program outputs the first 256 bytes of the monitor ROM (locations 0000H—00FFH) to output port 80H. This port address does not access an actual I/O device on the SDK-85; it is used for demonstration purposes only.

TABLE 16.1
SDK-85 Signal Connections

8085 Signal Name	*Logic Analyzer Input*	*Location on SDK-85*
A_0	bit 0	8212 (A6) pin 4
A_1	bit 1	8212 (A6) pin 6
A_2	bit 2	8212 (A6) pin 8
A_3	bit 3	8212 (A6) pin 10
A_4	bit 4	8212 (A6) pin 15
A_5	bit 5	8212 (A6) pin 17
A_6	bit 6	8212 (A6) pin 19
A_7	bit 7	8212 (A6) pin 21
A_8	bit 8	8085 (A11) pin 21
A_9	bit 9	8085 (A11) pin 22
A_{10}	bit 10	8085 (A11) pin 23
A_{11}	bit 11	8085 (A11) pin 24
A_{12}	bit 12	8085 (A11) pin 25
A_{13}	bit 13	8085 (A11) pin 26
A_{14}	bit 14	8085 (A11) pin 27
A_{15}	bit 15	8085 (A11) pin 28
AD_0	bit 16	8085 (A11) pin 12
AD_1	bit 17	8085 (A11) pin 13
AD_2	bit 18	8085 (A11) pin 14
AD_3	bit 19	8085 (A11) pin 15
AD_4	bit 20	8085 (A11) pin 16
AD_5	bit 21	8085 (A11) pin 17
AD_6	bit 22	8085 (A11) pin 18
AD_7	bit 23	8085 (A11) pin 19
$\overline{RD}$	Clock	8085 (A11) pin 32
$IO/\overline{M}$	Qualifier bit 0	8085 (A11) pin 34
S0	Qualifier bit 1	8085 (A11) pin 29
S1	Qualifier bit 2	8085 (A11) pin 33
GROUND	Ground input(s)	8085 (A11) pin 20

Source: Courtesy of Intel Corporation

```
Address  Contents           Instruction
                            ORG 2000H
2000H    31 C2 20           LXI SP,20C2H   ;INITALIZE STACK POINTER
2003H    21 00 00           LXI H,0000H    ;POINT TO FIRST ROM LOCATION
2006H    CD 11 20   LOOP:   CALL SUB1      ;PROCESS ONE BYTE
2009H    23                 INX H          ;POINT TO NEXT ROM LOCATION
200AH    7C                 MOV A,H        ;SEE IF POINTING TO 0100H
200BH    FE 01              CPI 01H
200DH    C2 06 20           JNZ LOOP       ;IF NOT, JUMP BACK FOR MORE
2010H    CF                 RST 1          ;ELSE, QUIT
2011H    7E         SUB1:   MOV A,M        ;GET BYTE FROM ROM
2012H    D3 80              OUT 80H        ;DO AN OUTPUT WRITE TO PORT 80H
2014H    C9                 RET            ;RETURN TO MAIN PROGRAM
```

2. Configuring the Logic Analyzer to Trace Program Execution

Turn on the logic analyzer power switch, then define the data format and trace specifications as follows:

Signal group A: input probes 0–15 (address bus)
Signal group B: input probes 16–23 (data bus)
Data format for both signal groups: hexadecimal, positive logic
Trigger word (group A portion): 2000H
Trigger word (group B portion): XXH
Qualifier bits (Q2–Q0): XXX
Clock slope: positive
Trace mode: start display with trigger word, delay = 000000

NOTE: The X's refer to "don't care" input conditions.

The trigger word in this example is the address of the first instruction in the program (2000H), with the data bus signals (group B input probes) defined as "don't cares." The analyzer must see the trigger word pattern to start the data capture process. After the trigger word is detected and stored, subsequent data words are sampled and stored in the logic analyzer memory under control of the Clock input signal. Since the Clock input to the analyzer is connected to the 8085 $\overline{RD}$ signal, and since a positive Clock slope is selected, the analyzer will read and store a 24-bit data word every time the $\overline{RD}$ signal goes from low to high. This signal transition occurs whenever a Memory Read or Opcode Fetch machine cycle is performed, as shown in Figure 16.1.

Notice that when $\overline{RD}$ goes from low to high, the data bus contains valid data fetched from program memory; also, the address bits are stable at that time.

3. Tracing Instruction Execution

Arm the logic analyzer (enable its data capture mode) by pressing the TRACE button. Next, execute the demonstration program. The logic analyzer should detect the trigger word, then sample and store an additional data word each time the Clock

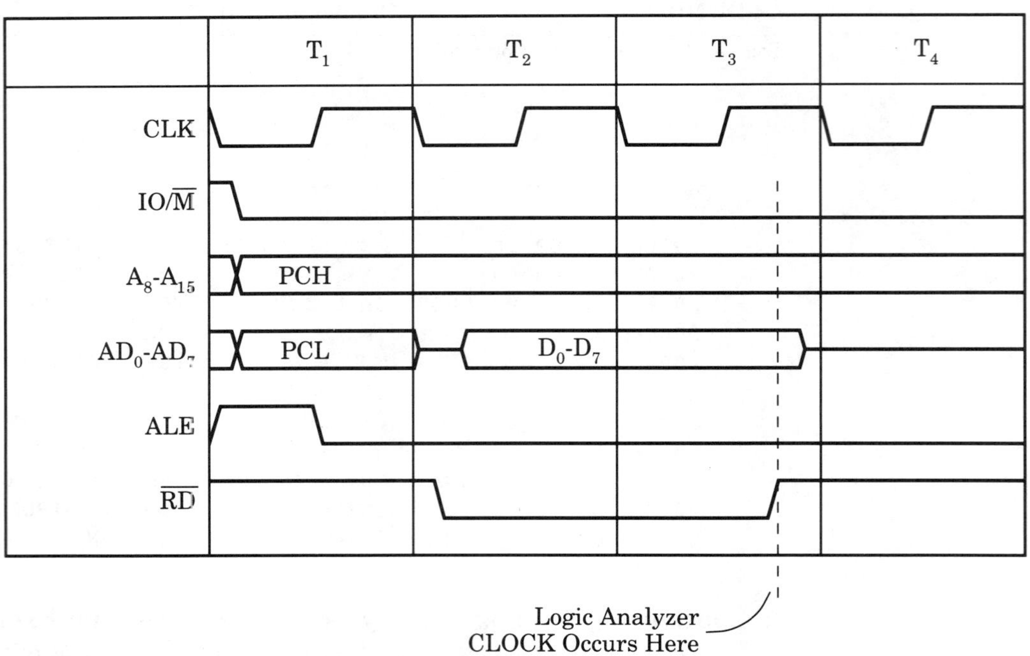

FIGURE 16.1
Opcode Fetch Machine Cycle
Source: Adapted from material copyrighted by Intel Corporation.

input detects the positive edge of the $\overline{RD}$ signal. Typically, the stored results are displayed in a 16-line listing format. Additional lines of information can be viewed by pressing the ROLL DISPLAY UP and ROLL DISPLAY DOWN buttons. The following list shows the results as they might appear on a typical logic analyzer display; the comments are included to describe the corresponding bus activity.

Group A Signals	*Group B Signals*		*Comments*
2000	31		
2001	C2	———	LXI SP,20C2H instruction
2002	20		
2003	21		
2004	00	———	LXI H,0000H instruction
2005	00		
2006	CD		
2007	11	———	CALL SUB1 instruction
2008	20		
2011	7E	———	MOV A,M instruction (subroutine in progress)
0000	3E	———	Read first data byte from ROM
2012	D3	———	OUT 80H instruction
2013	80		
2014	C9	———	RET instruction
20C0	09	———	Pop LS byte of return address off of stack
20C1	20	———	Pop MS byte of return address off of stack
2009	23	———	INX H instruction
200A	7C	———	MOV A,H instruction
200B	FE	———	CPI 01 instruction
200C	01		
200D	C2		
200E	06	———	JNZ LOOP instruction
200F	20		
2006	CD	———	Now, repeat the loop. . .
.	.		
.	.		
.	.		

Scroll through the data for the first three or four loop passes and note the values read from memory. Identify which data words correspond with Opcode Fetch cycles.

4. Tracing Only Opcode Fetch Machine Cycles

It is often desirable to display only opcode bytes, rather than all opcode, operand, and data bytes. This can be done using the analyzer trigger qualifier inputs. For this example, define the qualifier bits as follows:

Q0 (IO/$\overline{M}$): 0
Q1 (S0): 1
Q2 (S1): 1

Recall that IO/$\overline{M}$ is low while a memory access is made. S0 and S1 are the

8085 status signals used to identify the current machine cycle. These three signals are summarized as follows:

IO/$\overline{M}$	*S1*	*S0*	*Machine Cycle*
0	0	1	Memory Write
0	1	0	Memory Read
0	1	1	Opcode Fetch
1	0	1	I/O Write
1	1	0	I/O Read

Arm the logic analyzer, then run the demonstration program on the SDK-85. The analyzer should display these results:

Group A Signals	*Group B Signals*	*Comments*
2000	31	LXI SP,20C2H opcode
2003	21	LXI H,0000H opcode
2006	CD	CALL SUB1 opcode
2011	7E	MOV A,M opcode
2012	D3	OUT 80H opcode
2014	C9	RET opcode
2009	23	INX H opcode
200A	7C	MOV A,H opcode
200B	FE	CPI 01H opcode
200D	C2	JNZ LOOP opcode
2006	CD	CALL SUB1 opcode
.	.	
.	.	
.	.	

As you can see, this mode is well suited for tracing the flow of instructions in a program.

5. Tracing I/O Machine Cycles

I/O Read and Write cycles can be traced using the logic analyzer. Recall that I/O cycles are indicated when IO/$\overline{M}$ is high. An I/O Write machine cycle is illustrated in Figure 16.2.

To demonstrate the trace of an I/O write cycle, connect the analyzer Clock input to the $\overline{WR}$ signal on the 8085 (chip A15, pin 31 on the SDK-85). Change the trigger word to XX80 for group A, and XX for group B. Also, set the trigger qualifier bits as follows:

Q0 (IO/$\overline{M}$): 1
Q1 (S0): X
Q2 (S1): X

Arm the logic analyzer, then run the program on the SDK-85. The analyzer should display these results:

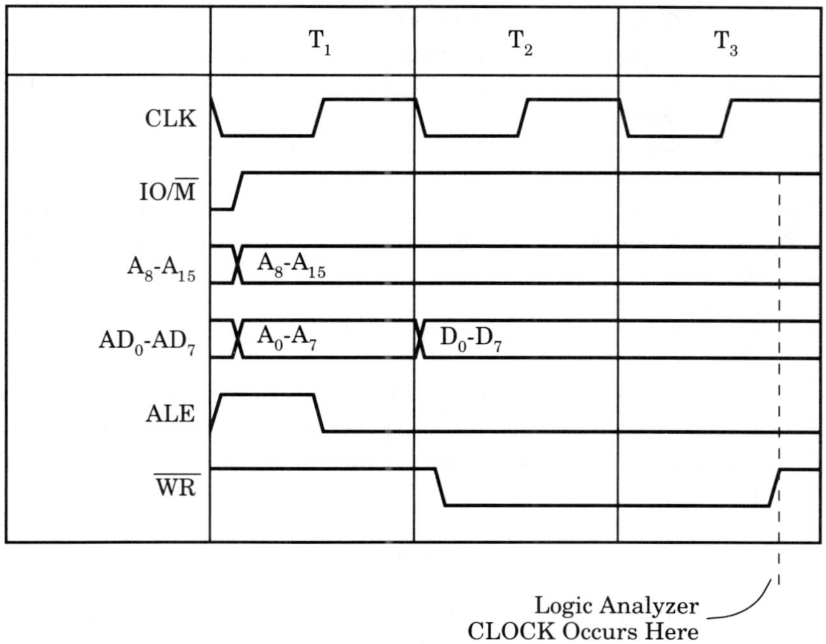

FIGURE 16.2
I/O Write Machine Cycle
Source: Adapted from material copyrighted by Intel Corporation.

Group A Signals	*Group B Signals*	*Comments*
8080	3E	First byte written to I/O port 80H
8080	00	Second byte written to I/O port 80H
8080	32	Third byte written to I/O port 80H
8080	00	Fourth byte written to I/O port 80H
8080	19	Fifth byte written to I/O port 80H
8080	C3	Sixth byte written to I/O port 80H
.	.	
.	.	
.	.	

Notice that the 8085 outputs the port address to both the upper eight and the lower eight address bits. Compare the data bus readings with the corresponding bytes contained in the monitor ROM.

6. Finding a Stuck Bit with the Logic Analyzer
Disconnect the logic analyzer probe from AD_3 on the 8085 chip. Connect that logic analyzer probe to +5 V. Arm the logic analyzer, then run the demonstration program. The analyzer should display these results:

Group A Signals	*Group B Signals*	*Comments*
8080	3E	First byte written to I/O port 80H
8080	08	Second byte written to I/O port 80H
8080	3A	Third byte written to I/O port 80H
8080	08	Fourth byte written to I/O port 80H
8080	19	Fifth byte written to I/O port 80H
8080	CB	Sixth byte written to I/O port 80H
.	.	
.	.	
.	.	

The displayed group B bits contain the error that was introduced, but it may not be immediately apparent. Change the data display format so that the Group B signals are displayed in *binary* form, instead of in hexadecimal. The display should now show:

Group A Signals	*Group B Signals*	*Comments*
8080	00111110	First byte written to I/O port 80H
8080	00001000	Second byte written to I/O port 80H
8080	00111010	Third byte written to I/O port 80H
8080	00001000	Fourth byte written to I/O port 80H
8080	00011001	Fifth byte written to I/O port 80H
8080	11001011	Sixth byte written to I/O port 80H
.	.	
.	.	
.	.	

You can now see much more clearly that group B bit 3 is always high. A binary display of the data is also a convenient way to monitor sensor bits, peripheral device status flags, and the results of bit manipulation instructions.

Reconnect the AD_3 signal of the 8085 to the logic analyzer and connect the $\overline{RD}$ signal to the analyzer Clock input before proceeding to the next step.

7. Viewing Data Activity Prior to a Trigger Event

It is often necessary to determine what events *preceded* a trigger word. For example, it may be helpful to know what condition caused a program to call a particular subroutine or caused it to generate a certain output signal. Many logic analyzers allow data that occurred *before* the trigger word to be stored and displayed. This concept is demonstrated in the following steps.

First, set the logic analyzer controls as follows:

Trigger word (group A portion): 2011H
Trigger word (group B portion): XXH
Clock slope: positive
Trace mode: trigger at end of display, Delay = 000005
Q0 (IO/$\overline{M}$): 0
Q1 (S0): 1
Q2 (S1): 1

This configuration will trace Opcode Fetch cycles, with the trigger word equal to the address of the subroutine. The end-display trace mode and the delay factor cause the trigger word to appear five locations from the end of the list of data samples. The events that preceded the trigger word can be observed, as well as the five events following it.

Arm the analyzer by pressing the TRACE button, then run the 8085 program as before. After the analyzer triggers, scroll to the end of the data list; the following information should be displayed there:

Group A Signals	*Group B Signals*	*Comments*
.	.	
.	.	
.	.	
xxxx	xx	Monitor program activity
2000	31	LXI SP,20C2H opcode
2003	21	LXI H,0000H opcode
2006	CD	CALL SUB1 opcode
2011	7E	MOV A,M opcode (trigger word)
2012	D3	OUT 80H opcode
2014	C9	RET opcode
2009	23	INX H opcode
200A	7C	MOV A,H opcode
200B	FE	CPI 01H opcode

Using this mode, you can observe the events that preceded a particular subroutine or other program sequence.

8. Viewing a Particular Pass Through a Loop

Programs that include looping structures can be traced easily using the "occurrence" feature of the logic analyzer. For example, the logic analyzer can capture and display the sequence of instructions that occurs beginning on the 20th pass through a loop. Similarly, the analyzer could follow the effects of a subroutine the 500th time it is called.

Connect the logic analyzer Clock signal to $\overline{WR}$ on the 8085 (pin 31), then set the logic analyzer as follows to demonstrate the occurrence mode:

Trigger word (group A portion): XX80H
Trigger word (group B portion): XX
Clock slope: positive
Trace mode: start display with trigger word, Delay = 000000, Occur = 000001
Q0 (IO/$\overline{M}$): 1
Q1 (S0): X
Q2 (S1): X

With these settings, the Occur parameter indicates that the logic analyzer will trigger on the first occurrence of the trigger word. Arm the analyzer, then execute the demonstration program. The results should be:

Group A Signals	*Group B Signals*	*Comments*
8080	3E	First byte written to I/O port 80H
8080	00	Second byte written to I/O port 80H
8080	32	Third byte written to I/O port 80H
8080	00	Fourth byte written to I/O port 80H
8080	19	Fifth byte written to I/O port 80H
.	.	
.	.	
.	.	

Change the Occur value to 000003, arm the analyzer, and run the program. This time, data capture will begin on the third I/O Write cycle. The displayed values should be:

Group A Signals	*Group B Signals*	*Comments*
8080	32	Third byte written to I/O port 80H
8080	00	Fourth byte written to I/O port 80H
8080	19	Fifth byte written to I/O port 80H
8080	C3	Sixth byte written to I/O port 80H
8080	F1	Seventh byte written to I/O port 80H
.	.	
.	.	
.	.	

Change the Occur value to 000250, arm the analyzer, then run the program. Explain the results.

Additional Activities

1. Many logic analyzers have additional features, including program disassembly, timing diagram, and data comparison modes. If your logic analyzer has these features, explore them using the demonstration program described in procedure step 1.
2. If your logic analyzer generates an external trigger pulse, connect it to the channel 1 input of a dual-trace oscilloscope. Configure the logic analyzer to trace the I/O Write cycles that occur in this program:

```
        ORG 2000H
        MVI A,55H
LOOP:   OUT 80H
        JMP LOOP
```

   Set the oscilloscope in the dual-trace mode, with channel 1 as the trigger source. Use the channel 2 input probe on the oscilloscope to observe the activity on the address bus, data bus, and $\overline{WR}$ signal while running this program. Record your observations and compare them with the results you expected.

Review Questions

1. A logic analyzer is attached to an 8085-based microcomputer. The trigger qualifier bits are connected as follows:

Q0 (IO/$\overline{M}$): 1
Q1 (S0): 1
Q2 (S1): 0

What machine cycle matches these qualifier conditions?

2. Study the user's manual for your logic analyzer, then answer these questions:
   - How many events can be stored in the memory of your logic analyzer?
   - What is the maximum permissible Clock signal frequency?
   - How many data and qualifier inputs does your logic analyzer allow?

EXPERIMENT 17

Interfacing Memory Circuits

Objectives

Memory components are basic parts of the architecture of a computer system, whether the system is a large mainframe machine or a small microcomputer. Most microcomputers include Read-Only Memory (ROM) that permanently stores information and Read-Write Memory (RAM) that temporarily stores user programs and data. After completing this experiment, you will be able to

- Design address-decoding logic to interface memory components to an 8085 microprocessor
- Construct a static RAM circuit and check its performance using a memory test program
- Interface an EPROM containing an 8085 program to a microcomputer

Reference Reading

Gaonkar, Ramesh S. *Microprocessor Architecture, Programming, and Applications with the 8085/8080A*. 2nd ed. Columbus, OH: Merrill, 1989. Sections 2.2, 3.3, and 17.3.

The MCS-80/85 Family User's Manual. Santa Clara, CA: Intel Corp., 1986. Pages 3–1 to 3–5, 6–10 to 6–23, and A1–8 to A1–10.

Materials Needed

8085 single-board computer
EPROM programmer
EPROM ultraviolet eraser
Breadboard with logic switches and LED indicators
6264LP (150 ns) 8K × 8 RAM
2764 (450 ns) 8K × 8 EPROM
74LS138 3-to-8 decoder

Discussion

Memory Address Decoding

8085-based systems use control signals to permit proper data transfer between the microprocessor and its attached peripherals. The $IO/\overline{M}$ signal distinguishes I/O devices from memory devices, while the $\overline{RD}$ and $\overline{WR}$ signals select either Read or Write operations. In addition, most peripheral systems use address-decoding logic to define the address of the peripheral. This decoding is performed either with combinational logic or with decoder ICs.

Figure 17.1 shows a 74LS138 used as an address decoder in a memory circuit interfaced to an 8085. A specific decoder output is active (low) when the $IO/\overline{M}$ signal is low and the selection address of that output is applied. In this circuit, each decoder output line selects a specific 2K × 8 block of addresses, as shown. The Output Enable ($\overline{OE}$) line of the RAM controls Memory Read operations; the Write Enable ($\overline{WE}$) line controls Write cycles. Since the EPROM is a Read-Only device, it uses only the $\overline{OE}$ input; no $\overline{WE}$ input is necessary.

RAM and EPROM Control Signals

The 6264LP 8K × 8 RAM and the 2764 8K × 8 EPROM are popular memory components that are easy to interface to most microprocessors. Figure 17.2 describes the pin numbers and signal definitions for these two devices.

In the following procedure, you will interface a 6264LP 8K × 8 static RAM and a 2764 8K × 8 EPROM to your 8085 single-board microcomputer system. After using simple testing procedures to verify the performance of this memory system,

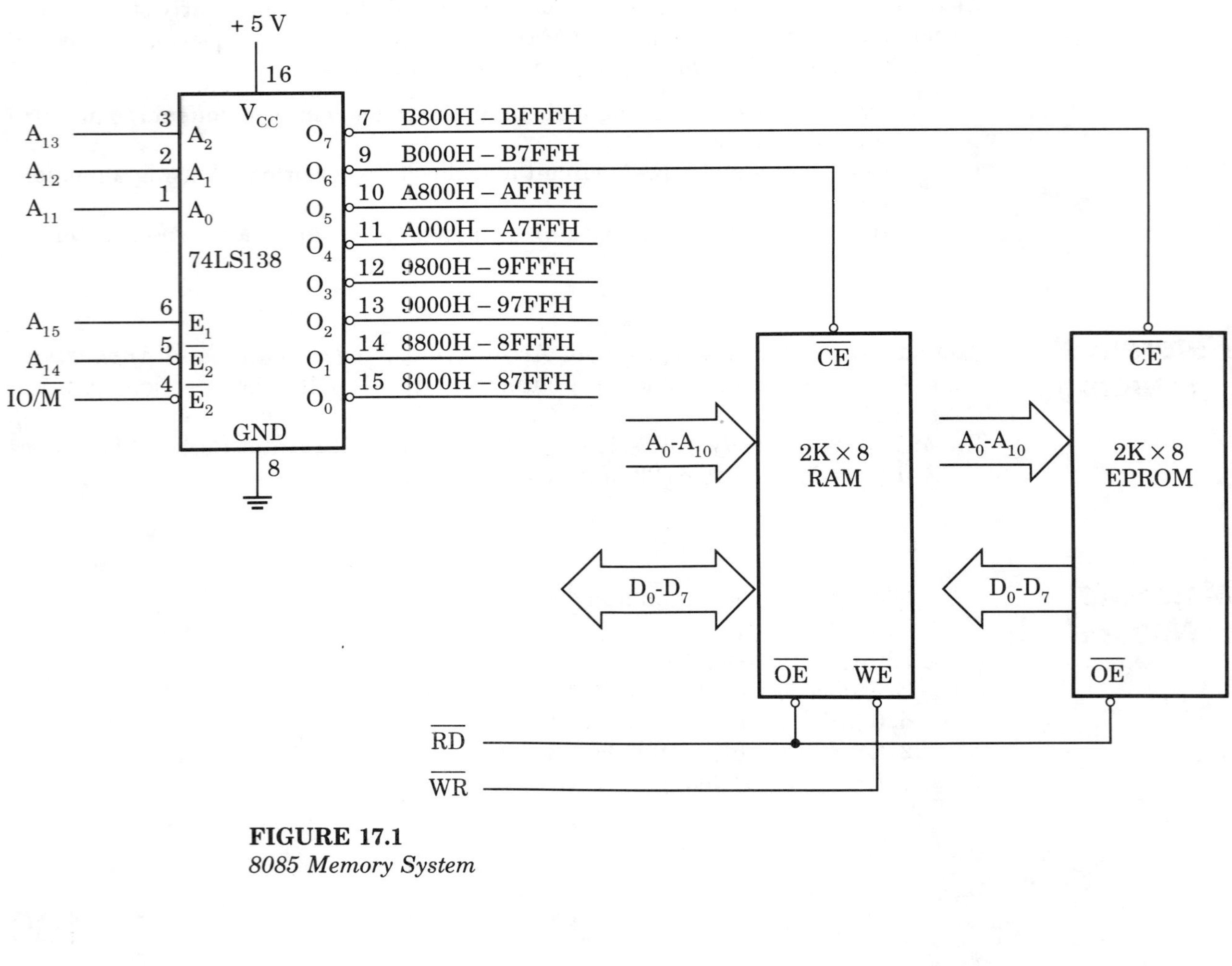

FIGURE 17.1
8085 Memory System

HM6264P – 15
PIN CONFIGURATION

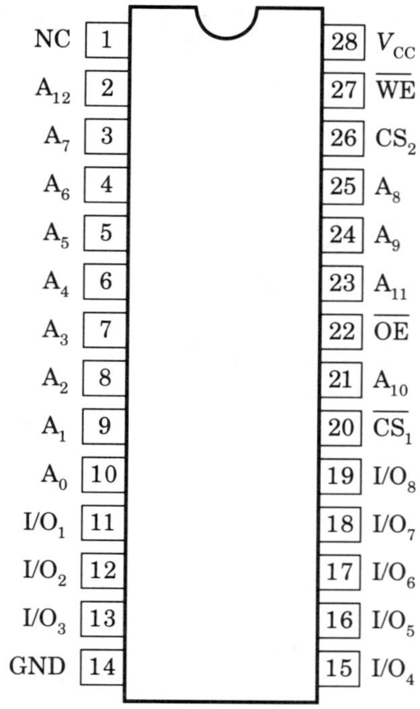

Truth Table

$\overline{CS_1}$	CS_2	$\overline{WE}$	$\overline{OE}$	Mode	I/O Pins
H	X	X	X	Not Selected	High Z
X	L	X	X	Not Selected	High Z
L	H	L	H	WRITE	D_{in}
L	H	H	L	READ	D_{out}

(a)

2764
PIN CONFIGURATION

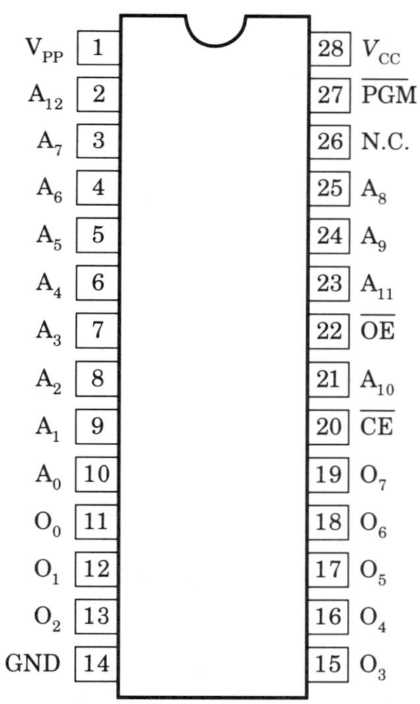

Truth Table

$\overline{CE}$	$\overline{OE}$	$\overline{PGM}$	V_{PP}	Mode	Output Pins
L	L	H	V_{CC}	READ	D_{out}
H	X	X	V_{CC}	STANDBY	High Z

(b)

FIGURE 17.2
Pin Configuration and Truth Tables for (a) Hitachi HM6264P-15 RAM and (b) Intel 2764 EPROM
Source: (a) Adapted with permission of Hitachi America, Ltd., (b) Pin configuration reprinted by permission of Intel Corporation, copyright 1983. Table adapted from material copyrighted by Intel Corporation.

you will write a program to test the RAM circuit for wiring errors and defective components.

Procedure

1. Address Decoding Logic
Design an add-on memory system for your single-board computer. Use a 74LS138 1-of-8 decoder, a 6264LP CMOS RAM, and a 2764 EPROM. Configure the address decoder to place the RAM at memory locations E000H–FFFFH and the EPROM at locations 8000H–9FFFH.

HARDWARE NOTE: The addresses from 8000H to FFFFH in the SDK-85 microcomputer are in "expansion memory" space. The bus expansion buffer chips A1–A7 must be installed to use this expansion area. If you are using a different type of single-board computer, your instructor will supply the necessary memory expansion details.

2. RAM Hardware
Connect the address decoder and RAM portions of the memory circuit to your single-board computer. Do not place the EPROM in the circuit at this time. Perform initial tests on the RAM circuit using the Substitute Memory function on your single-board computer. If the RAM circuit is working properly, you should be able to view and alter the contents of any RAM location.

3. EPROM Hardware
Test the EPROM portion of your memory system by programming a 2764 EPROM to contain this simple test program:

```
          ORG 8000H
UPDDT     EQU 036EH       ;DATA FIELD DISPLAY ROUTINE ADDRESS
          LXI SP,20C2H
          MVI A,00H       ;CLEAR COUNT
FOREVER:  PUSH PSW        ;SAVE COUNT VALUE
          CALL UPDDT      ;DISPLAY COUNT IN DATA FIELD
          LXI B,0000H     ;DELAY LOOP INDEX
DELAY:    DCX B           ;DELAY LOOP STARTS HERE
          MOV A,B
          ORA C
          JNZ DELAY
          POP PSW         ;RESTORE DISPLAY COUNT
          INR A           ;INCREMENT IT
          JMP FOREVER     ;REPEAT UNTIL RESET OCCURS
```

To program the EPROM, you should first assemble the program using the 8085 cross assembler. Next, transfer the assembled object file into your EPROM programmer system. Follow the instructions for your EPROM programmer to program the EPROM with this information.

Insert the 2764 EPROM into your memory circuit, then inspect the program code in the EPROM using the Substitute Memory function on your computer. If the EPROM data are accessible, as they should be, execute the program and note the results.

4. RAM Circuit Testing
It would be very time-consuming to detect all possible errors in the RAM circuit using the simple Substitute Memory test performed in step 2. The flowchart shown

in Figure 17.3 illustrates a RAM test algorithm, known as the walking-ones test, that can expedite the RAM testing process, and can systematically detect many common wiring errors and faulty components.

This algorithm initially clears all RAM locations. Next, it checks the first RAM location to verify that it contains all zeros; if it does, then the binary test pattern (TESTPAT) 00000001 is stored there. If the location does not contain all zeros, then ERROR A is produced. The sequence continues by checking the second location; if it contains all zeros, then 00000010 is stored there. This procedure continues until all 8K bytes in memory are filled, as follows:

RAM Location	*Binary Contents*
E000H	00000001
E001H	00000010
E002H	00000100
E003H	00001000
E004H	00010000
E005H	00100000
E006H	01000000
E007H	10000000
E008H	00000001
.	.
.	.
.	.
FFFEH	01000000
FFFFH	10000000

The procedure now reads each value from RAM and compares it with what should be there, starting at the first location. If a discrepancy is found, ERROR B is produced.

If no errors are detected so far, the memory is again cleared, the test pattern TESTPAT is shifted left by one bit, and the process is repeated. In this manner, each bit of each location in memory is tested to see if it can store a 1 while all other bits in all locations remain unchanged. This procedure effectively locates addressing problems, RAM data bits that are stuck high or low, and data bits that are shorted together or left floating.

Write an 8085 program to implement the walking-ones memory test algorithm. To indicate the condition of the RAM being tested, the program should display one of these messages on the LED display of your single-board computer:

Message	*Description*
PASS	All locations pass the memory test.
xxxx 0A	Location xxxx produced ERROR A. This error indicates that the location did not clear properly or that the contents of the location were modified when data were written to another address.
xxxx 0B	Location xxxx produced ERROR B. This error indicates that the location did not maintain the data bit pattern that was originally stored there.

When one of these three conditions is met, the appropriate message should remain on the display, and the program should be "trapped" in an endless loop.

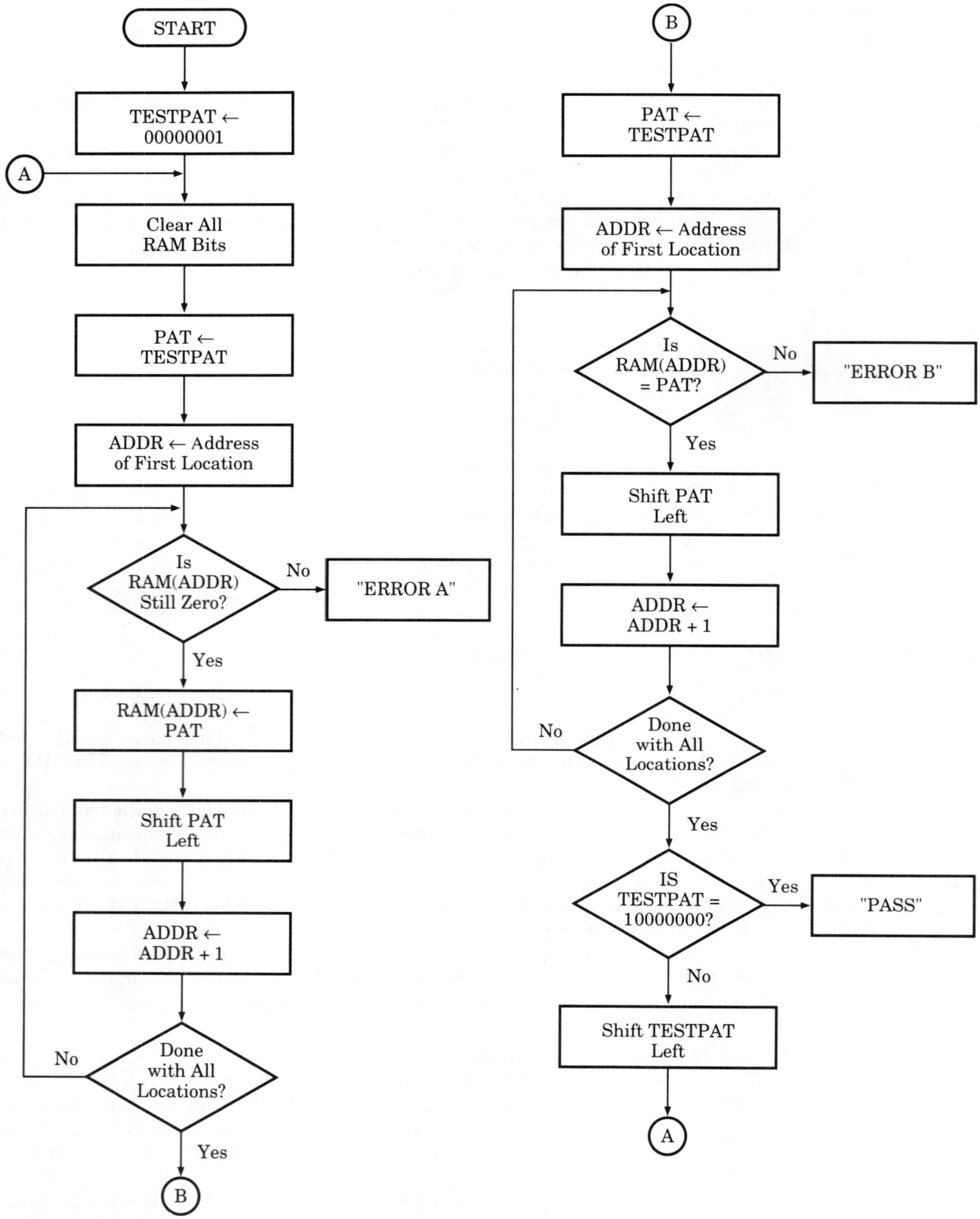

FIGURE 17.3
Flowchart for RAM Test Program

Test the ability of your program to produce the ERROR A message by temporarily disconnecting address line A_{10} on the RAM and connecting that RAM pin high. Run the memory test program to verify the results. Remember to reconnect the A_{10} line before proceeding to the next step.

The ERROR B error may be induced by removing the data line D_1 from the RAM temporarily and connecting pins D_0 and D_1 on the RAM. Also, connect a 10 kΩ resistor between D_1 on the computer and the system ground. This "pull-down" resistor pulls the floating D_1 line low and prevents ERROR A from occurring. Again, run the memory test program and verify the results.

Additional Activities

1. Calculate the timing relationships present in your memory circuit. Compare the timing requirements of the 8085 with the access times of the 2764 and 6264-15 devices. Include in your calculations the propagation delay through the address decoder. Draw timing diagrams to support your answer.
   NOTE: Refer to data sheets for the 2764, 6264-15, 74LS138, and 8085 for signal-timing details.
2. Design an EPROM programmer circuit to program a 2764 EPROM. Include in your design the necessary power supply switching logic and sufficient RAM to store the data being programmed. Interface the programmer to your single-board computer, then test its performance.
   NOTE: Refer to a 2764 data sheet for the programming mode electrical and timing requirements.

Review Questions

1. Design an address decoder circuit to control the following devices:
   - 2K x 8 RAM addressed at 8000H–87FFH
   - 2K x 8 RAM addressed at 8800H–8FFFH
   - 8K x 8 EPROM addressed at 9000H–AFFFH
   - 8K x 8 EPROM addressed at B000H–CFFFH
2. Explain how the walking-ones RAM test program detects each of these faults:
   a. A single bit in RAM that is stuck high
   b. A single bit in RAM that is stuck low
   c. An address bit on the RAM chip that is not connected to the 8085
   d. A data bit on the RAM chip that is not connected to the 8085
3. What would happen if the address decoder selected both the RAM and the EPROM at the same time and a $\overline{RD}$ signal occurred?

EXPERIMENT 18

Interfacing TTL I/O Circuits

Objectives

Programmable I/O devices such as the 8155 and the 8355 are more powerful and more expensive than necessary for many applications. In those instances, simpler input and output circuits using inexpensive TTL (transistor-transistor logic) integrated circuits can accomplish the required interface. After completing this experiment, you will be able to

- Construct the necessary address decoding logic to interface I/O ports to an 8085 microprocessor
- Interface an input port to read data input signals and an output port to control output devices
- Control the average power applied to a DC load using pulse-width modulation

Reference Reading

Gaonkar, Ramesh S. *Microprocessor Architecture, Programming, and Applications with the 8085/8080A*. 2nd ed. Columbus, OH: Merrill, 1989. Sections 2.3, 2.5, 4.1, 4.5 and 4.6.

The MCS-80/85 Family User's Manual. Santa Clara, CA: Intel Corp., 1986. Pages 3–1 to 3–5 and 6–10 to 6–23.

Materials Needed

8085 single-board computer
Breadboard with logic switches and LED indicators
Oscilloscope
74LS138 3-to-8 decoder
74LS244 octal 3-state buffer
74LS374 octal D latch
TIP102 NPN Darlington transistor
1 kΩ resistor
#47 6.3 V lamp

Discussion

I/O Port Hardware

Figure 18.1 shows a simple input and output port interfaced to the 8085. The 74LS138 serves not only as the address decoder for the circuit, but also as a gating circuit that combines the IO/$\overline{M}$, $\overline{RD}$, and $\overline{WR}$ control signals. Some of the 74LS138 outputs produce I/O Read signals, while other outputs produce I/O Write signals.

Figure 18.2a shows the timing relationships for an I/O Read machine cycle using this circuit. Notice that the data are placed on the data bus by the 74LS244 when IO/$\overline{M}$ is high, $\overline{RD}$ is low, A_{15} is high, A_{14} is low, and A_{13} is low. The data bus returns to a 3-state condition when $\overline{RD}$ goes back high.

Figure 18.2b depicts the timing diagram for an I/O Write cycle. The O_5 output of the 74LS138 is low when IO/$\overline{M}$ is high, $\overline{WR}$ is low, A_{15} is high, A_{14} is low, and A_{13} is low. The 74LS374 latches data on the low-to-high transition of the CP (clock) input; this occurs when the $\overline{WR}$ signal goes from low to high.

Driving High-Current DC Loads

Microcomputers use special interface hardware to control electrical loads such as lamps, valves, relays, and solenoids. The logic-level output from an I/O port typically can drive only a small current into a load; additional circuitry, however, can control load currents of several amperes.

Figure 18.3 shows a driver circuit that can control a variety of DC loads. Using the specified component values, the circuit can handle DC loads of up to 2 A. The control of this large output current is possible because of the high current gain of the TIP102 Darlington transistor; it provides a typical DC current gain of 5000. The 1 kΩ base resistor limits the base current to about 2 mA, which is within the 74LS374 I_{OH} (output current when the output is high) specification of 2.6 mA.

If the TIP102 is mounted on an adequate heat sink, it can control load currents up to 8 A. Slightly more base current (about 4 mA) is required to produce this high load current, so the base resistor must be reduced to 470 Ω. The 74LS374 can supply the 4 mA base current; although 4 mA is above its specified I_{OH} value of 2.6 mA, it is still much lower than the available output short-circuit current (I_{OS}) of 30 mA.

The TIP102 includes an internal clamping diode to protect itself from voltage spikes caused by inductive loads. While this internal protection is adequate for many applications, an external clamping diode is recommended across any load that is heavily inductive.

Procedure

1. Construct the circuit shown in Figure 18.1. Connect the eight input port lines to logic switches on the breadboard. Connect the eight output port lines to LED indicators. Be sure to connect a ground wire between the breadboard and the single-board computer. Check all wiring carefully before proceeding.
2. Determine the address ranges at which the input and output portions of the circuit are accessible.
3. Write a simple program to continually input 8-bit data from the input port and output the data to the corresponding lines on the output port. Test your program by executing it on your single-board computer.
4. A microcomputer controls the brightness of a series of indicator lamps on an industrial control panel. The computer adjusts the brightness of each indicator lamp to compensate for changing ambient lighting conditions. The system uses a *pulse-width modulation (PWM)* technique; the duty cycle of a power source

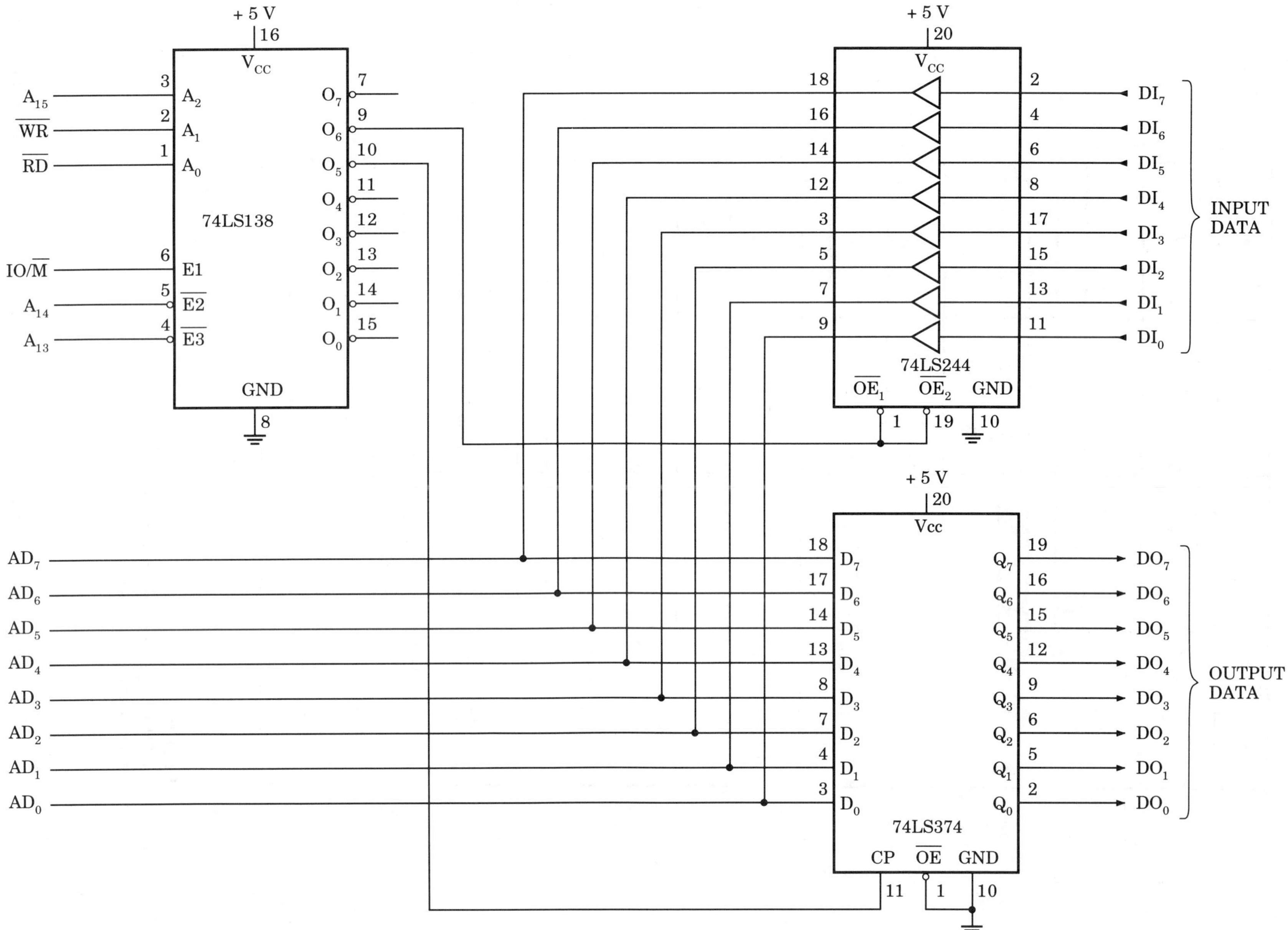

FIGURE 18.1
TTL Input/Output Port Circuit

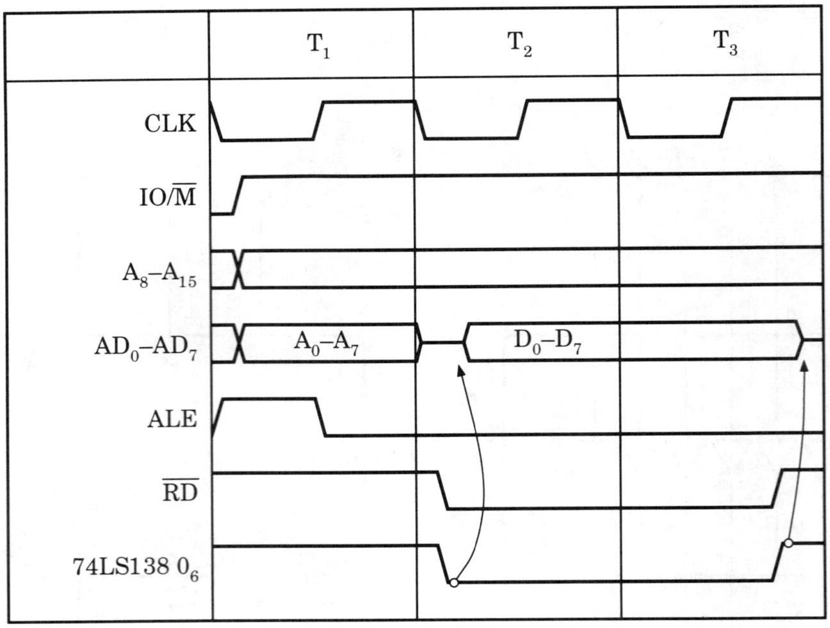

(a)

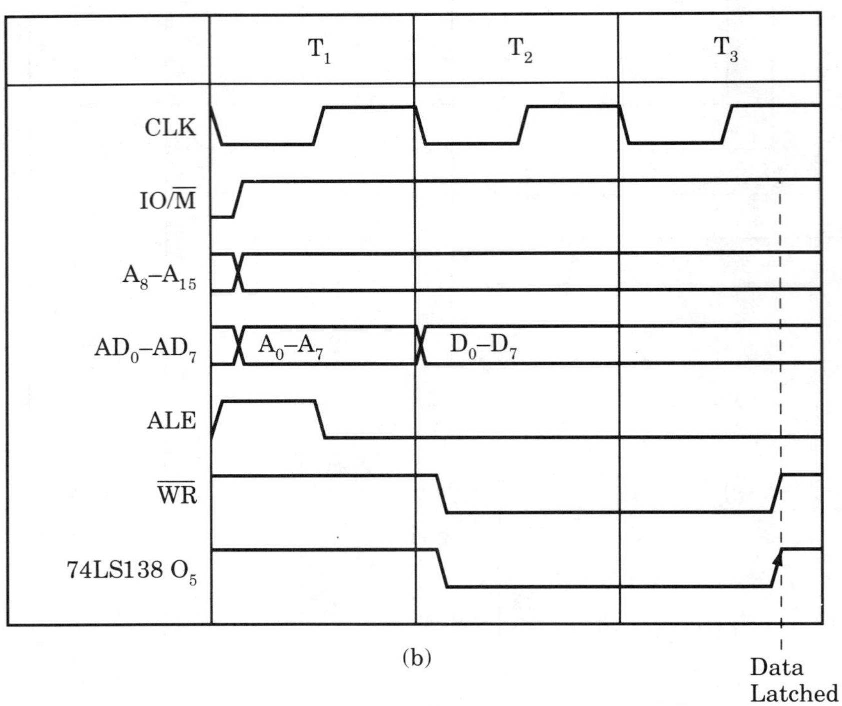

(b)

FIGURE 18.2
(a) I/O Read Timing, (b) I/O Write Timing
Source: Adapted from material copyrighted by Intel Corporation.

varies to change the average power applied to the lamps. Figure 18.4 shows the power control waveforms for 20% and 70% duty cycle operation.

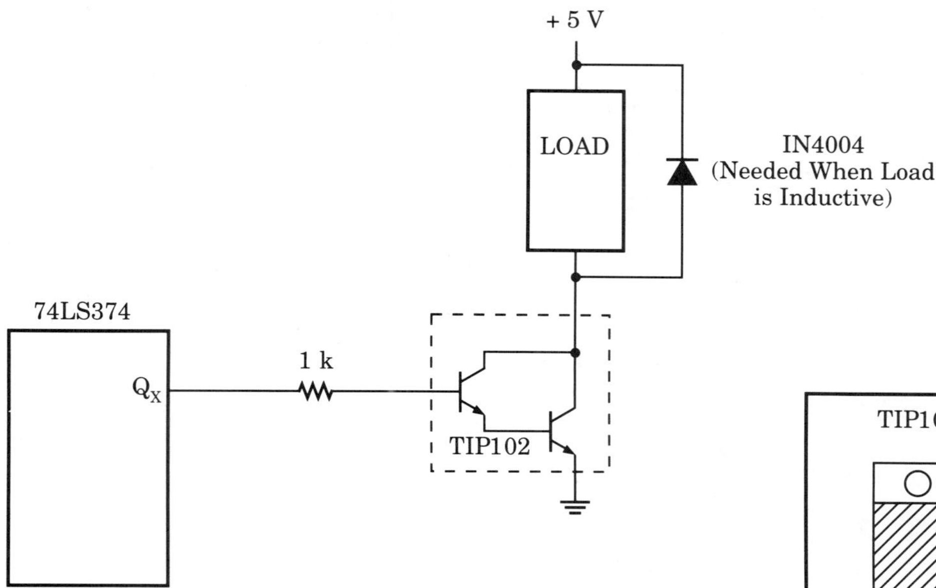

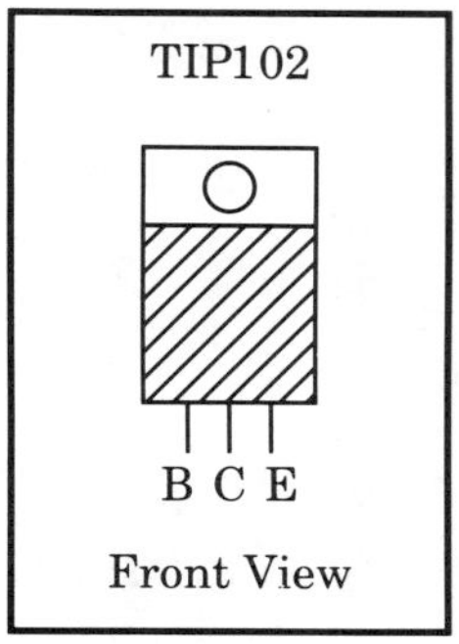

FIGURE 18.3
DC Load Driver Circuit

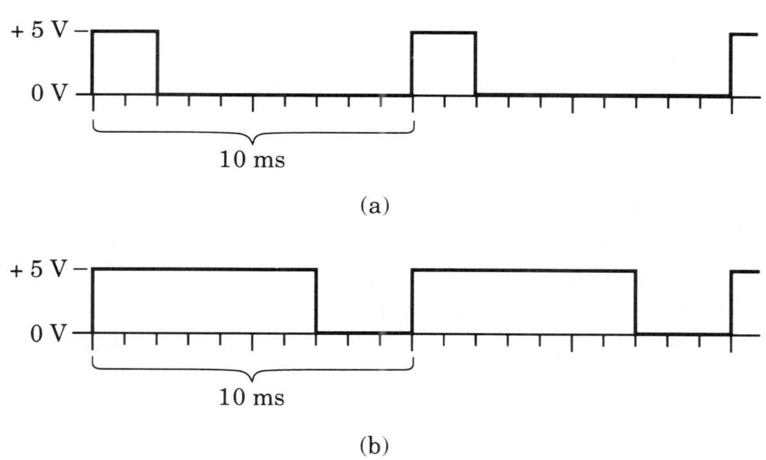

FIGURE 18.4
Pulse-Width Modulation Waveforms: (a) 20% Duty Cycle, (b) 70% Duty Cycle

Implement the lamp control system by connecting the DC load control circuit shown in Figure 18.3 to bit 0 of the output port. Use a #47 lamp for the load; the clamping diode is not needed for this application. Test the hardware using the program you wrote in step 3.

Write a program to pulse-width modulate the power applied to the indicator lamp. Control the duty cycle of the power source by applying a 4-bit BCD number to input port bits 0–3. The control number should produce the following results:

Input	*Results*
0000	Lamp is off.
0001	Lamp duty cycle is 10%.
0010	Lamp duty cycle is 20%.
0011	Lamp duty cycle is 30%.
0100	Lamp duty cycle is 40%.
0101	Lamp duty cycle is 50%.
0110	Lamp duty cycle is 60%.
0111	Lamp duty cycle is 70%.
1000	Lamp duty cycle is 80%.
1001	Lamp duty cycle is 90%.
≥1010	Lamp is constantly on.

The program should continually monitor the 4-bit input number and produce an output with the appropriate duty cycle. Test your program for each possible input case while monitoring the output port signal with an oscilloscope. Sketch the waveform you observe for each case.

Additional Activities

1. The address-decoding logic shown in Figure 18.1 is only partially decoded. Show the additional logic needed to fully decode the input port and output port addresses.
2. The windshield wiper control in a new automobile design contains a microprocessor to vary the speed of the wiper motor. A 4-bit binary code controls the speed in ten steps, ranging from off (0000) to fully on (1010). Simulate this control application by connecting a small DC motor as a load in the circuit shown in Figure 18.3. Connect a clamping diode across the motor to protect the TIP102 transistor.

Review Questions

1. What I/O activity selects the six unused outputs of the 74LS138 in Figure 18.1?
2. What advantage does I/O-mapped I/O (also known as direct I/O) have over memory-mapped I/O?
3. What is the purpose of the clamping diode in the circuit shown in Figure 18.3?
4. What voltage would be read by a DC averaging-type voltmeter connected to each signal in Figure 18.4?

EXPERIMENT 19

Stepper Motor Control

Objectives

Stepper motors are digitally controlled motors that transform digital signals into mechanical rotation. A microprocessor can control the speed and direction of a stepper motor digitally. After completing this experiment, you will be able to

- Construct interface hardware to control a stepper motor
- Use optocouplers to isolate current transients from the microcomputer system
- Control the speed and direction of a stepper motor using a microcomputer

Reference Reading

Stepper motor data sheet.

Materials Needed

8085 single-board computer
Breadboard
+15 V, 2 A power supply
7406 hex inverter (open collector)
Four 4N26 optocouplers
Four TIP102 NPN Darlington transistors
Four 1N4004 diodes
Two 10 Ω 10 W resistors
Four 470 Ω resistors
Four 10 kΩ resistors
Stepper motor, Superior Electric M061-FD302 or similar type

Discussion

Stepper Motor Characteristics

Stepper motors rotate in discrete steps, rather than continuously as ordinary motors do. Stepper motors divide each shaft rotation into a specific number of increments; typical stepper motors divide one rotation into 1.8-degree, 2-degree, or 5-degree steps. Motor movement is further divided into *half steps* to give even better control of the shaft position.

The stepper motor used in this experiment moves in 1.8-degree increments; in other words, 200 steps produce one complete shaft revolution. This motor can also operate in a half-step mode, in which there are 400 0.9-degree intervals per revolution.

Stepper motor windings are selectively energized and de-energized to produce the desired shaft response. The stepper motor used in this experiment contains four windings that are sequenced as shown in Table 19.1 to produce full steps. Note that the rotation direction is changed from clockwise to counterclockwise by reversing the sequence in which the windings are energized.

The stepper motor produces half steps using the sequence shown in Table 19.2. Half-stepping allows the motor shaft to be positioned with more resolution; also, it allows the motor to turn more rapidly.

The time needed for a stepper motor to move from one step to the next depends on the electromechanical characteristics of the motor. Typical stepper motors require between 3 and 30 ms to move from one step to the next. The Superior Electric MO61-FD302 stepper motor requires 4.2 ms for one step to be completed. Attempting to step at a faster rate results in "missed" steps and erratic operation.

TABLE 19.1
Stepper Motor Winding Sequence To Produce Full Steps

	Winding			
Step	*A*	*B*	*C*	*D*
1	On	Off	On	Off
2	On	Off	Off	On
3	Off	On	Off	On
4	Off	On	On	Off
1	On	Off	On	Off

CW ↓ ↑ CCW

TABLE 19.2
Stepper Motor Winding Sequence To Produce Half Steps

	Winding			
Step	*A*	*B*	*C*	*D*
1	On	Off	On	Off
2	On	Off	Off	Off
3	On	Off	Off	On
4	Off	Off	Off	On
5	Off	On	Off	On
6	Off	On	Off	Off
7	Off	On	On	Off
8	Off	Off	On	Off
1	On	Off	On	Off

CW ↓ ↑ CCW

Stepper Motor Control Hardware

A microcomputer can digitally control the current through the four stepper motor windings to define the motor speed and direction. Figure 19.1 shows a typical stepper motor driver circuit.

In this circuit, the four output port bits drive 7406 open collector inverters. Each inverter controls the input LED of a 4N26 optocoupler. When an inverter input is at a logic 1 state, the corresponding output is low and the optocoupler LED is turned on. The 4N26 LED turns on the phototransistor output stage, which in turn keeps the TIP102 base voltage below the value needed to turn on. Thus, the stepper motor winding is turned off.

A logic 0 on the input of the 7406 turns off the optocoupler LED and output transistor. The 10 kΩ pull-up resistor then supplies the base current needed to turn on the TIP102, and the motor winding is turned on. This design ensures that all stepper windings are off when the microcomputer is reset. Since the reset action defines all programmable ports on the microcomputer as inputs, the 7406 inputs float to the logic 1 state and keep the motor windings off.

The optocouplers isolate the high-current +15 V power supply from the +5 V power supply. This isolation prevents voltage spikes (caused by inductive load switching) that may be present on the +15 V power supply from being coupled to the digital logic circuit; the isolated supplies permit the digital logic circuitry to operate with higher reliability.

The two 10 Ω power resistors drop the supply voltage down to the 5.9 V needed by the motor windings; the resistors also improve the response of the motor by decreasing the L/R time constant of the motor winding. For other stepper motor types, compute the resistor size using the formula

$$R = \frac{V_{supply} - V_{winding} - V_{CE}}{I_{winding}}$$

where V_{supply} is the power supply voltage, $V_{winding}$ is the DC winding voltage, V_{CE} is the collector–to–emitter voltage at the required winding current, and $I_{winding}$ is the winding current. Using the MO61-FD302 and TIP102 specifications, the resistor value is computed as follows:

$$R = \frac{15\text{ V} - 5.9\text{ V} - 0.75\text{ V}}{0.88\text{ A}} = 9.5\ \Omega$$

Select a 10 Ω, 10 W resistor, which is the closest standard size.

Procedure

1. If your stepper motor comes equipped with a motor driver circuit board, connect the board to an output port on your microcomputer. Otherwise, construct the stepper motor circuit shown in Figure 19.1, and connect it to an output port.
2. Write an 8085 assembly language program to step the motor in a *clockwise* sequence using the logic shown in Figure 19.2. Use the full-step codes shown in Table 19.1. Test your program and note the results.
3. Modify your stepper motor control program to rotate the motor in the counter-clockwise direction.
4. Reduce the time delay between steps until the motor no longer starts reliably or turns smoothly. Calculate the exact step rate at that point.

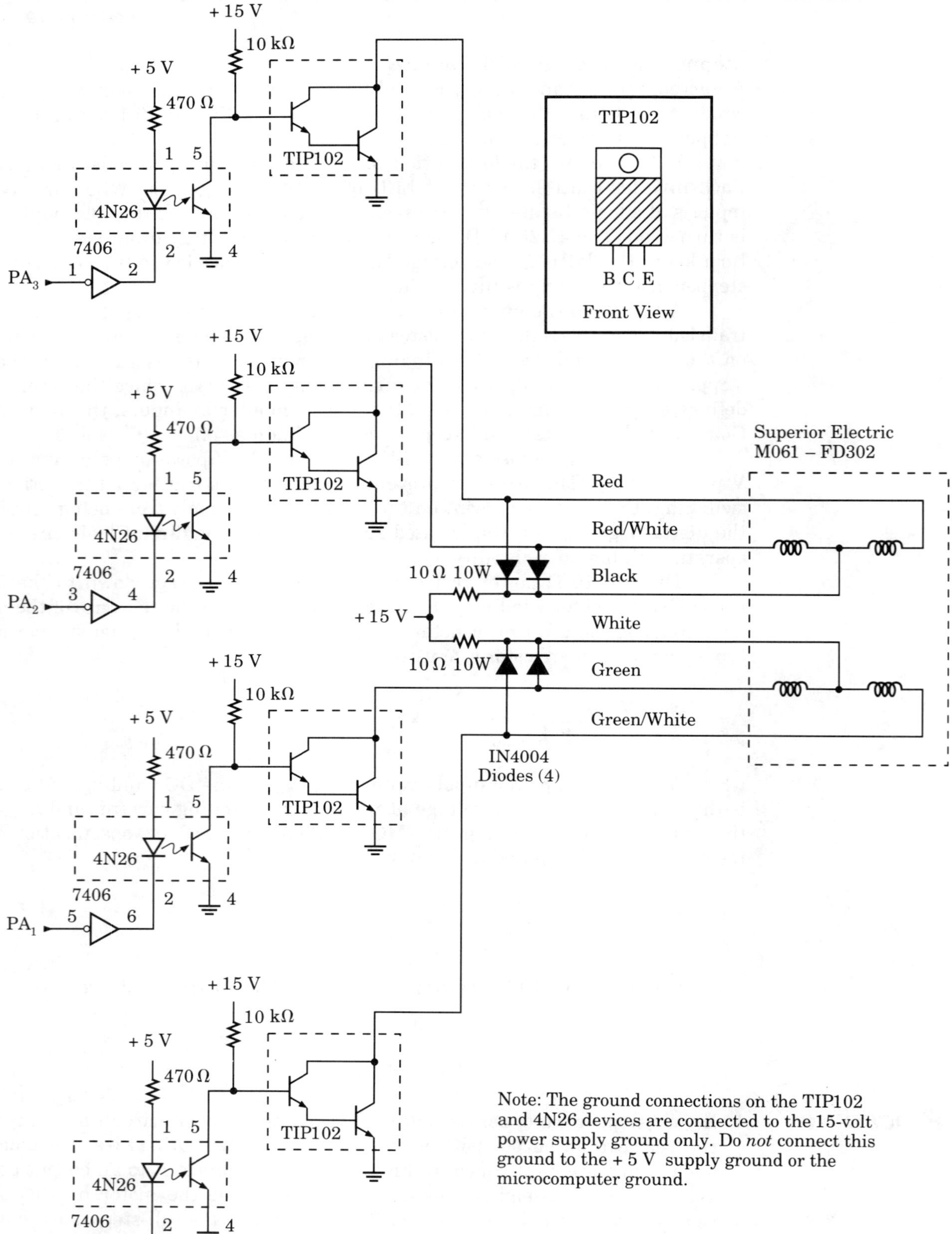

Note: The ground connections on the TIP102 and 4N26 devices are connected to the 15-volt power supply ground only. Do *not* connect this ground to the + 5 V supply ground or the microcomputer ground.

FIGURE 19.1
Stepper Motor Driver Circuit

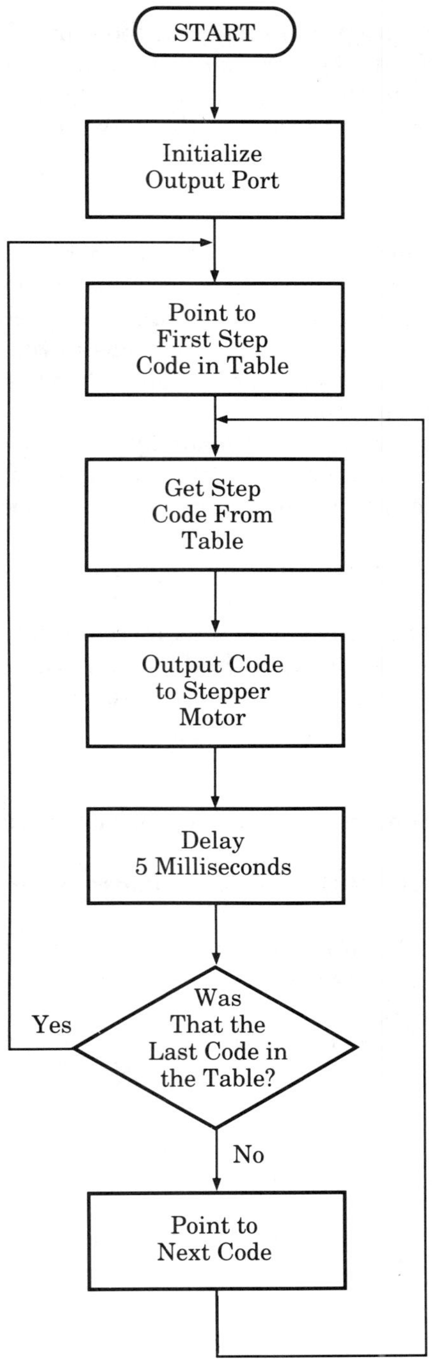

FIGURE 19.2
Flowchart for Full-Step Rotation

5. Repeat steps 2–4 for the half-step sequence in Table 19.2. Compare the half-step and full-step response characteristics.
6. A stepper motor in a chemical processing plant regulates a valve that controls the flow of a liquid into a storage tank. The stepper motor turns 20 counter-clockwise rotations to change the valve position from fully closed to fully open.

Write and test an 8085 program to regulate the liquid flow in the pipe. Your program should read a BCD number (00–20) from the microcomputer keyboard, then open or close the valve to that position. The program should ignore invalid input commands, such as a command to open the valve to position 21.

Additional Activities

1. Write a universal subroutine to rotate the stepper motor in either direction, at a specified speed, by a specific number of steps. Design the subroutine so that register B passes the direction code, with 00 indicating clockwise rotation and 01 indicating counterclockwise rotation. Register C passes the speed factor between 1 and 100, representing 1–100 steps per second. Register pair DE passes the number of motor steps to the subroutine.
2. Stepper motors turn large mechanical loads by rotating slowly at first, then increasing speed gradually. Similarly, an abrupt stop may be undesirable when stopping the load, so the stepper motor must reduce speed gradually before stopping.

   Write a program to start and stop the stepper motor gradually. Design the program to start the motor rotation when the 1 key is pressed on the keyboard. The motor rotation should begin slowly, then increase until it is a constant 200 steps per second. The program should stop the motor when the 0 key is pressed; the motor speed should diminish until the motor comes to a complete stop.

Review Questions

1. Explain the role of each component in the stepper motor drive circuit (see Figure 19.1).
2. What sequence of steps rotates the stepper motor counterclockwise in half-step increments?
3. A stepper motor interfaced to a microcomputer is not rotating as it should, but instead is only "humming." What is one likely reason for this problem?

EXPERIMENT 20

8085 Interrupts

Objectives

Peripheral devices use interrupts to request attention from the microprocessor. The 8085 contains several interrupt inputs that are suited for a variety of applications. After completing this experiment, you will be able to

- Use the 8085 INTR input and a priority encoder to handle multiple interrupts
- Use the RST6.5 interrupt input as a power failure detector

Reference Reading

Gaonkar, Ramesh S. *Microprocessor Architecture, Programming, and Applications with the 8085/8080A*. 2nd ed. Columbus, OH: Merrill, 1989. Sections 12.1–12.3.

The MCS-80/85 Family User's Manual. Santa Clara, CA: Intel Corp., 1986. Pages 2–3 to 2–5.

Materials Needed

8085 single-board computer
Breadboard with three debounced switches
Logic probe
Function generator (60 Hz square wave)
Two 74123 dual retriggerable monostable multivibrators
74LS148 priority encoder
74LS240 octal inverting buffer
Three 3.9 kΩ resistors
1.8 MΩ resistor
Three 0.01 μF capacitors
0.1 μF capacitor

Discussion

8085 Interrupt Structure

The 8085 includes five interrupt inputs; they are summarized here in decreasing order of priority:

TRAP: TRAP is a nonmaskable interrupt that must go from low to high and stay high to be recognized. It causes the program to branch to location 0024H.

RST7.5: The 8085 controls this maskable interrupt using the EI, DI, and SIM instructions described in the next section. This interrupt is triggered on the rising edge of an input signal; it remains latched until acknowledged. RST7.5 causes the program to branch to location 003CH.

RST6.5: This maskable interrupt is controllable by the EI, DI, and SIM instructions. When triggered by a high level, it causes the program to branch to location 0034H.

RST5.5: This maskable interrupt is controllable by the EI, DI, and SIM instructions. When triggered by a high level, it causes the program to branch to location 002CH.

INTR: This interrupt is controlled by the EI and DI instructions. When triggered by a high level on the INTR input pin, the $\overline{\text{INTA}}$ output from the 8085 controls external circuitry that places an RST instruction on the data bus.

8085 Interrupt Control Instructions

The following instructions control the interrupt logic in the 8085:

Instruction	*Description*
EI	Enables Interrupts.
DI	Disables Interrupts.
SIM	Set Interrupt Mask. Uses contents of the accumulator to define RST7.5, RST6.5, and RST5.5 mask conditions (Figure 20.1a).
RIM	Read Interrupt Mask. Loads the accumulator with the current status of the interrupt logic (Figure 20.1b).

SDK-85 Interrupt Configuration

The SDK-85 microcomputer uses several interrupts to control various machine processes. The remaining interrupts are available to the user. Table 20.1 describes each 8085 interrupt and its function on the SDK-85.

Since the interrupt vector addresses defined by the 8085 are located in the SDK-85 monitor ROM, an interrupt request causes the SDK-85 to jump to a ROM location where a JMP instruction is stored. This JMP instruction forces the program to go to a RAM location, where the user may place a JMP instruction to the appropriate interrupt service routine. The specific RAM addresses are given in Table 20.1.

Procedure

1. VECT INT Key (RST7.5) Demonstration

Enter the following program into the SDK-85. If you are using a different type of microcomputer, your instructor will supply the necessary program modifications.

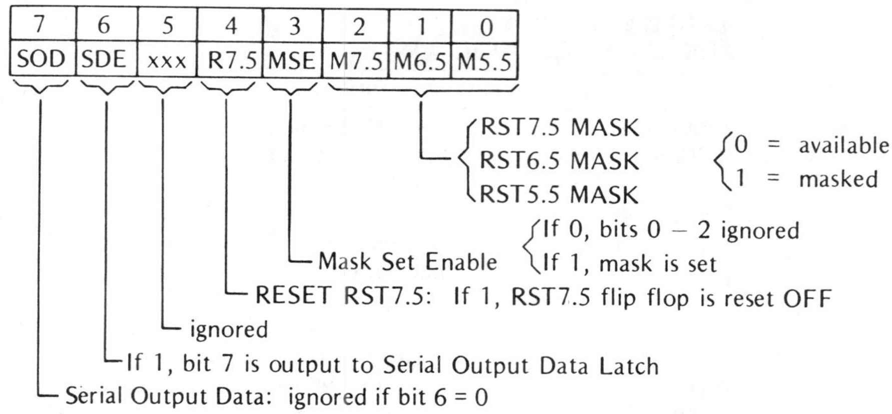

(a)

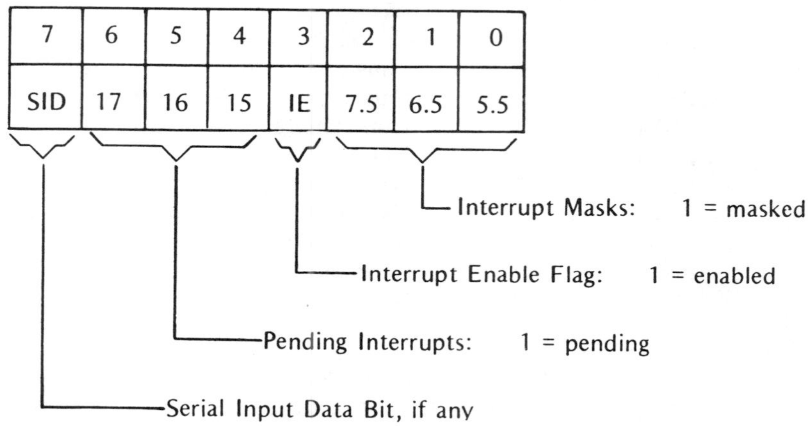

(b)

FIGURE 20.1
(a) Accumulator Bit Pattern Used by SIM, (b) Accumulator Bit Pattern After RIM
Source: Reprinted by permission of Intel Corporation, copyright 1979.

```
UPDAD  EQU 0363H         ;UPDAD SUBROUTINE ADDRESS
       ORG 2000H         ;MAIN PROGRAM
       LXI SP,20C2H      ;INITIALIZE STACK POINTER
       MVI A,00011011B   ;UNMASK RST7.5
       SIM
       LXI D,0000H       ;INITIAL DISPLAY VALUE
       EI                ;ENABLE INTERRUPTS
       JMP $             ;STAY HERE IN ENDLESS LOOP
       ORG 2050H         ;INTERRUPT SERVICE ROUTINE
       PUSH D            ;SAVE REGISTER PAIR D
       CALL UPDAD        ;DISPLAY REGISTER PAIR D
       POP D             ;RESTORE REGISTER PAIR D, THEN
       INX D             ; INCREMENT THAT VALUE
       EI                ;ENABLE INTERRUPTS FOR NEXT TIME
       RET
       ORG 20CEH         ;SDK-85 JMP INSTRUCTION TO SEND
       JMP 2050H         ; PROGRAM TO SERVICE ROUTINE
```

TABLE 20.1
SDK-85 Interrupt Details

8085 Interrupt	*Description*
TRAP	Used by the single-step feature.
RST7.5	Connected to VECT INTR key. Causes jump to 20CEH in user RAM.
RST6.5	Available to user on I/O connector J1-20. Causes jump to 20C8H in user RAM. NOTE: Jumper pins 3, 4, and 5 must be disconnected to use this interrupt input. When not using RST6.5, connect pins 3 and 4 if the SDK-85 has expansion buffers installed; otherwise, connect pins 3 and 5. These jumpers keep RST6.5 inactive when it is not used.
RST5.5	Used by 8279 keyboard/display controller IC.
INTR	Available to user on I/O connector J1-18. The INTA (interrupt acknowledge) signal is available on I/O connector J2-16. NOTE: Jumper pins 20 and 21 must be disconnected to use this interrupt input; connect the two pins at all other times to keep the INTR input low.
RST7	Causes jump to 20CBH in user RAM.
RST6	Causes jump to 20C5H in user RAM.
RST5	Causes jump to 20C2H in user RAM.
RST4	Not available.
RST3	Not available.
RST2	Not available.
RST1	"Warm start." Returns control to monitor program without modifying registers.
RST0	"Cold start." Same effect as pressing RESET key.

Execute the program and note the results when the VECT INTR key is pressed. You should see the address field of the display count each time the VECT INTR key is pressed. Since this key is not debounced, several counts may accumulate each time the key is pressed or released. Explain why this occurs.

2. Conditioning an RST6.5 Interrupt Signal

Connect the circuit shown in Figure 20.2. Disconnect the SDK-85 RST6.5 input signal jumper, as described in Table 20.1. If a debounced switch is not available on your breadboard, build a debounced switch circuit (see Figure 5.4).

The monostable multivibrator is configured to produce an 11 μs pulse when the debounced switch produces a rising edge. This pulse is wide enough to be recognized by the 8085, but it is not so wide that it will be recognized more than once. Test the circuit by monitoring the monostable multivibrator output with a logic probe as the switch is activated.

Modify the program given in step 1 to make it respond to the RST6.5 interrupt. Test the program by activating the debounced switch several times. The displayed count should increment once each time the switch is activated.

Remove the monostable multivibrator from the RST6.5 input. Connect the debounced switch directly to the RST6.5 pin. Execute the program again and note what happens. Explain your observations.

3. A Power Failure Detector

Computers often use interrupts to detect serious system problems. One common example is a backup power system that switches on automatically when power from the AC power line is interrupted. By monitoring the 60 Hz line frequency signal, the

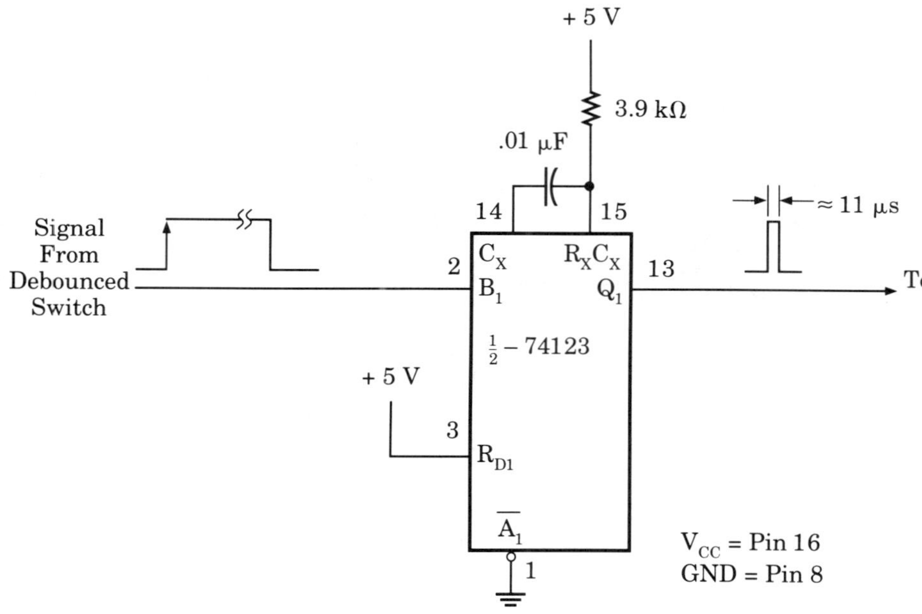

FIGURE 20.2
RST6.5 Signal Conditioning

computer can detect a power failure the instant it occurs and can respond by turning on a backup generator or battery pack.

The circuit in Figure 20.3 shows a very simple method of generating an interrupt when a 60 Hz signal stops.

The 74123 is a *retriggerable* monostable multivibrator, which means that the output pulse will be extended indefinitely so long as a trigger input occurs at time intervals less than the pulse width. With the values shown, the pulse width of the first monostable multivibrator is 50 ms, which is considerably longer than the 16.67 ms period of the 60 Hz input signal. The Q_1 output will remain high so long as the 60 Hz input is present.

If the 60 Hz input disappears and allows the Q_1 output to go low, the second monostable multivibrator triggers; this produces an 11 μs pulse that activates the RST6.5 interrupt.

Connect the hardware as shown in Figure 20.3. Produce the 60 Hz 0-to-+5 V signal with a function generator. Write a program to display a hexadecimal count sequence on the address field of the display. This count sequence should continue until the 60 Hz signal stops; the message FAIL should then appear on the display and stay there until the computer is reset.

4. Prioritized Interrupts Using the INTR Input

Figure 20.4 shows how three peripheral devices can independently interrupt the 8085 using the INTR interrupt input. When one or more of the three switches is activated, the 74LS148 priority encoder raises its E_0 output, causing the 8085 INTR line to go high. The 74LS148 also outputs a 3-bit code corresponding to the highest priority input that is active. In response to the INTR signal, the $\overline{\text{INTA}}$ output of the 8085 goes low; this action turns on the 74LS240, which puts the opcode for the appropriate RST instruction on the data bus.

Construct this circuit, and check the wiring carefully before proceeding. Remember to remove the SDK-85 INTR jumper (See Table 20.1). NOTE: Since the

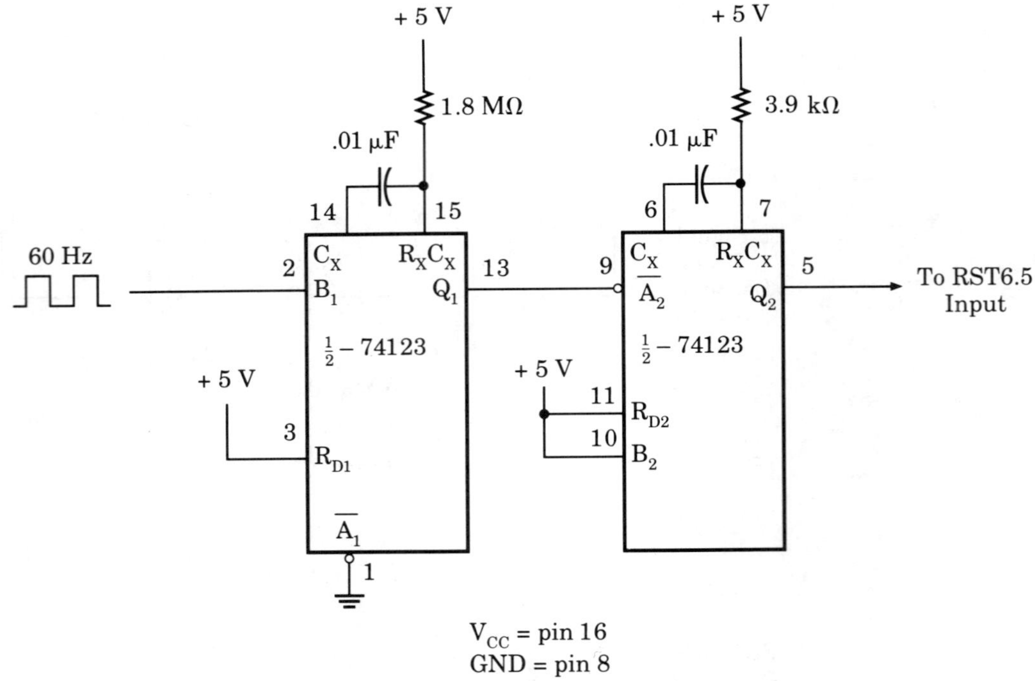

FIGURE 20.3
Power Failure Detection Circuit

SDK-85 allows the user to utilize only the RST5, RST6, and RST7 interrupts, the circuit is limited to only three input signals.

Write an 8085 program to use the three interrupt inputs as the control lines of an up/down counter. The counter should increment when switch 7 is activated, and it should decrement when switch 6 is pressed. Switch 5 should clear the count to zero. The display should initially show the count 0000. Design the program to continually wait in a loop for the next interrupt.

Additional Activities

1. The oil in an industrial engine is changed once every 100 hours of operation. The elapsed time is determined by a digital clock circuit that outputs a single 10 μs pulse each hour. Design an interrupt-driven system to count these pulses and produce the message OIL on the display after 100 pulses occur.
2. Design a digital frequency counter by connecting a 1 Hz pulse to one interrupt input, and the unknown frequency to a second interrupt input. Show the frequency of the unknown signal on the single-board computer display. Compare the performance of your system with a "real" frequency counter.

Review Questions

1. Why must the RST5.5 and RST6.5 interrupt inputs be short pulses? How does RST7.5 differ in this respect?
2. In Figure 20.4, what hexadecimal opcode is placed on the data bus when the inputs $\overline{I_5}$ and $\overline{I_6}$ are simultaneously active?
3. What pulse width must be produced by the first retriggerable monostable multivibrator in Figure 20.3 if the circuit is to detect when a signal frequency has dropped below 20 Hz?

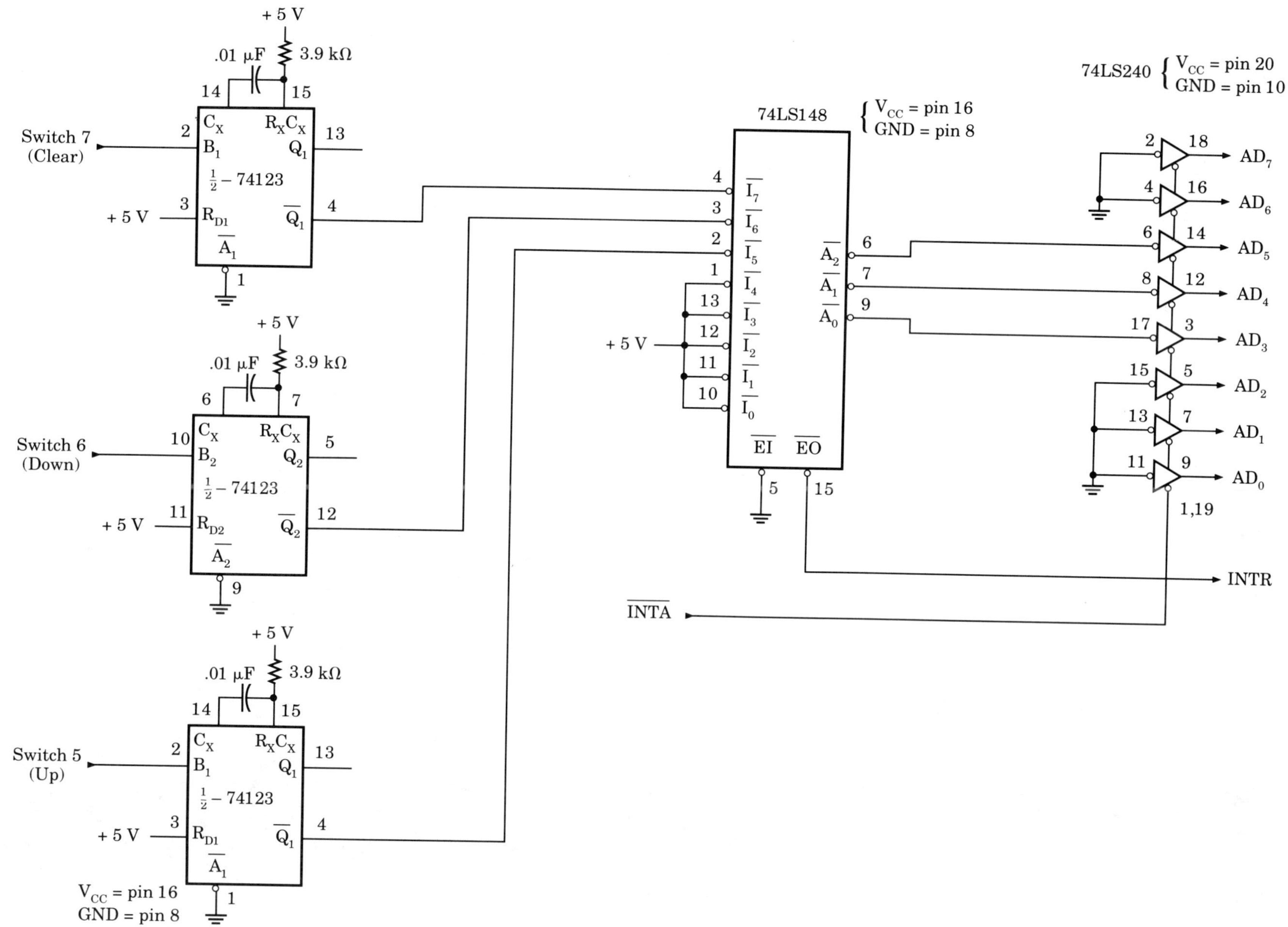

FIGURE 20.4
Prioritized Interrupt Circuit

EXPERIMENT 21

The 8255A Programmable Peripheral Interface

Objectives

The Intel 8255A programmable peripheral interface device interfaces easily to the 8085 microprocessor. It can control a variety of peripheral devices using 24 I/O lines and versatile operating modes. After completing this experiment, you will be able to

- Interface an 8255A to an 8085-based microcomputer
- Use the 8255A in the simple I/O mode
- Use the 8255A bit set/reset (BSR) mode for bit manipulation
- Use the 8255A in the interrupt-driven strobed input mode

Reference Reading

Gaonkar, Ramesh S. *Microprocessor Architecture, Programming, and Applications with the 8085/8080A*. 2nd ed. Columbus, OH: Merrill, 1989. Section 15.1.

Materials Needed

8085 single-board computer
Breadboard with logic switches, LED indicators, and one debounced switch
8255A-5 programmable peripheral interface
74LS138 3-to-8 decoder

Discussion

8255A Control Word

The 8255A is a general-purpose, parallel I/O device that is programmable for simple I/O, interrupt I/O, handshaking, or bidirectional data transfer. These modes are defined by an 8 bit control word, shown in Figure 21.1.

The 8255A has 24 I/O lines, grouped as three 8-bit ports. Ports A and B are configured independently as input or output ports. Port C is divided into two 4-bit groups; each group can be configured as an input port, an output port, or handshake signals. The following sections describe several of the 8255A operating modes.

Mode 0: Simple I/O

Mode 0 defines ports A, B, and C as simple input or output ports. No handshake or interrupt capabilities are provided. The following program segment demonstrates mode 0 operation. Notice how the EQU directives define the address of the 8255A.

```
PORTA    EQU 80H          ;8255 "BASE" ADDRESS. PORT A ADDRESS
PORTB    EQU PORTA+1      ;PORT B ADDRESS
PORTC    EQU PORTA+2      ;PORT C ADDRESS
CONTROL  EQU PORTA+3      ;CONTROL REGISTER ADDRESS
         ORG 2000H
         MVI A,10010001B  ;I/O MODE 0, PORT A IS INPUT PORT, PORT B IS
                          ; OUTPUT PORT, PORT C (UPPER) IS OUTPUT PORT,
                          ; PORT C (LOWER) IS INPUT PORT
         OUT CONTROL      ;SEND CONTROL WORD TO 8255A
         IN PORTA         ;READ PORT A BITS, THEN
         OUT PORTB        ; OUTPUT THEM TO PORT B
```

Bit Set/Reset (BSR) Mode

Bit 7 of the 8255A control word selects either the I/O mode or the bit set/reset (BSR) mode. Use the BSR mode to set or reset individual bits on port C. Figure 21.2 shows the control word format for the BSR mode.

The following program configures ports A, B, and the upper half of port C as input ports. The lower half of port C is defined as an output port. The program demonstrates manipulation of the lower port C bits using the BSR mode.

```
PORTA    EQU 80H          ;8255'S "BASE" ADDRESS. PORT A ADDRESS
PORTB    EQU PORTA+1      ;PORT B ADDRESS
PORTC    EQU PORTA+2      ;PORT C ADDRESS
CONTROL  EQU PORTA+3      ;CONTROL REGISTER ADDRESS
         ORG 2000H
         MVI A,10011010B  ;I/O MODE 0, PORT A, B, AND PORT C (UPPER)
                          ; ARE INPUT PORTS. PORT C (LOWER) IS
                          ; OUTPUT PORT
         OUT CONTROL      ;SEND CONTROL WORD TO 8255A
         MVI A,00000101B  ;SET PORT C BIT 2
         OUT CONTROL
         MVI A,00000110B  ;RESET PORT C BIT 3
         OUT CONTROL
```

Mode 1: I/O with Handshaking

In mode 1, ports A and B are used for parallel I/O; port C bits are handshake signals. Mode 1 also provides interrupt generation logic to allow the 8255A to be used for interrupt-driven data transfers. While mode 1 is usable in both strobed input or strobed output applications, only the strobed input mode is discussed in this experiment.

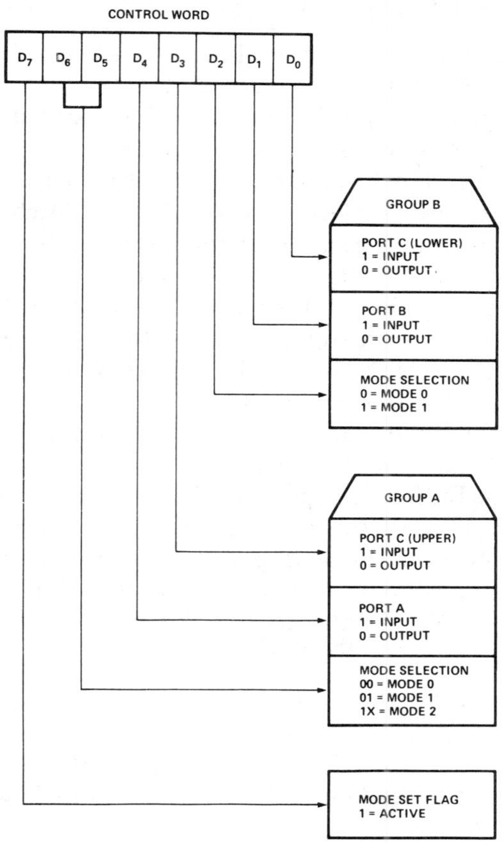

FIGURE 21.1
8255A I/O Mode Control Word
Source: Reprinted by permission of Intel Corporation, copyright 1981.

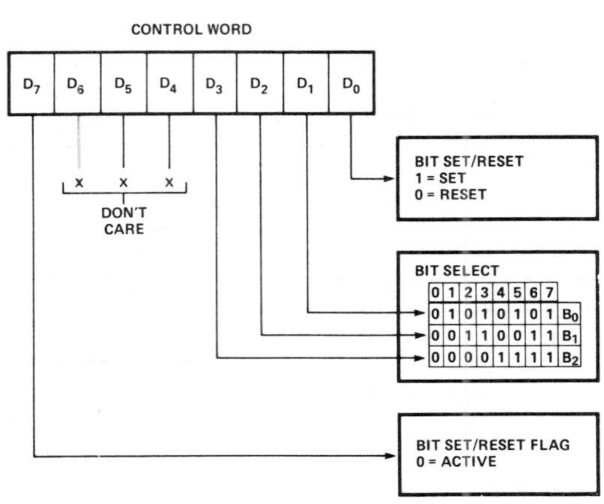

FIGURE 21.2
8255A BSR Mode Control Word
Source: Reprinted by permission of Intel Corporation, copyright 1981.

For strobed input operation, port C pins are defined as follows:

PC_7: Used as input or output bit (not handshake signal). Direction is defined by bit 3 of control word (see Figure 21.1).
PC_6: Used as input or output bit (not handshake signal). Direction is defined by bit 3 of control word (see Figure 21.1).
PC_5: IBF_A (Input Buffer Full, port A). Output from the 8255A indicates that a data byte has been strobed into port A input latch.
PC_4: STB_A (Strobe Input, port A). Active-low input to the 8255A that strobes data on port A into the port A input latch.
PC_3: $INTR_A$ (Interrupt Request, port A). Output from the 8255A goes high if STB and IBF signals are high, and the internal $INTE_A$ (Interrupt Enable) flip-flop is set. NOTE: the $INTE_A$ flip-flop is controlled by setting or resetting PC_4 using the BSR mode.
PC_2: STB_B (Strobe Input, port B). Active-low input to the 8255A that strobes data on port B into port B input latch.
PC_1: IBF_B (Input Buffer Full, port B). Output from the 8255A indicates that a data byte has been strobed into port B input latch.
PC_0: $INTR_B$ (Interrupt Request, port B). Output from 8255A goes high if STB_B and IBF_B signals are high, and the $INTE_B$ (Interrupt Enable) flip-flop is set. NOTE: the $INTE_B$ flip-flop is controlled by setting or resetting PC_2 using the BSR mode.

Figure 21.3 illustrates the timing waveforms for mode 1 operation.

For strobed input operation, mode 1 status information is obtained by reading port C. The status bits are used when controlling the 8255A in a polled I/O application. The status bits read on port C are defined as follows:

PC_7: I/O bit
PC_6: I/O bit
PC_5: IBF_A (Interrupt Buffer Full, port A)
PC_4: $INTE_4$ (Interrupt Enable flag, port A)
PC_3: $INTR_A$ (Interrupt Request, port A)
PC_2: $INTE_B$ (Interrupt Enable flag, port B)
PC_1: IBF_B (Interrupt Buffer Full, port B)
PC_0: $INTR_B$ (Interrupt Request, port B)

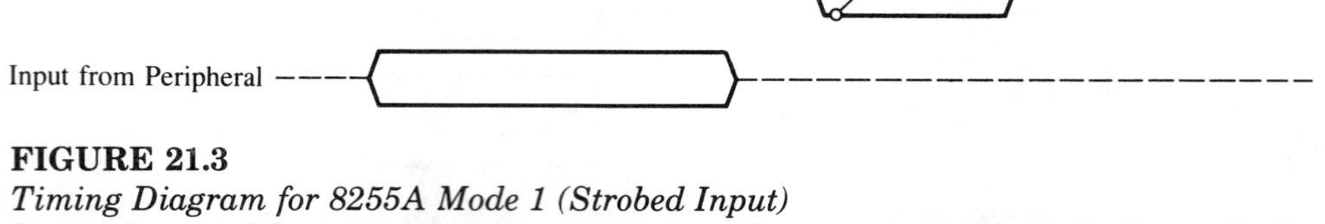

FIGURE 21.3
Timing Diagram for 8255A Mode 1 (Strobed Input)
Source: Reprinted from *Microprocessor Architecture, Programming, and Applications with the 8085/8080A*, Second Edition by Ramesh Gaonkar. Copyright 1989 by Merrill Publishing Company. Courtesy of Merrill Publishing Company. Adapted from material copyrighted by Intel Corporation.

The following sample program configures port A as an input port operating in mode 1, and port B as an output port in mode 0. Port C bits PC_7 and PC_6 are configured as inputs. The program sets $INTE_A$ and enables the 8085 interrupt logic. The interrupt service routine and masking steps are not shown.

```
PORTA    EQU 80H          ;8255'S "BASE" ADDRESS. PORT A ADDRESS
PORTB    EQU PORTA+1      ;PORT B ADDRESS
PORTC    EQU PORTA+2      ;PORT C ADDRESS
CONTROL  EQU PORTA+3      ;CONTROL REGISTER ADDRESS
         ORG 2000H
         MVI A,10111000B  ;I/O MODE, PORT A IS STROBED INPUT PORT,
                          ; PORT B IS SIMPLE OUTPUT PORT, PORT C
                          ; BITS 6 AND 7 ARE INPUT BITS
         OUT CONTROL      ;SEND CONTROL WORD TO 8255A
         MVI A,00001001B  ;SET PC4 (INTEA)
         OUT CONTROL      ;SEND BSR CONTROL WORD TO 8255A
         EI               ;ENABLE 8085 INTERRUPTS, THEN
                          ; WAIT FOR INPUT TO BE STROBED
```

Mode 2: Bidirectional I/O

Mode 2 uses port A as a bidirectional port, with port C providing handshake signals. This mode is particularly useful when interfacing two computers to each other, allowing the computers to communicate with each other through parallel data transfers.

Procedure

1. Mode 0 I/O Demonstration

Connect the 8255A to your microcomputer as shown in Figure 21.4. Connect port A to eight logic switches and port C to eight LED indicators. Remember to connect a ground wire between your microcomputer and the breadboard.

Write a program to initialize the 8255A with ports A and B configured as mode 0 input ports and with both halves of port C configured as outputs. The program should read the logic switches on port A and output these bits to port C.

Execute the program and note the results displayed on the LEDs as you change the position of the logic switches. Each switch on port A should control the corresponding LED on port C.

2. BSR Mode Application

Use the 8255A BSR mode to simulate a 74LS138 3-to-8 decoder integrated circuit. Use the three least significant bits of port A as the 3-bit binary selection input of the decoder. Use port C as the eight decoder output lines. Remember that the 74LS138 decoder has active-low outputs. For example, if the binary selection input of the decoder is 011, then output bit 3 is low, while the other seven outputs are high.

3. Mode 1 Strobed Input Application

Keep the eight port A lines connected to the eight logic switches, but remove all connections to port C. Connect PC_4 to the *active-low* output of a debounced switch on your breadboard; this signal is the STB_A input to 8255A. Connect PC_3 to the RST6.5 interrupt input on your microcomputer; this signal is the $INTR_A$ output from the 8255A that will interrupt the 8085 microprocessor.

Write an interrupt-driven program that will continually read and display the eight logic switch bits under the control of the debounced switch. Each time the

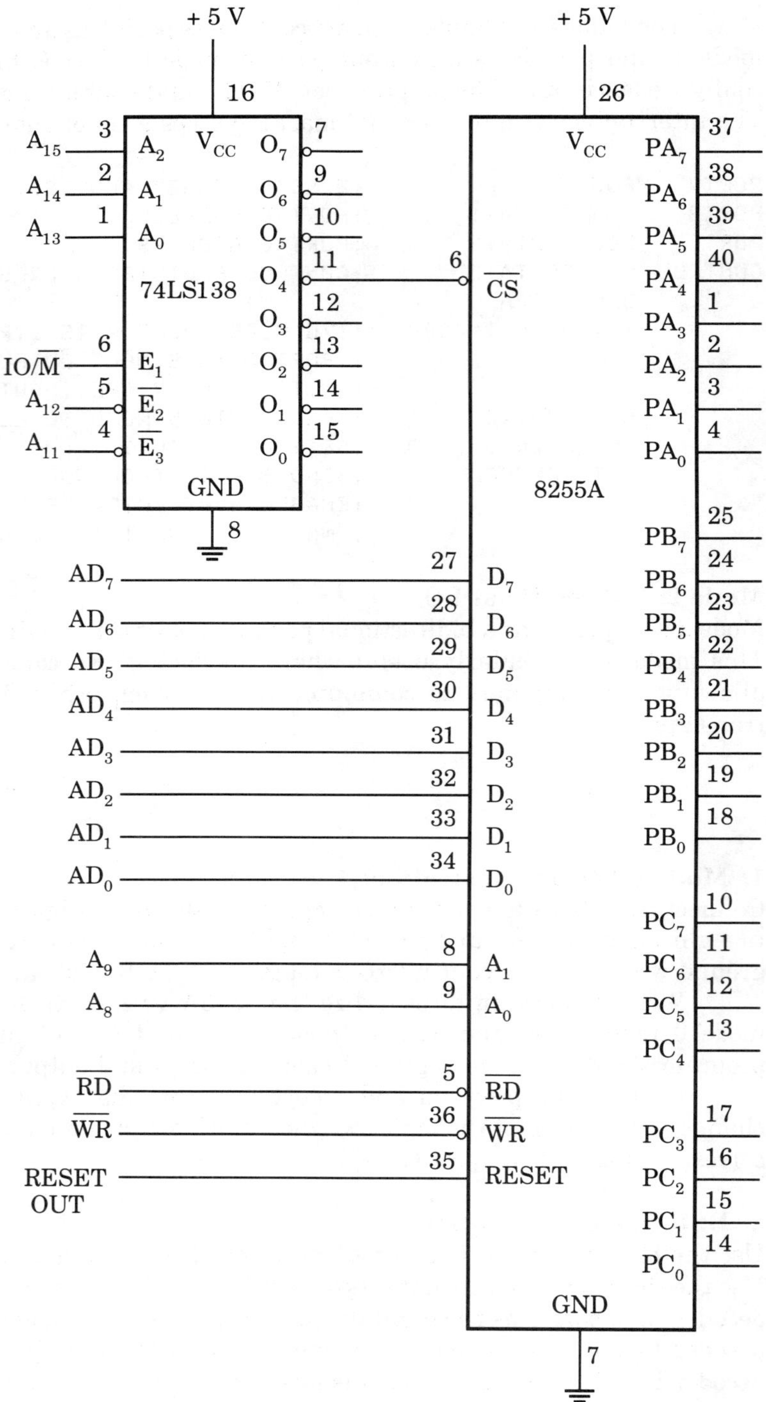

FIGURE 21.4
8255A Interfaced to 8085 Signals

debounced switch is activated, the switch data should be read, then output to the LED display on the microcomputer.

Additional Activities

1. Use the 8255A BSR mode to produce a 100 Hz, 20% duty cycle rectangular waveform on PC_2.
2. A microcomputer reads an 8-bit binary value from a transducer once each second and stores the data in an array in memory. Implement this data-recording system using the 8255A strobed input mode. Use a 1 Hz square wave to strobe the data into the 8255A input latch. Limit your program so that it reads and stores data for 30 s, then stops.

Review Questions

1. Compare the features of the 8255A with those of the 8355 and 8155 devices. What are some of the advantages and disadvantages of each device?
2. What 8255A control word is needed to set bit PC_6?
3. What 8255A control word is needed to configure port A as a simple output port, port B as a strobed input port, and port C bits 6 and 7 as inputs?
4. Show how to change the address decoding in Figure 21.4 so that the 8255A is accessible at addresses B0H–B3H.

EXPERIMENT 22

Computer-to-Computer Data Transfer

Objectives

Two computers can exchange data using parallel data ports and handshaking. Parallel data transfer techniques are inherently faster than serial methods and are ideal for transferring information from one computer to another. Parallel data transfer techniques are also used to interface computers to printers, disk drives, and other peripheral devices. After completing this experiment, you will be able to

- Interface a personal computer to an 8085-based single-board computer
- Transfer data in Intel HEX file format from a personal computer to the memory of an 8085 single-board computer

Reference Reading

Gaonkar, Ramesh S. *Microprocessor Architecture, Programming, and Applications with the 8085/8080A*. 2nd ed. Columbus, OH: Merrill, 1989. Section 14.2.

The MCS-80/85 Family User's Manual. Santa Clara, CA: Intel Corp., 1986. Pages 6–26 to 6–37.

Materials Needed

8085 single-board computer
Personal computer with parallel printer port
Cable to connect personal computer to 8085 single-board computer (see Figure 22.1a)

Discussion

If you use a personal computer (PC) to cross-assemble your 8085 programs, you already have the hardware needed to download machine language program files from the PC to your 8085-based single-board microcomputer. The PC can output the data file generated by your cross assembler program to a parallel printer port; the 8255A or 8155 programmable I/O device on your single-board computer can receive and store this information. The following sections describe the hardware and the data file format needed to complete this interface.

Parallel Data Transfer Hardware

Personal computers transfer data to parallel printers in 8-bit parallel form using handshaking signals to control the flow of data. The data sent by the PC can be received by an 8255A or 8155 configured in the strobed input mode. The 8255A strobed input mode was described in Experiment 21; the 8155 can be configured for strobed input operation in a similar manner. The 8155 strobed input handshaking waveform is identical to that of the 8255A, as was shown in Figure 21.3. When operated in ALT 3 mode (refer to Figure 11.1b), the handshake pin assignments for port A of the 8155 are as follows:

PC_0: Port A INTR (Interrupt)
PC_1: Port A BF (Buffer Full)
PC_2: Port A $\overline{STB}$ (Strobe)

Figure 22.1a shows the signal connections needed to interface the standard parallel printer port on a personal computer to an 8155. The PAPER END, $\overline{\text{ACKNOWL}}$, SELECT, and $\overline{\text{ERROR}}$ signals are normally controlled by the printer. In this application, however, these signals are not used; instead, we deactivate them by tying them to appropriate logic levels.

Figure 22.1b illustrates the handshaking signal action that controls data transfers between the parallel printer port on the PC and the 8155. Note that the INTR signal indicates that a byte has been strobed into the 8155 input latch. This signal can serve as an interrupt input to the 8085; it can also be tested by polling bit 0 of the 8155 status register (see Figure 11.1c).

Intel HEX File Format

Personal computers use the Intel HEX file format to exchange data with EPROM programmers, emulators, and other peripheral devices. Each information record consists of ASCII characters representing the record length, memory load address, data, and checksum. Here is a byte-by-byte description of the Intel HEX file format:*

Byte 1: Record mark. The ASCII colon (:) character signals the start of each record.

Byte 2: Record length. Two ASCII characters representing a hexadecimal number (00H–10H) describe the number of data bytes in the record. Notice that this is *not* the number of hexadecimal digits in the record. Up to 16 data bytes may appear in one record. A record length of 00H indicates the End-of-File (EOF) condition.

Bytes 4–7: Load address. These four ASCII characters represent the hexadecimal memory address where the data in that record are to be stored. The

*Adapted from material copyrighted by Intel Corporation.

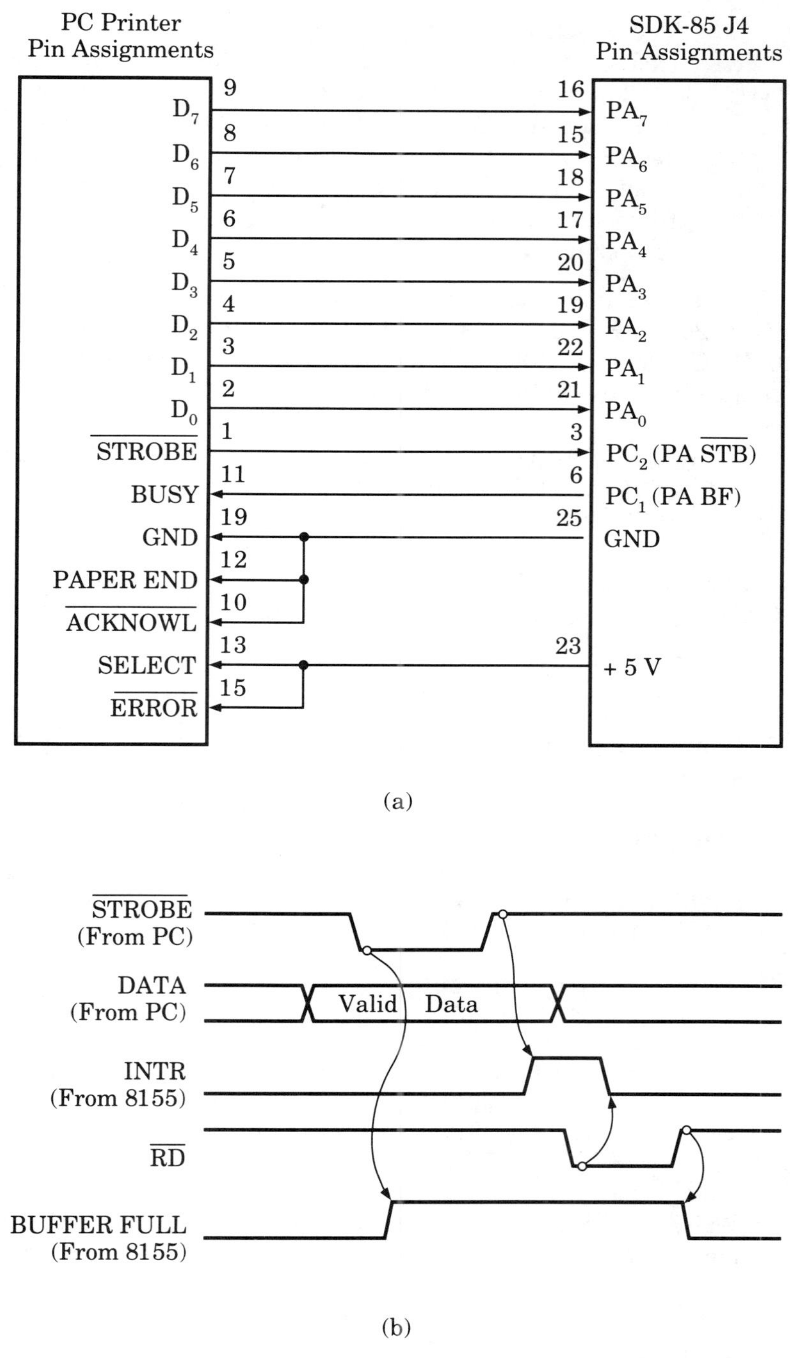

FIGURE 22.1
(a) Parallel Printer Port Interface to 8155, (b) Handshaking Signal Timing

first data byte is stored in the location referenced by the load address; the remaining data bytes are placed in subsequent locations.

Bytes 8 and 9: Record type. These two ASCII characters are always 00 except for the EOF record; the EOF record type is 01.

Bytes 10 to 10 + 2 × (record length) − 1: Data. Each 8-bit data byte is represented by two ASCII characters (0–9, A–F). These two characters form hexadecimal values 00H–FFH.

Bytes 10 + 2 × (record length) to 10 + 2 × (record length) + 1: Checksum.

The checksum is the negative of the sum of all bytes in the record, excluding the colon, evaluated modulus-256. When receiving a record, add all 2-digit bytes in the record while ignoring carries out of the 8-bit sum. Next, add the 2-digit checksum byte; the result should equal zero.

Bytes 12 + 2 × (record length) to 12 + 2 × (record length) + 1: Carriage return and line feed. These two ASCII characters follow each record in the file. The ASCII code for the carriage return is 0DH; the code for the line feed character is 0AH.

For example, if memory locations 2000H–2015H contained the bytes 31H, C2H, 20H, 3EH, 04H, D3H, 20H, CDH, 3DH, 20H, FEH, 3AH, C2H, 20H, 0EH, 00H, CDH, 47H, 20H, B7H, CAH, and 34H, then a printout of the HEX file containing these values would look like this:

```
:1020000031C2203E04D320CD3D20FE3AC2200E0036
:06201000CD4720B7CA34E1
:00000001FF
```

Note that the first record contains 16 data bytes, the second record contains 6 data bytes, and the third record is an End-of-File indicator.

Procedure

1. Connect a personal computer to the 8155 on your single-board computer, as shown in Figure 22.1a.
2. Create an Intel HEX file representation of the following program using your cross assembler:

```
RDKBD  EQU 02E7H        ;KEYBOARD SUBROUTINE ADDRESS
UPDDT  EQU 036EH        ;DISPLAY UPDATE SUBROUTINE ADDRESS
       ORG 2080H
       LXI SP,20C2H
       MVI A,08H        ;UNMASK KEYBOARD INTERRUPT
       SIM
LOOP:  CALL RDKBD       ;READ CHARACTER FROM KEYBOARD
       MVI B,00H        ;TURN OFF DOT
       CALL UPDDT       ;THEN DISPLAY IT
       JMP LOOP         ;REPEAT FOREVER
```

3. Write an 8085 subroutine to initialize the 8155 as a strobed input port suitable for interfacing to a personal computer. Use a polling technique to monitor the 8155 INTR flag.
4. Write an 8085 subroutine that polls the INTR status flag, then reads one byte from strobed input port A and returns the byte in the accumulator. Test the subroutine by calling it from a main program; next, on a PC using the MS-DOS operating system, type the command

   COPY filename.HEX PRN

   to copy the HEX file to the printer port. The 8155 should accept the first character in the file, the colon (:) character. Verify this by examining the contents of the accumulator.
5. Design an 8085 program to receive a complete HEX file from the personal computer. The program should store all received data bytes in the appropriate "load addresses" in memory. Draw a flowchart before writing any program code

to ensure that all bytes in the file are processed properly. Test your program by transferring the HEX file created in step 2, then examining memory locations starting at 2080H. Finally, execute the test program.

Additional Activities

1. Interface two single-board computers to allow two-way data communications. Use the 8155 or 8255A port A on one machine to communicate with port A on the other; connect port B on each machine in a similar manner. Design software to allow characters entered on the keyboard of one computer to be output to the display LEDs on the other.
2. Write a BASIC program to generate an Intel HEX file. The program should then output the file contents to the single-board computer using the parallel printer port. Use your 8085 HEX file "receiver" program to receive and store these data in the proper memory locations in the single-board computer.

   Add logic to your receiver program to allow the downloaded program bytes to be executed when the command characters Eaaaa are received from the PC, where aaaa is the 4-digit hexadecimal starting address of the program. For example, E2080 would execute a program beginning at memory location 2080H.

Review Questions

1. What HEX file records would be used to represent the 7-byte HEX data file containing the values F2H, 27H, B2H, 09H, 72H, 4FH, and E3H? Assume that the first data byte is stored in location 2050H.
2. What types of data errors would a simple checksum scheme *not* detect? Give examples.

EXPERIMENT 23

The 8253 Programmable Interval Timer

Objectives

The Intel 8253 programmable interval timer can generate precision time delays and count input pulses; it does these tasks with a minimum of software overhead. After completing this experiment, you will be able to

- Interface an 8253 programmable interval timer to an 8085-based single-board computer
- Program the 8253 as a precision timer
- Program the 8253 as an event counter

Reference Reading

Gaonkar, Ramesh S. *Microprocessor Architecture, Programming, and Applications with the 8085/8080A*. 2nd ed. Columbus, OH: Merrill, 1989. Section 15.4.

Materials Needed

8085 single-board computer
Breadboard with one debounced logic switch
Oscilloscope
Frequency counter
8253-5 programmable interval timer
74LS74 dual D-type flip-flop
74LS138 3-to-8 decoder

Discussion

The 8253 contains three 16-bit counters, each of which includes a clock input line, a gate control input signal, and an output line. The three counter stages can be independently programmed in one of six modes, as shown in Figure 23.1.

In this experiment, only mode 0 (interrupt on terminal count) and mode 3 (square-wave generator) are used. These two modes are summarized as follows:

Mode 0: Interrupt on Terminal Count. A 16-bit binary or BCD count value is loaded into a counter stage when the first pulse is applied to the clock input line. The counter output line goes low when that first pulse occurs. Each successive input pulse decrements the count value by 1 until the counter reaches zero; at that time, the output line goes high and remains high until the counter is reloaded by the program.

Mode 3: Square-Wave Generator. The output line produces a square wave

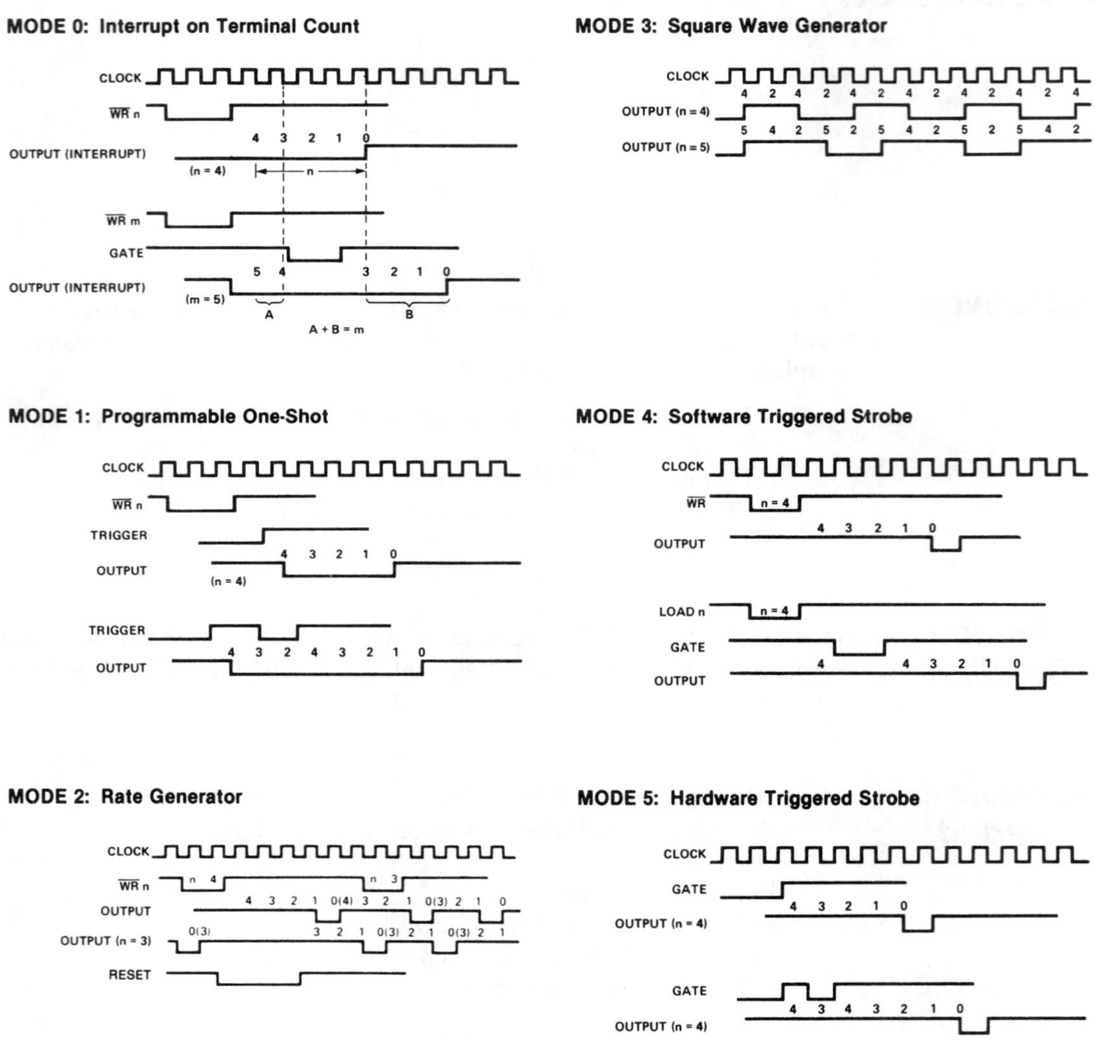

FIGURE 23.1
8253 Timing Diagrams
Source: Reprinted by permission of Intel Corporation, copyright 1981.

with a period equal to the counter value times the period of the input clock signal. As shown in Figure 23.1, if the count value is an even number, the output waveform is symmetrical. If the count value is an odd number, the output waveform is high for one clock period more than it is low.

The three counter stages are configured by a single 8-bit control word, shown in Figure 23.2.

Bits 7 and 6 select the desired counter stage; bits 4, 3, and 2 select the operating mode; and bit 0 selects binary or BCD counting. Bits 5 and 4 control the sequence used to load a value into a counter or to read a value from a counter. Bits 5 and 4 also allow the count value to be latched so that it may be read without the possibility of the count changing during the reading process. When these two bits are loaded with 00, the contents of the counter are latched and may be retrieved by simply reading from the appropriate counter address.

Procedure

1. Square-Wave Generation

Connect the circuit shown in Figure 23.3 to your single-board microcomputer. Determine the address range in which the 8253-5 will be selected.

Since the 8253-5 maximum clock rate is 2.6 MHz, the 74LS74 D flip-flop is needed to reduce the CLK signal frequency to an acceptable value. Connect the 1.536 MHz signal to the CLK_0 input line. Tie the $GATE_0$ input line high to enable counting. Attach the OUT_0 line to the inputs of your oscilloscope and frequency counter.

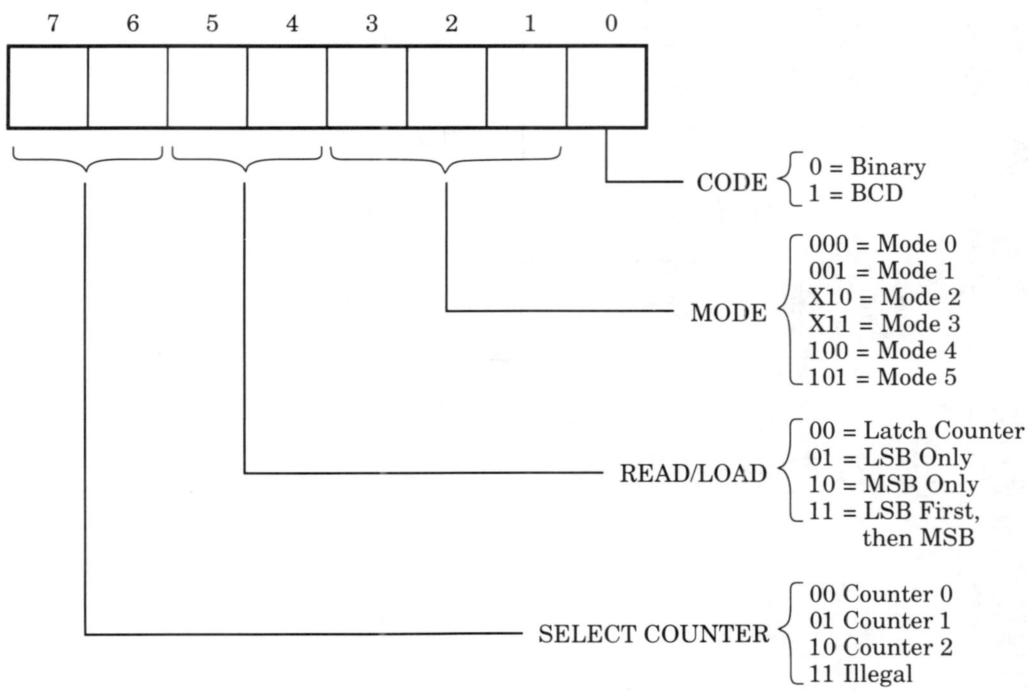

FIGURE 23.2
8253 Control Word Format
Source: Adapted from material copyrighted by Intel Corporation.

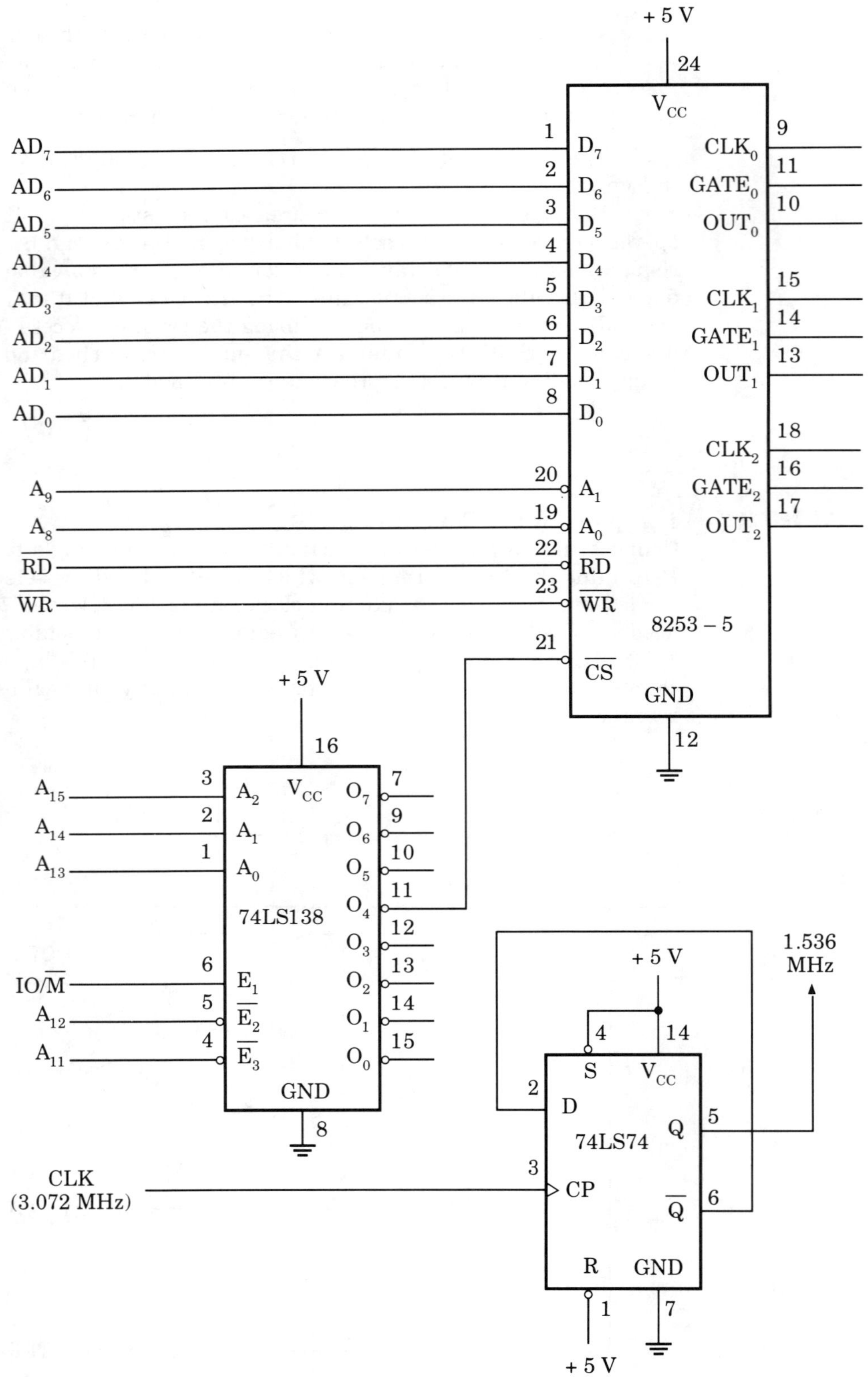

FIGURE 23.3
8253 Interfaced to 8085 Signals

Enter the following program into your microcomputer. This program places the 8253-5 into the square-wave generation mode and produces an output frequency of 1000 Hz by dividing the CLK frequency 3.072 MHz by 1536. Execute the program and note the results displayed on your oscilloscope and frequency counter.

```
CTR0    EQU xxH          ;CHANNEL 0 ADDRESS (DETERMINED PREVIOUSLY)
CTR1    EQU CTR0+1       ;CHANNEL 1 ADDRESS
CTR2    EQU CTR0+2       ;CHANNEL 2 ADDRESS
MODE    EQU CTR0+3       ;CONTROL REGISTER ADDRESS

        ORG 2000H
        MVI A,00110110B  ;CTR 0, MODE 3, BINARY, LSB FIRST, MSB LAST
        OUT MODE
        LXI H, 1536D     ;COUNTER VALUE
        MOV A,L
        OUT CTR0         ;OUTPUT LEAST SIGNIFICANT BYTE FIRST

        MOV A,H
        OUT CTR0         ;THEN OUTPUT MOST SIGNIFICANT BYTE
        RST 1            ;STOP PROGRAM
```

2. Delay Time Generation

Several pumps in a petroleum refinery are controlled using an 8085-based microcomputer. One of the pumps must turn on exactly 20 s after another process begins. An 8253-5 connected as shown in Figure 23.4 creates this time interval. The output of CTR_2 controls the pump actuator.

Cascade the three counter stages as shown in Figure 23.4. Notice that each gate control input is tied high to allow counting to occur. Connect the output of CTR_2 to an LED indicator on your breadboard. Write a program that will configure the 8253-5 to generate a 20 s delay, using mode 0 for each of the three counter stages. At the end of the 20 s delay time, the LED should turn on.

3. Event Counting

An 8253-5 can be used to count events, such as the number of items moving by on an assembly line. To demonstrate this application, connect a debounced switch to the CLK_0 input and tie the $GATE_0$ input high. Write a program to count the number of switch closures and display that 4-digit BCD value on the LED display of your microcomputer. Your program should continually read the counter value "on the fly," using the counter-latching command.

Since the counter value decrements each time an input pulse occurs, your program must initialize the counter to 9999; the present CTR_0 value is then subtracted from 10000 to produce the accumulated number of switch pulses. The number 10000 is used, since the first count pulse received by the 8253-5 causes the counter value to be loaded, but not decremented. Thus, the first pulse that occurs loads 9999 into CTR_0, and the value 0001 (10000 minus 9999) is displayed. The second pulse causes CTR_0 to decrement to 9998 and causes the display to show 0002,

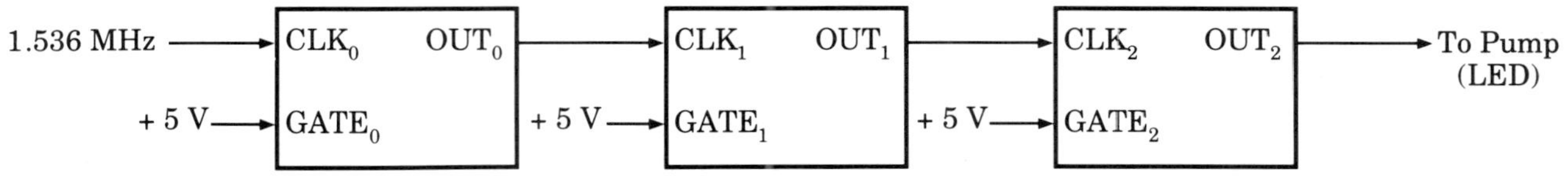

FIGURE 23.4
Block Diagram of 8253 Used for Time-Delay Generation

etc. This BCD subtraction can be performed by subtracting first from 9999, then adding (in BCD) 0001. In this way, the decimal subtraction step will not require the complicated 10's complement method you used in Experiment 9.

Additional Activities

1. Configure 8253-5 CTR_0 as a baud-rate generator using the square-wave mode (mode 3). The baud-rate frequency is to be selected by pressing one of six keys on the keyboard of your microcomputer. The LED display on the microcomputer should indicate the selected frequency as follows:

Key Pressed	*Display*
1	0300
2	0600
3	1200
4	2400
5	4800
6	9600

2. Design a frequency counter using the 8253-5. Apply the unknown frequency f_x to CLK_2. Generate a 1 s timebase signal by cascading CTR_0 and CTR_1. At the beginning of this 1 s interval, CTR_2 should be set to 9999. At the end of the 1 s interval, CTR_2 will contain a value equal to $10000 - f_x$. (The minuend is 10000, not 9999, because the first input pulse loads the counter but does not decrement it.)

   Test your results by comparing them with readings obtained with a commercial frequency counter.

Review Questions

1. What count value must be loaded into the 8253-5 to produce a 60 Hz square wave? Assume that a 1.536 MHz signal source is available, as shown in Figure 23.3.
2. If CTR_0, CTR_1, and CTR_2 are configured in mode 3, what is the maximum output signal period that can be generated on the OUT_2 line of Figure 23.4? NOTE: The *maximum* counter value is 65536, which occurs when the count value 0000H is loaded.

EXPERIMENT 24

Software-Generated Serial I/O

Objectives

Serial data communication between a computer and a peripheral device is usually accomplished with a UART (Universal Asynchronous Receiver/Transmitter) integrated circuit. However, in many small systems, hardware costs can be reduced using software-based serial I/O techniques. After completing this experiment, you will be able to

- Write subroutines to serially send and receive ASCII characters
- Interface an 8085-based single-board computer to a serial video terminal
- Write programs to serially send and receive blocks of data

Reference Reading

Gaonkar, Ramesh S. *Microprocessor Architecture, Programming, and Applications with the 8085/8080A*. 2nd ed. Columbus, OH: Merrill, 1989. Sections 16.1 and 16.2.

Materials Needed

8085 single-board computer
Breadboard
Oscilloscope
ASCII video terminal with serial RS-232C I/O connector
Serial I/O cable
MAX232 RS-232C driver/receiver
Five 10 μF, 16 V capacitors

Discussion

Asynchronous Serial Data Format

Asynchronous serial data communication between a computer and a peripheral device must conform to a standardized timing and electrical signal format. For example, the ASCII character 5 (35H hexadecimal) transmitted at 1200 baud with even parity would appear as shown in Figure 24.1.

Each ASCII character is framed by a single start bit and one or two stop bits. A start bit is always a logic 0 or SPACE level, while a stop bit is always a logic 1 or MARK level. The RS-232C electrical standard defines a logic 0 as a voltage level between +3 and +15 V, and a logic 1 as a voltage level between −3 and −15 V. The parity bit may or may not be used, depending on the application.

Serial Interface to a Video Terminal

Figure 24.2 illustrates the connections needed for serial data communication between a single-board microcomputer and an RS-232C serial video terminal.

The MAX232 is a specialized integrated circuit that contains two RS-232C drivers, two receivers, a +5 to +10 V voltage doubler, and a +10 to −10 V voltage inverter. Since this device operates on a single +5 V power supply, it reduces the total system cost by eliminating the need for separate +12 and −12 V power supplies.

The video terminal pin numbers shown are standard for all RS-232C peripheral devices configured as data terminal equipment (DTE). Refer to the user's manual for your video terminal to verify these connection requirements.

Software to Transmit and Receive Serial Characters

The flowcharts shown in Figure 24.3 describe how to send and receive serial characters. Both subroutines process ASCII characters containing one start bit, seven data bits, one parity bit, and one stop bit. The delay time intervals depend on the baud rate of the serial transmission.

The RECEIVE subroutine waits for the beginning of a start bit, then examines the input signal again one-half bit period later to make sure the signal is still low; this logic prevents a momentary noise spike from being interpreted as a valid start bit.

Procedure

1. Serial Transmitter Demonstration

Connect the circuit shown in Figure 24.2 to your single-board microcomputer. On the SDK-85, use the 8355 ports A and B. Connect the video terminal as shown, and

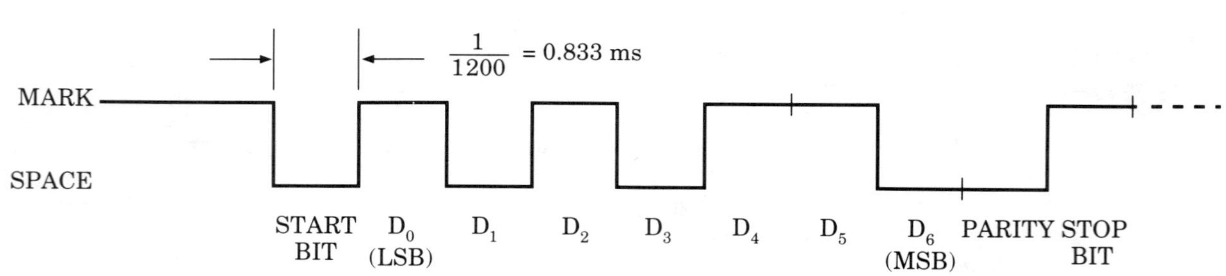

FIGURE 24.1
ASCII Character 5 at 1200 Baud with Even Parity

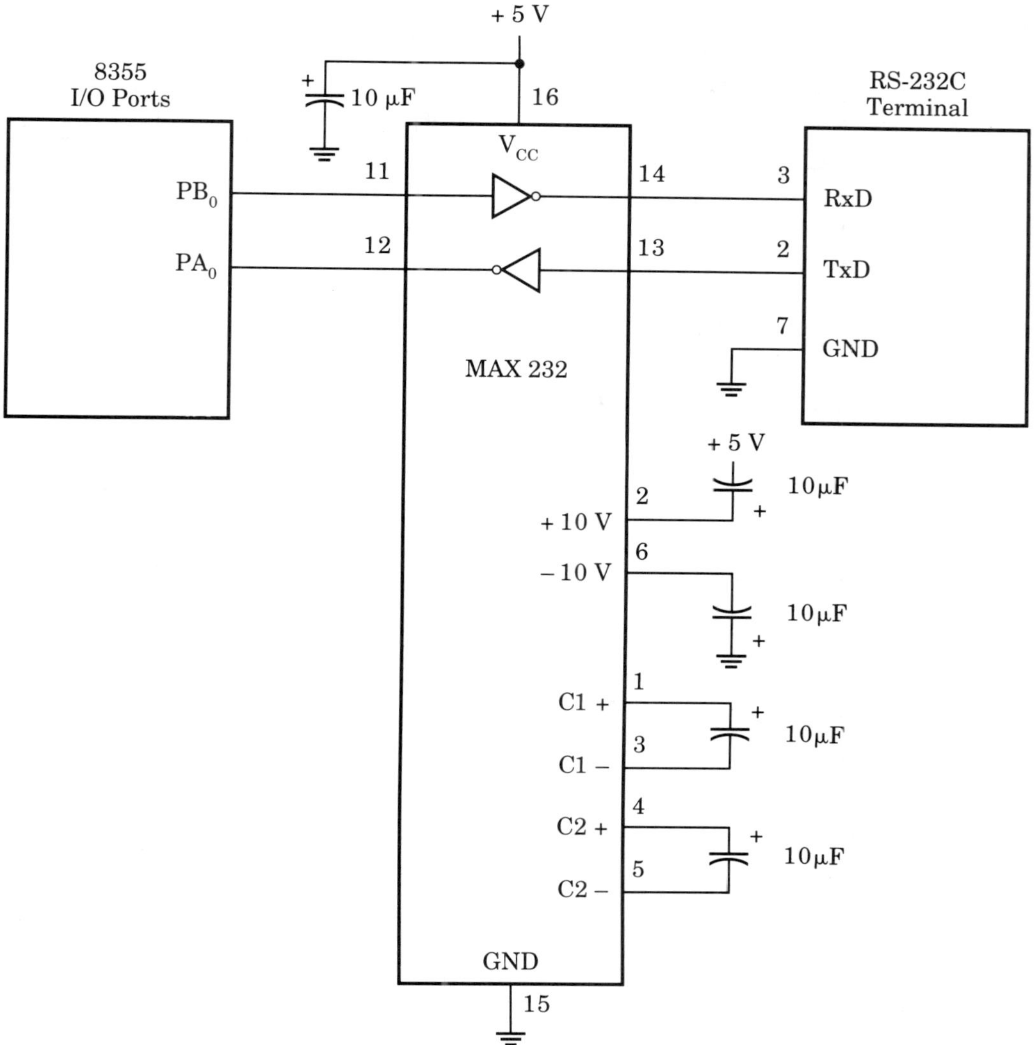

FIGURE 24.2
RS-232C Video Terminal Interface

set it for 1200 baud operation, one stop bit, no parity, and 8-bit data; in this experiment, we will not use the parity bit for error detection.

Write the SEND and RECEIVE subroutines for your single-board microcomputer. Test the SEND routine by calling it repeatedly in a loop, as follows:

```
      CALL INIT    ;INITIALIZE 8355 PORTS
      MVI A,'A'    ;PUT ASCII "A" CHARACTER (41H) INTO ACCUMULATOR
LOOP: CALL SEND    ;SEND THE CHARACTER
      JMP LOOP     ;REPEAT FOREVER
```

This program should send a series of A's to the screen of the video terminal. Use the oscilloscope to measure and record the waveform at the output of the MAX232 driver. Compare this waveform with the one shown in Figure 24.1.

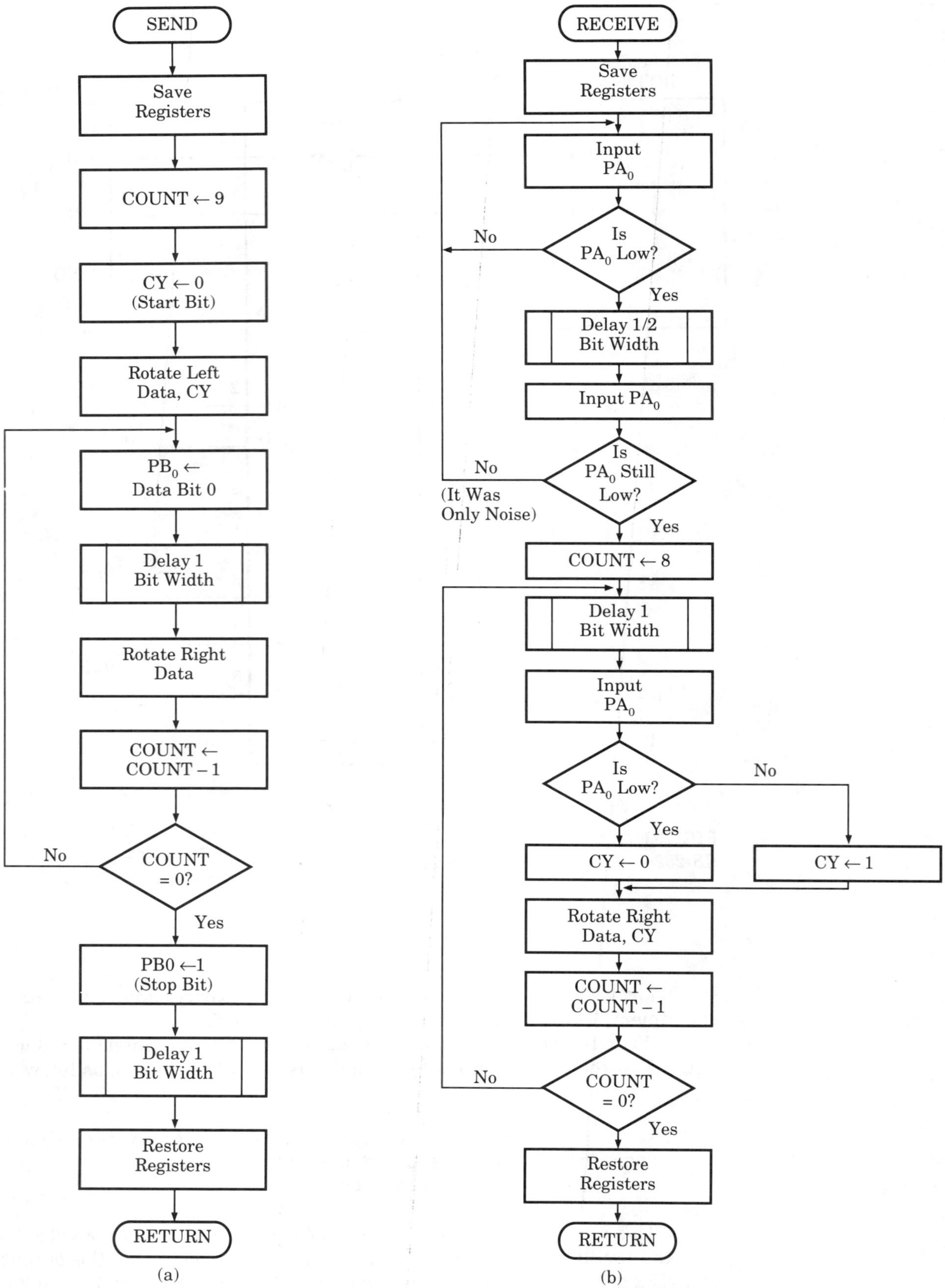

FIGURE 24.3
Flowcharts for (a) SEND Subroutine and (b) RECEIVE Subroutine

2. Serial Receiver Demonstration
Test the RECEIVE subroutine using this test program:

```
UPDDT  EQU 036EH        ;SDK-85 DISPLAY SUBROUTINE ADDRESS
       CALL INIT        ;INITIALIZE 8355 PORTS
AGAIN: CALL RECEIVE     ;GET A SERIAL CHARACTER
       CALL UPDDT       ;OUTPUT IT ON LED DISPLAYS
       JMP AGAIN
```

Each time a key on the terminal is pressed, the corresponding ASCII code should appear on the LED display.

3. Character String Transmission Application
Write an 8085 program to send a block of ASCII characters to the screen of the video terminal. The program should send the characters that are stored beginning at memory location 2080H; the process should end when an ASCII NUL character (00H) is encountered.

4. Data Entry Application
A word processor program stores ASCII characters in memory, then sends these characters to a disk file when a SAVE command is issued. Simulate the action of a word processor by writing an 8085 program that will read characters from the video terminal keyboard, display them on the screen, and store them in an array in memory. The program should read, display, and store characters until an ASCII CONTROL-C character (03H hexadecimal) is encountered. At that time, the program should transmit the entire array of characters to the screen.

Additional Activities

1. Connect two single-board microcomputers to allow two-way serial data communications. Connect the TxD and RxD signals on the first computer to the RxD and TxD signals, respectively, on the second machine. Remember to connect a ground wire between the two computers.

   Write software to allow the first computer to send the contents of memory locations 0000H–001FH to the second machine serially. The second computer should store these values in locations 2090H–20AFH. Upon receiving this string of characters, the second computer should respond by transmitting the ASCII character X (hexadecimal code 58H). After receiving the X character, the first computer should respond by displaying the message PASS.
2. Change the software delay times in your SEND and RECEIVE subroutines to allow communication at 2400 baud. Change the baud-rate setting on the video terminal to 2400, then verify the operation of your revised program. Repeat this procedure for baud rates of 4800 and 9600.
3. Connect your single-board computer and serial interface hardware to a serial pen plotter. Using commands found in the user's manual for the plotter, write a program to plot the ASCII waveform diagram shown in Figure 24.1.

Review Questions

1. What is the width of each bit in Figure 24.1 if the character is transmitted at 4800 baud?
2. What voltage is associated with an RS-232C MARK level? With a SPACE level?
3. Why is the one-half bit width delay included in the RECEIVE subroutine? What would happen if it were removed?

EXPERIMENT 25

The 8251A Programmable Communication Interface

Objectives

The software-generated serial I/O method developed in Experiment 24 has a low hardware cost, but offers little flexibility. Changes in data word format or other operating characteristics can require major changes in the software. A more flexible alternative to using this software-intensive method is the *universal synchronous/asynchronous receiver/transmitter,* or USART. After completing this experiment, you will be able to

- Interface an 8251A to an 8085-based single-board computer
- Control a serial ASCII video terminal with the 8251A
- Serially transfer ASCII data between a personal computer and an 8085-based single-board computer

Reference Reading

Gaonkar, Ramesh S. *Microprocessor Architecture, Programming, and Applications with the 8085/8080A*. 2nd ed. Columbus, OH: Merrill, 1989. Section 16.4

The MCS-80/85 Family User's Manual. Santa Clara, CA: Intel Corp., 1986. Pages 6–49 to 6–65.

Materials Needed

8085 single-board computer
Breadboard
Frequency counter
Oscilloscope
Personal computer with one serial I/O port
Serial I/O cable
8251A USART

74LS90 BCD counter
74LS93 binary counter
74LS138 3-to-8 decoder
MAX232 RS-232C driver/receiver
6-position SPST DIP switch
Five 10 μF, 16 V capacitors

Discussion

The 8251A programmable communication interface is a versatile device designed to support both asynchronous and synchronous data communication. It interfaces easily to the 8085 microprocessor and can accommodate many data word and baud-rate combinations. It is well suited for a variety of applications. In this experiment, only the asynchronous features are considered. In the asynchronous mode, the 8251A operates with baud rates up to 19.2 kbaud. Character lengths of five to eight bits with one or two stop bits are possible. Odd or even parity can be used, or parity can be disabled.

The 8251A Control and Status Registers

The 8251A is configured by first sending it a *mode word,* then giving it a *command word*. The mode word, shown in Figure 25.1, specifies the number of data bits, the number of stop bits, and the parity bit requirements. The mode word also specifies the baud-rate factor; the baud-rate factor divides the external transmit clock and receiver clock signals by a constant (either 16 or 64 for asynchronous applications) to determine the transmitted and received data baud rates.

Figure 25.2 shows the command word. It is used to enable the transmitter and receiver logic and to reset error flags. It is also used to control the handshaking output lines $\overline{RTS}$ and $\overline{DTR}$.

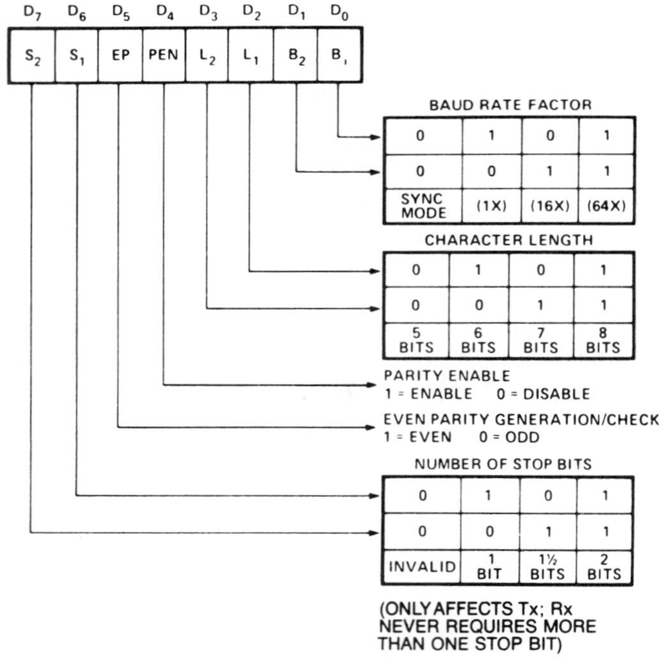

FIGURE 25.1
8251A Mode Instruction Format
Source: Reprinted by permission of Intel Corporation, copyright 1981.

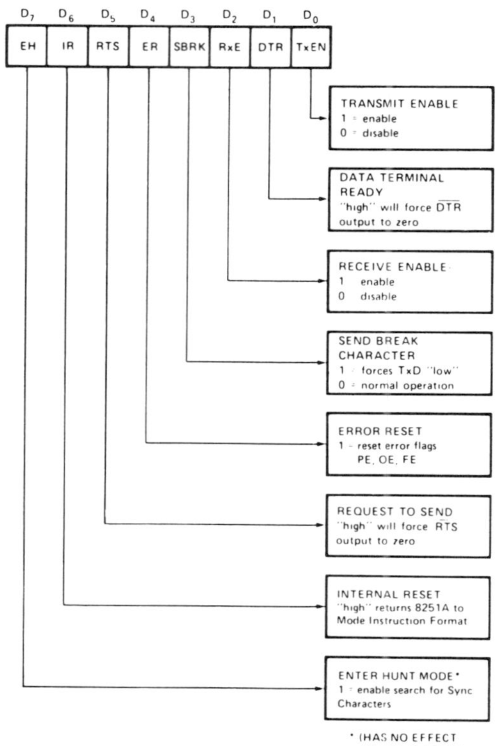

Note: Error Reset must be performed whenever RxEnable and Enter Hunt are programmed.

FIGURE 25.2
8251A Command Instruction Format
Source: Reprinted by permission of Intel Corporation, copyright 1981.

Figure 25.3 illustrates the 8251A status register. This read-only register indicates the three error conditions detectable by the 8251A: framing error, receiver overrun error, and parity error. The status register also includes the RxRDY bit that goes high when a character has been received and is ready to be read by the microprocessor.

The TxRDY flag goes high to indicate that the microprocessor can send another character to the 8251A. The TxEMPTY flag differs from the TxRDY flag in that the former is active when there are no more characters in either stage of the double-buffered transmitter.

Interfacing an 8251A to the Single-Board Microcomputer

Figure 25.4 shows how to connect an 8251A to a video terminal. Since no handshaking is used in this application, the $\overline{\text{DSR}}$ and $\overline{\text{CTS}}$ inputs to the 8251A are tied low to enable them permanently.

The 8251A is selected using the $\overline{\text{CS}}$ and C/$\overline{\text{D}}$ input pins. The C/$\overline{\text{D}}$ line, when high, selects a control word (either the command word or the mode word when writing) or the status word (when reading). When C/$\overline{\text{D}}$ is low, receiver or transmitter data are read or written, respectively.

The 74LS90 and 74LS93 counter ICs allow the user to select the baud rate by closing one of the six switches. These six signal frequencies, in conjunction with the 16× or 64× baud-rate factors, allow communication rates of 300, 600, 1200, 2400,

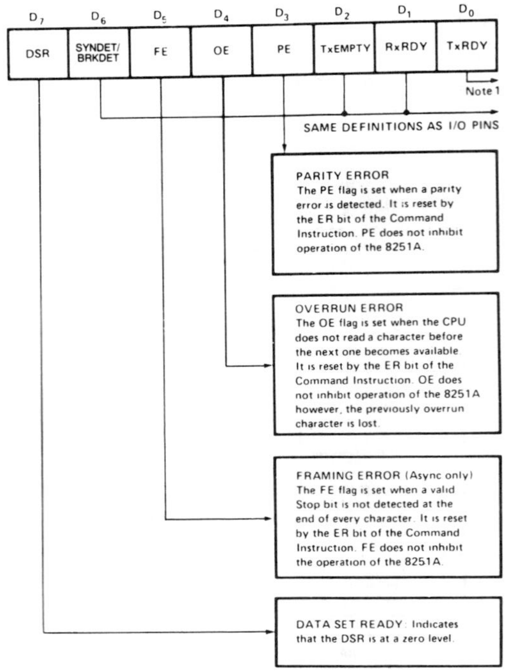

Note 1: TxRDY status bit has different meanings from the TxRDY output pin. The former is not conditioned by $\overline{CTS}$ and TxEN; the latter is conditioned by both $\overline{CTS}$ and TxEN.

i.e. TxRDY status bit = DB Buffer Empty

TxRDY pin out = DB Buffer Empty $\cdot (\overline{CTS} = 0) \cdot (TxEN = 1)$

FIGURE 25.3
8251A Status Register Format
Source: Reprinted by permission of Intel Corporation, copyright 1981.

4800, and 9600 baud, as shown in Figure 25.4. These two counter ICs could, of course, be replaced by an 8253 programmable timer or by the timer section of an 8155, but then the baud rate could not be changed by the user without altering software.

Procedure

1. Serial Transmitter Demonstration
Connect the circuit shown in Figure 25.4. Verify the output frequency on each of the 74LS90 and 74LS93 counter switches. Connect the video terminal as shown, and set it for 8-bit data, no parity, and one stop bit.

Determine the hardware addresses corresponding to the command word, mode word, status word, and transmitted and received data. Next, write a subroutine to initialize the 8251A for compatibility with the video terminal settings. Use the 16 × baud-rate factor and set the appropriate baud-rate switch to produce a 19.2 kHz signal on the transmitter and receiver clock input pins (TxC and RxC, respectively). Check this signal frequency with an oscilloscope or frequency counter before continuing.

Write a subroutine called UWRITE to send the ASCII character in the accumulator to the 8251A. The subroutine should use a polling technique to check

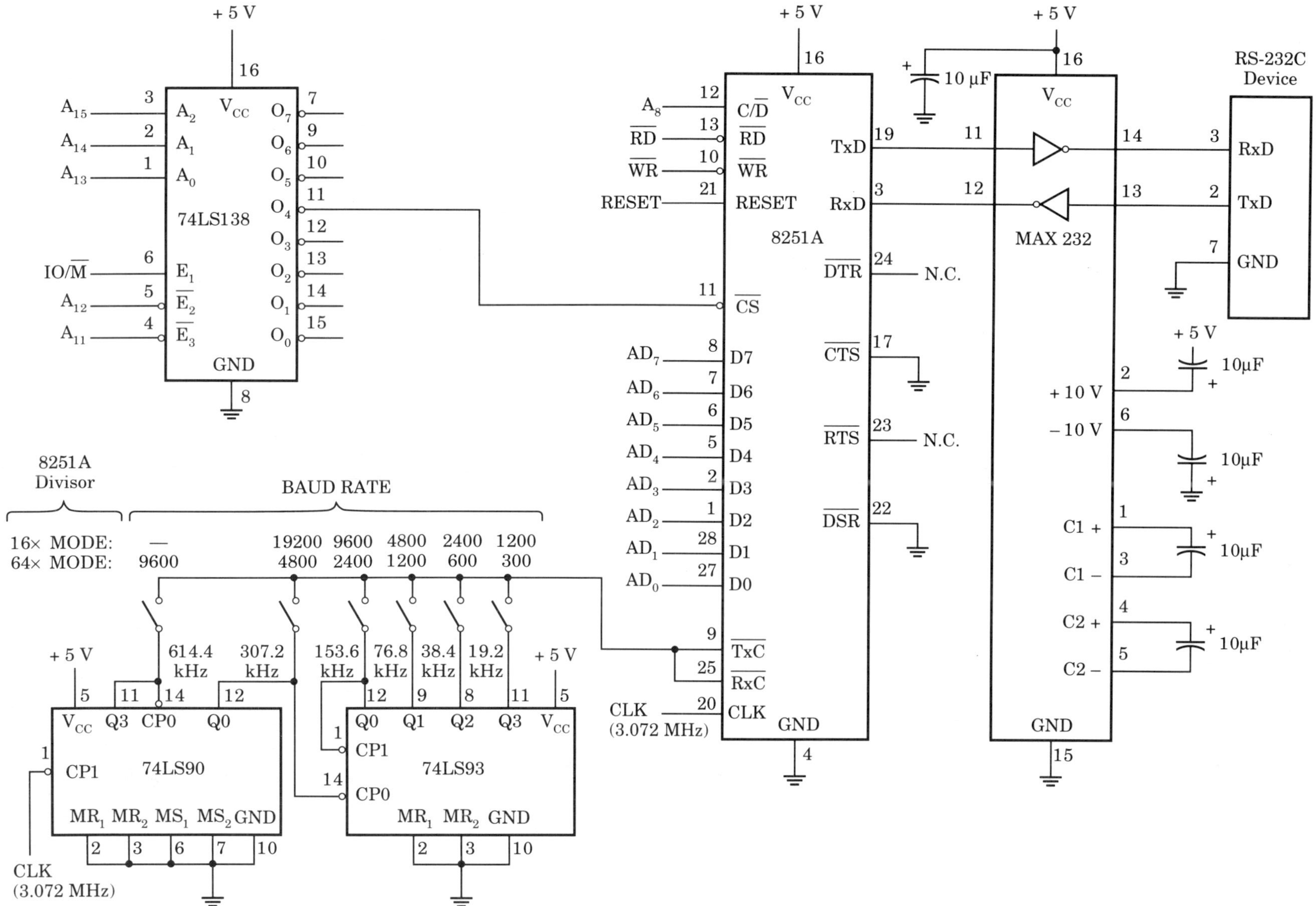

FIGURE 25.4
8251A Interfaced to 8085 Signals

the TxRDY flag to determine when the 8251A is ready to send a character. Test your subroutine by calling it repeatedly in a loop, as follows:

```
        CALL INIT     ;INITIALIZE 8251A
LOOP:   MVI A,'A'     ;PUT ASCII "A" (41H) INTO ACCUMULATOR
        CALL UWRITE   ;SEND THE CHARACTER
        JMP LOOP      ;REPEAT FOREVER
```

This program should send a series of A's to the screen of the video terminal.

2. Serial Receiver Demonstration

Write a subroutine called UREAD to read one character from the 8251A and return it in the accumulator. Your subroutine should poll the RxRDY flag until it goes high, indicating that a character can be read from the 8251A receiver register. Test the UREAD subroutine using this test program:

```
UPDDT  EQU 036EH       ;SDK-85 DISPLAY SUBROUTINE ADDRESS
       CALL INIT       ;INITIALIZE 8251A
AGAIN: CALL UREAD      ;READ A CHARACTER FROM THE 8251A
       CALL UPDDT      ;OUTPUT IT ON LED DISPLAYS
       JMP AGAIN       ;REPEAT FOREVER
```

Each time a key on the terminal is pressed, the corresponding ASCII code should appear on the LED display.

3. Transmitting ASCII Data from a Personal Computer to the 8251A

The serial I/O port on a personal computer may be used to transmit data to an 8085-based single-board computer. The following program, written in BASICA for IBM–PC-compatible personal computers, transmits the ASCII characters INTEL 8085 out of serial port COM1:

```
10 'SERIAL INTERFACE TO TRANSMIT STRING OF CHARACTERS
20 OPEN "COM1:1200,N,8,1,RS,DS,CD,CS,LF" AS #1
30 PRINT #1,"INTEL 8085"
40 CLOSE #1
50 END
```

Line 20 in the program configures the communications port COM1 for 1200 baud communication, no parity, eight data bits, and one stop bit. It also suppresses the RTS handshake output and ignores the DSR, CD, and CTS handshake inputs. A carriage return (CR) and a line feed (LF) character follow the transmission of the string in line 30.

NOTE: If you are using a different version of BASIC, or if you are using a computer that is not IBM-PC compatible, your instructor will explain the modifications needed for this program to work properly on your computer.

Write an 8085 program that will use the 8251A to read and store each serial character it receives. The program should store the received characters in memory beginning at location 2080H; it should stop when a carriage return character (0DH) is encountered.

Test the BASICA program and the 8085 program by connecting the personal computer in place of the video terminal. Next, run your 8085 receiver program. Finally, execute the BASICA program to transmit the data; check the memory contents in your single-board computer to verify the results.

4. Transmitting Data from the 8251A to the Personal Computer
The following BASICA program reads a string of characters from the serial port of the personal computer and displays them on the screen:

```
10 'SERIAL INTERFACE TO RECEIVE STRING OF CHARACTERS
20 OPEN "COM1:1200,N,8,1,DS,RS,CS,CD" AS #1 LEN=1
30 X$ = ""
40 WHILE X$<>CHR$(13) : 'DO UNTIL CR ENCOUNTERED
50   IF LOC(1) > 0 THEN X$ = INPUT$(1,#1) : PRINT X$;
60 WEND
70 CLOSE #1
80 END
```

Line 50 in the program tests for characters in the COM1 input buffer; if a character is present in the buffer, the character is read and displayed. The program continues to read characters until a carriage return is encountered; then it stops.

Write an 8085 program to initialize the 8251A and transmit the array of characters beginning at location 2080H. The program should terminate after sending a carriage return character (0DH). Test your program using the following data created by the DB directive:

```
ORG 2080H
DB 'YOU HAVE SUCCEEDED!',0DH
```

Additional Activities

1. Modify the data transfer program you developed in Experiment 22 so that the data are received serially using an 8251A. Use the following BASICA program to serially transmit the HEX file generated by the cross assembler:

```
10 'SERIAL FILE TRANSMITTER PROGRAM
20 OPEN "I",1,"B:FILENAME.HEX"
30 OPEN "COM1:1200,N,8,1,RS,DS,CD,CS,LF" AS #2
40 WHILE NOT EOF(1)
50   INPUT #1,X$  : 'GET ONE RECORD FROM DATA FILE
60   PRINT X$     : 'PRINT IT ON THE VIDEO SCREEN
70   PRINT #2,X$  : 'SEND IT TO SERIAL PORT COM1
80 WEND
90 END
```

   Your 8085 receiver program should store the data bytes in appropriate memory locations, as described in Experiment 22.
2. Design a system in which the 8251A receives data from the personal computer at 300 baud and simultaneously relays the same information to the video terminal at 1200 baud. Connect the hardware, then write and test the software necessary to perform this task.

Review Questions

1. The TxC input of an 8251A is connected to a 153.6 kHz signal, while the RxC input frequency is 38.4 kHz. If the baud-rate factor is 16X, what is the transmitter baud rate? What is the receiver baud rate?
2. What is a receiver overrun error, and how can it be avoided?
3. What mode word value is needed to configure the 8251A for 9600 baud, seven data bits, even parity, and one stop bit? Assume that the TxC and RxC inputs are connected to a 614.4 kHz signal.

EXPERIMENT 26

Digital-to-Analog Conversion

Objectives

The digital-to-analog (D/A) converter produces an analog voltage proportional to a digital input value. D/A converters are widely used in many applications, ranging from industrial motor control to music synthesis. After completing this experiment, you will be able to

- Interface an 8-bit D/A converter to an 8085-based single-board computer
- Produce unipolar and bipolar voltage outputs from a current output D/A converter
- Generate complex waveforms with a D/A converter
- Control the speed and direction of a DC motor using a D/A converter

Reference Reading

Gaonkar, Ramesh S. *Microprocessor Architecture, Programming, and Applications with the 8085/8080A*. 2nd ed. Columbus, OH: Merrill, 1989. Section 13.1

Materials Needed

8085 single-board computer
Breadboard
Oscilloscope
Digital voltmeter (preferably with 4 1/2 digit display)
12 V dual-output, 2 A power supply
MC1408 D/A converter
741 operational amplifier
TIP102 NPN Darlington transistor
TIP106 PNP Darlington transistor
Two 1N4004 diodes

1 kΩ resistor
Two 2.4 kΩ resistors
Three 10 kΩ, 10-turn potentiometers
47 pF ceramic disk capacitor
Two 0.1 μF ceramic disk capacitors
Small permanent-magnet DC motor

Discussion

The D/A converter is used to convert the digital output from a computer into an analog voltage or current. The analog output signal can control the speed of a motor, the flow of fuel into an engine, or the gain of an audio amplifier. The D/A can also synthesize complex waveforms; speech and music synthesis are two well-known examples of this application.

The circuit shown in Figure 26.1 is an 8-bit D/A converter that converts an 8-bit digital quantity into a proportional unipolar analog output voltage. The output voltage is given by the equation

$$V_{out} = \left(\frac{D_{in}}{256}\right)\left(\frac{(R_1)(V_{ref})}{R_{14}}\right)$$

where D_{in} is the digital input value, ranging from 0 to 255. R_1 and R_{14} are resistance values, and V_{ref} is the applied reference voltage.

With the potentiometer (R_1) set at midrange (5 kΩ), the maximum output voltage of the circuit is

$$V_{out} = \left(\frac{255}{256}\right)\left(\frac{(5\text{ k}\Omega)(5\text{ V})}{2.4\text{ k}\Omega}\right) = 10.376\text{ V}$$

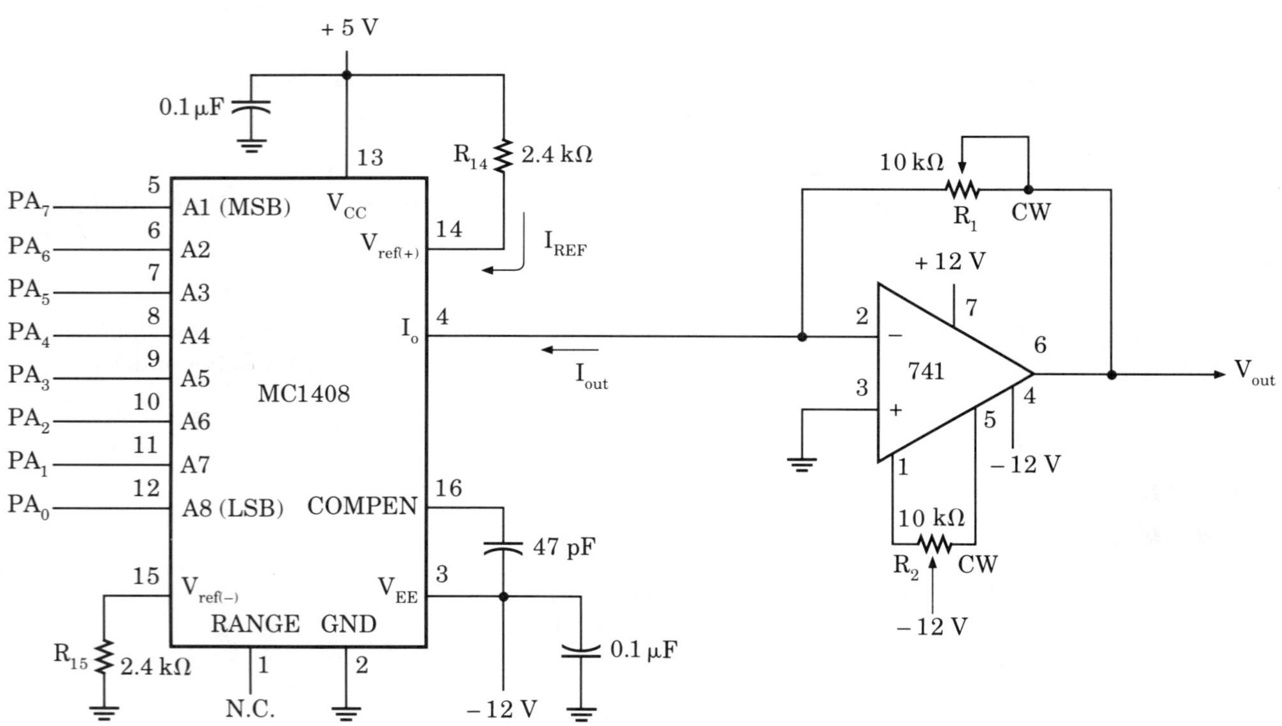

FIGURE 26.1
D/A Converter with Unipolar Output

The resolution of this circuit is given by the equation

$$V_{out} = \left(\frac{1}{256}\right)\left(\frac{(5\ k\Omega)(5\ V)}{2.4\ k\Omega}\right) = 0.0407\ V$$

Thus, with each 1-bit increase in the digital input word, the output voltage increases by 40.7 mV.

The D/A converter circuit in Figure 26.2 provides a *bipolar* output voltage. The current through R_B drives the operational amplifier output voltage in the negative direction. This current is added with the I_{out} current of the D/A converter, and the resulting current can drive the output of the operational amplifier in either the positive or the negative direction.

The output voltage for this circuit is given by the equation

$$V_{out} = \left(\frac{(R_1)(V_{ref})}{R_{14}}\right)\left(\frac{D_{in}}{256}\right) - \left(\frac{(R_1)(V_{ref})}{R_B}\right)$$

For the values used in Figure 26.2, with R_1 and R_B set at 4.8 kΩ, the output voltage is

$$V_{out} = \left(\frac{(4.8\ k\Omega)(5\ V)}{2.4\ k\Omega}\right)\left(\frac{D_{in}}{256}\right) - \left(\frac{(4.8\ k\Omega)(5\ V)}{4.8\ k\Omega}\right)$$

$$= \left(\frac{(10\ V)(D_{in})}{256}\right) - 5\ V$$

The code producing this bipolar output is known as *offset binary;* typical output values for this circuit are summarized as follows:

Digital Input	*Analog Output*
00000000	−5.000 V
00000001	−4.961 V
00000010	−4.922 V
01111111	−0.039 V
10000000	0.000 V
10000001	+0.039 V
11111110	+4.922 V
11111111	+4.961 V

The output of the 741 operational amplifier is buffered by the two Darlington transistors. These transistors allow the circuit to drive high-current bipolar loads; heat sinking may be needed for the transistors at higher power levels.

Procedure

1. Unipolar D/A Converter Circuit Calibration

Connect the unipolar D/A circuit (see Figure 26.1) to port A of the 8355 on your single-board microcomputer. Set the gain control (R_1) to maximum resistance, and set the zero-adjust potentiometer (R_2) to midrange.

Write and execute a simple program to output the digital value 00H to the D/A converter. Using a digital voltmeter, adjust R_2 until V_{out} is 0.000 V. This adjustment nulls the input offset voltage of the operational amplifier.

Change your test program to output FFH to the D/A. Execute the program, then adjust R_1 until V_{out} is 2.550 V. Recheck the zero adjustment by sending a 00H

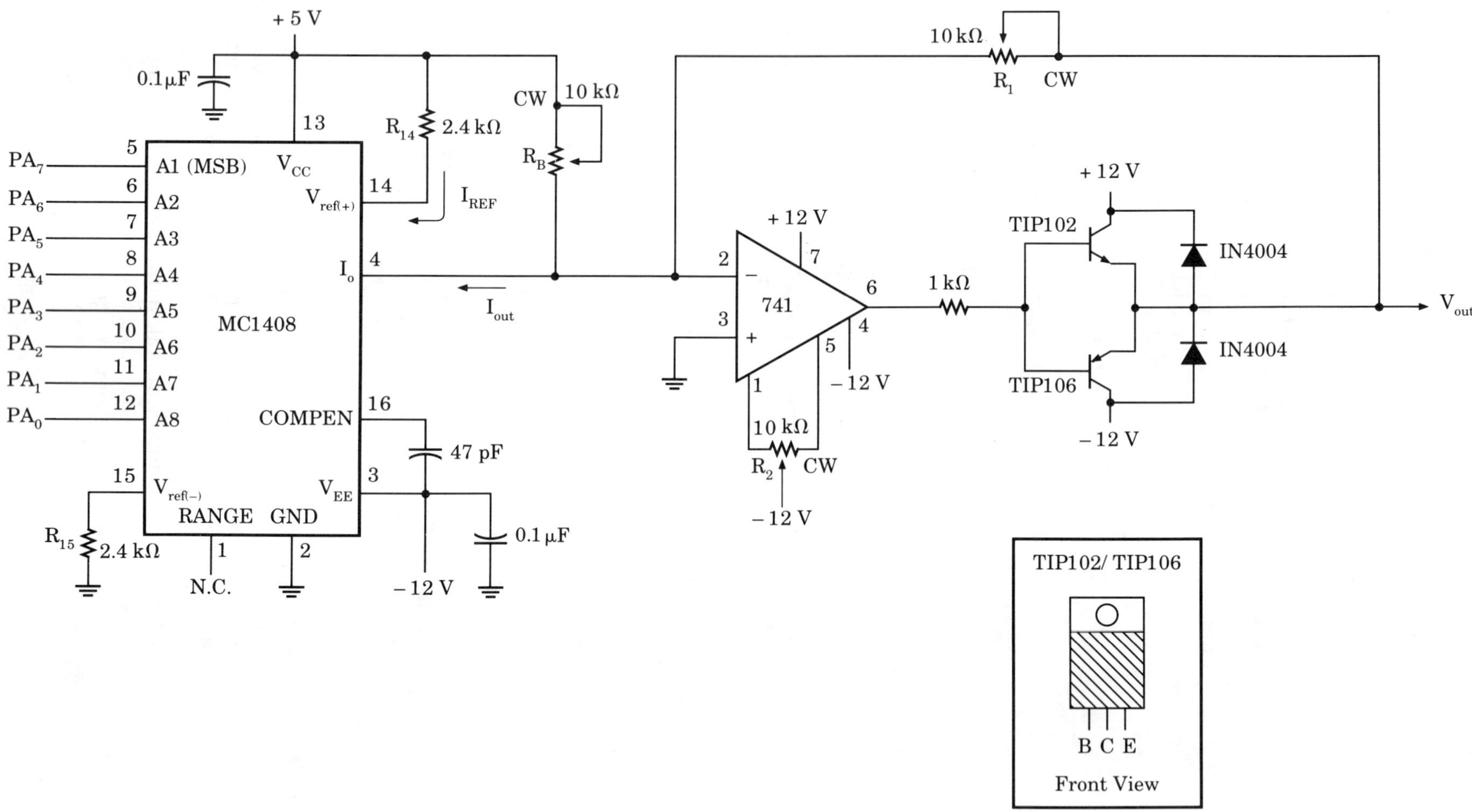

FIGURE 26.2
D/A Converter with Bipolar High-Current Output

to the D/A converter and repeat the adjustments to R_2 and R_1 if necessary. The output is now scaled to provide 10 mV resolution; in other words, each single-bit increase in the input word produces a 10 mV increase in the output voltage.

Output the following eight digital values to the D/A converter and record the corresponding analog output voltage for each case:

00H, 01H, 40H, 7FH, 80H, C0H, FEH, FFH

NOTE: The output voltage produced by this circuit depends on the reference voltage. Using the +5 V digital power supply for a reference as in Figure 26.1 is acceptable only if the supply is well regulated and filtered. In Experiment 27, a precision reference voltage circuit is introduced that is independent of power supply fluctuations. Use that approach when using D/A converters in precision applications.

2. Sawtooth Waveform Generation

Write an 8085 assembly language program to output an 8-bit binary count sequence to the D/A converter circuit. Execute the program. Observe the output voltage with the oscilloscope; the voltage should “ramp up” from 0.00 to +2.55 V, then repeat. Sketch this output waveform, carefully indicating the amplitude and frequency characteristics.

3. Bipolar D/A Circuit Calibration

Add the components shown in Figure 26.2 to create a D/A circuit with a bipolar output voltage. Output the digital value 80H to the D/A converter; set R_1 for maximum resistance, then adjust R_B for a V_{out} of 0.000 V.

Output 00H to the D/A converter and adjust R_1 for an output of −5.000 V. Recheck the zero adjustment by sending the value 80H to the D/A converter; repeat the adjustments to R_2 and R_1 if necessary.

Output the following digital values to the D/A converter, and record the corresponding analog output voltage for each case:

00H, 01H, 40H, 7FH, 80H, 81H, C0H, FEH, FFH

4. DC Motor Control Using the D/A Converter

Select a small DC motor to be used with the bipolar D/A converter. A permanent-magnet “toy” motor will work nicely. Motors of this type typically operate on voltages of 1.5–6 V, with stall currents of 2 A or less. Since the power transistors may dissipate several watts of power as the current demand increases, mount them on a suitable heat sink to cool them.

Output the digital value 00H to the D/A converter, then adjust the gain control (R_1) to set the maximum output voltage to a value compatible with the motor rating. Attach the motor to the D/A converter. Observe its speed and direction characteristics as each of these digital values is sent to the circuit:

00H, 40H, 80H, C0H, FFH

5. Bipolar Waveform Synthesis

D/A converters can synthesize complex waveforms using lookup table techniques. In waveform synthesis applications, the digital representation of a waveform is stored in a lookup table, and each value is retrieved and output to the D/A converter under control of a microprocessor. This technique is used for music synthesis and voice synthesis, as well as for many other industrial applications.

The following equation describes a sinusoidal waveform with 100 Hz frequency and 5 V peak amplitude:

$$V_{out} = 5 \sin(200\pi t)$$

Compute voltage values for one cycle of this waveform, using 0.5 ms time increments. Determine the 8-bit digital code needed to produce each of these voltage levels, then store these digital numbers in a lookup table. Finally, write software to output the lookup table values through the D/A converter. Your program should delay 0.5 ms between output steps to produce a 100 Hz waveform.

Execute your program and observe the resulting waveform with an oscilloscope. Note the positive and negative peak amplitudes, as well as the frequency of the signal.

Additional Activities

1. A video graphics display system uses two D/A converters to produce images on a cathode-ray tube (CRT). The first D/A converter drives the horizontal beam deflection circuit, while the second D/A converter drives the vertical deflection circuit. Both D/A converters produce a unipolar 0 to +5 V output.

   Simulate the video graphics display system by connecting two D/A converters to ports on your microcomputer. Set an oscilloscope in the X-Y mode; connect the first D/A converter output to the X input of the oscilloscope, and the second one to the Y input. Write a control program to make this hardware draw a square on the screen.

   For a more challenging assignment, use the hardware to draw a circle on the screen. Use two lookup tables, one for the vertical D/A converter and one for the horizontal D/A converter.
2. Using the bipolar D/A converter (see Figure 26.2), synthesize the damped sinusoidal waveform produced by the equation

   $$V_{out} = 5e^{-25t} \sin(100\pi t)$$

   Your program should produce an output at 2.0 ms increments from 0 to 120 ms, then repeat. Generate the hexadecimal lookup table values using BASIC. Download these table values directly from your personal computer into your single-board computer (see Experiments 22 and 25). Execute your program and sketch the resulting output waveform.

Review Questions

1. What is the resolution of the unipolar D/A converter in Figure 26.1 if the output voltage is 1.852 V when the digital input is 4FH?
2. What is the output voltage of the bipolar D/A converter (see Figure 26.2) if the digital input value is 9CH? Assume that the D/A converter is calibrated so that 00H produces −5.000 V, 80H produces 0.000 V, and FFH produces 4.961 V.
3. How will the resolution of the D/A converter of Figure 26.2 change if the value of R_1 is changed from 4.8 kΩ to 9.6 kΩ?

EXPERIMENT 27

Analog-to-Digital Conversion

Objectives

The analog-to-digital (A/D) converter produces a digital output word proportional to an analog input voltage. A/D converters are used in many applications in which an analog signal corresponding to a physical quantity must be monitored and processed by a digital system. After completing this experiment, you will be able to

- Interface an 8-channel, 8-bit A/D converter to an 8085-based single-board computer
- Build a temperature measurement system using a solid-state temperature sensor device

Reference Reading

Gaonkar, Ramesh S. *Microprocessor Architecture, Programming, and Applications with the 8085/8080A*. 2nd ed. Columbus, OH: Merrill, 1989. Section 13.2.

Materials Needed

8085 single-board computer
Breadboard
Digital voltmeter (preferably with 4 1/2 digit resolution)
12 V dual power supply
Laboratory thermometer (Fahrenheit scale)
ADC0809 A/D converter
74LS04 hex inverter
74LS93 binary counter
74LS138 3-to-8 decoder
LM1458 dual operational amplifier
LM335 temperature sensor

LM336-5.0 precision voltage reference
Two 6.8 kΩ resistors
Two 18 kΩ resistors
Three 10 kΩ, 10-turn potentiometers
100 kΩ, 10-turn potentiometer
Three 0.1 μF ceramic disk capacitors

Discussion

Interfacing the ADC0809 A/D Converter

In many data acquisition applications, several different analog signals must be monitored; the ADC0809 is an 8-channel A/D converter that is ideal for this task. Using an 8-bit successive approximation conversion technique, it completes a conversion cycle in approximately 100 μs. Figure 27.1 shows an ADC0809 interfaced to the 8085 microprocessor control signals.

One of the eight analog input channels is selected by placing a 3-bit address on pins ADD A, ADD B, and ADD C; the address is latched when the Address Latch Enable (ALE) input goes from low to high. A conversion cycle begins when the START input goes from high to low. This sequence allows the ALE and START inputs to be tied together so that a single pulse can latch the channel address and start the conversion.

The End-of-Conversion (EOC) signal goes low between one and eight clock cycles after the rising edge of the START input signal. The EOC output remains low until the conversion is complete (approximately 100 μs for the circuit shown in Figure 27.1), at which time it goes high. The microprocessor can poll the EOC line to determine when a conversion cycle is finished, or it can use EOC as an interrupt input. In many applications, EOC is not monitored; instead, a software delay is used to allow the conversion cycle to finish before reading the output data.

The Output Enable (OE) line controls the flow of A/D data onto the system bus. When OE is high, data are placed onto the bus; when OE is low, the data lines are in a 3-state condition.

The operation of the ADC0809 circuit is summarized as follows:

- Output the input channel number to the appropriate I/O address. This strobes the ALE and START lines to latch the address and begin another conversion.
- Wait 100 μs.
- Input the A/D data from the proper I/O address.

Using the LM335 Precision Temperature Sensor

A/D converters are often used in temperature measurement applications. The circuit shown in Figure 27.2 produces a 20 mV/°F output over the temperature range 0°F to +212°F. The LM335 is a precision temperature sensor integrated circuit that produces a 10 mV/°K output voltage. From this relationship, the following voltage equation results:

$$V_T = -10 \text{ mV} \left(\frac{5}{9} (°F - 32) + 273.15 \right)$$

Since the LM335 operates over a temperature range of −40°C to +100°C, it is well suited to measure temperatures in the range of 0°F to +212°F. A temperature of 0°F produces a V_T output of 2.554 V, while a 212°F temperature produces a 3.732 V output. R_3 calibrates the LM335 output. The LM335 is designed to be

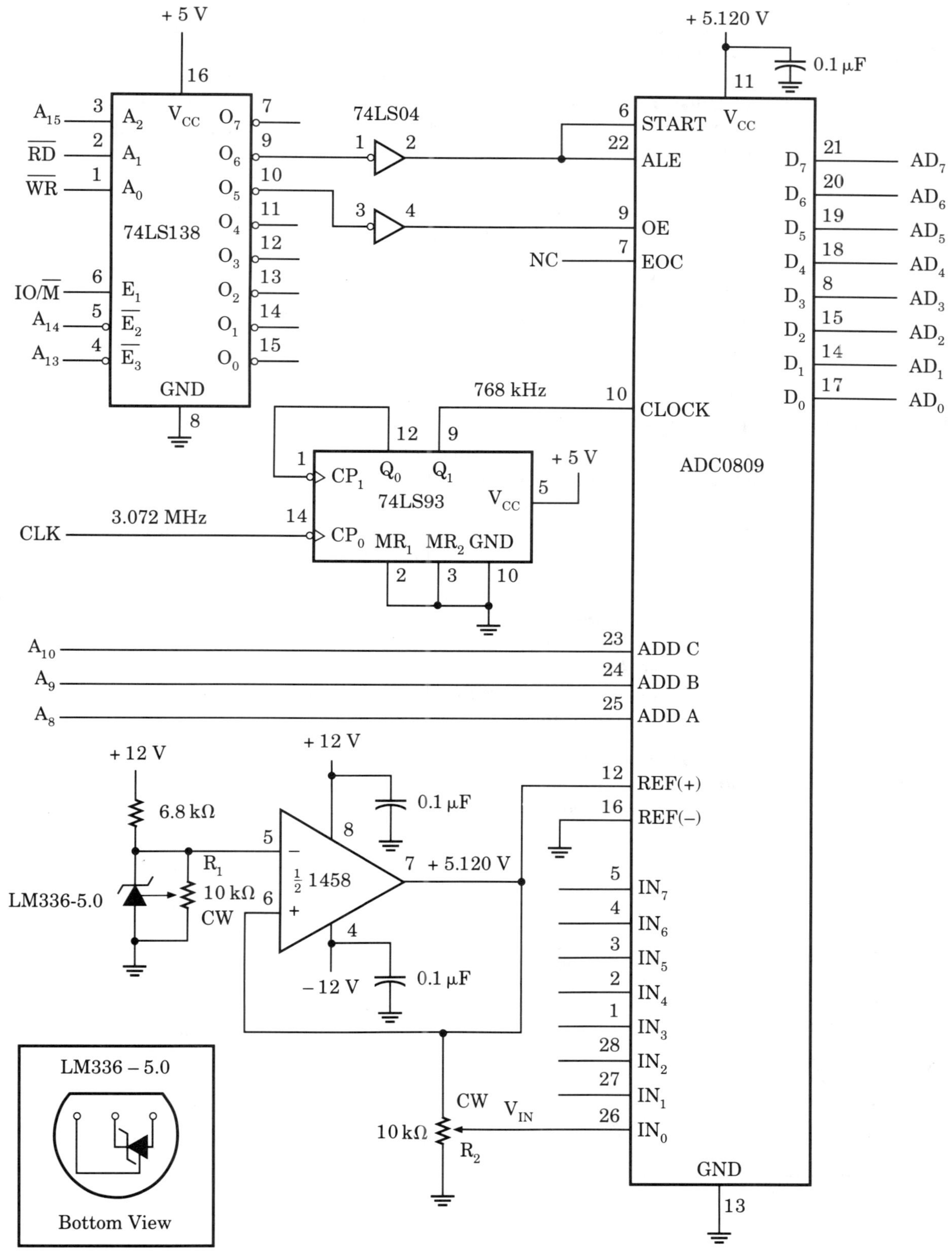

FIGURE 27.1
ADC0809 A/D Converter Interface

calibrated at one temperature and produce accurate results (typically within 1°C) over the entire operating temperature range.

The remaining circuit components in Figure 27.2 scale the output voltage to produce the required 20 mV/°F response. R_4 adjusts voltage V_2 to +2.554 V. The operational amplifier is configured as a summing amplifier that adds the LM335 output to the +2.554 V offset to produce the output voltage

$$V_{out} = -\frac{R_5}{18\ k\Omega}(V_2 + V_1)$$

If R_5 is adjusted to 64.8 kΩ, V_T is 0.0 V at 0°F and +4.24 V at 212°F. The values of the two 18 kΩ resistors should be closely matched to produce accurate results.

Procedure

1. Testing the A/D Converter Hardware

Construct the 5.120 V reference voltage section of Figure 27.1. Adjust R_1 until the operational amplifier output produces +5.120 V.

Carefully connect the remaining circuit components to your single-board microcomputer, as shown in Figure 27.1. Use caution when connecting signals to the ADC0809 IC; the device will be damaged if these precautions are not followed:

- Never apply an input signal to an analog input channel (IN_0–IN_7) unless V_{cc} is present.
- Always turn the analog input signal sources off before turning off V_{cc} on the ADC0809.
- Never allow an analog input channel to go negative or to become more positive than V_{cc}.

Determine the input and output port addresses needed to access the A/D converter hardware. Next, write an 8085 subroutine named CONVERT that will perform an A/D conversion on input channel IN_0. The subroutine should return the

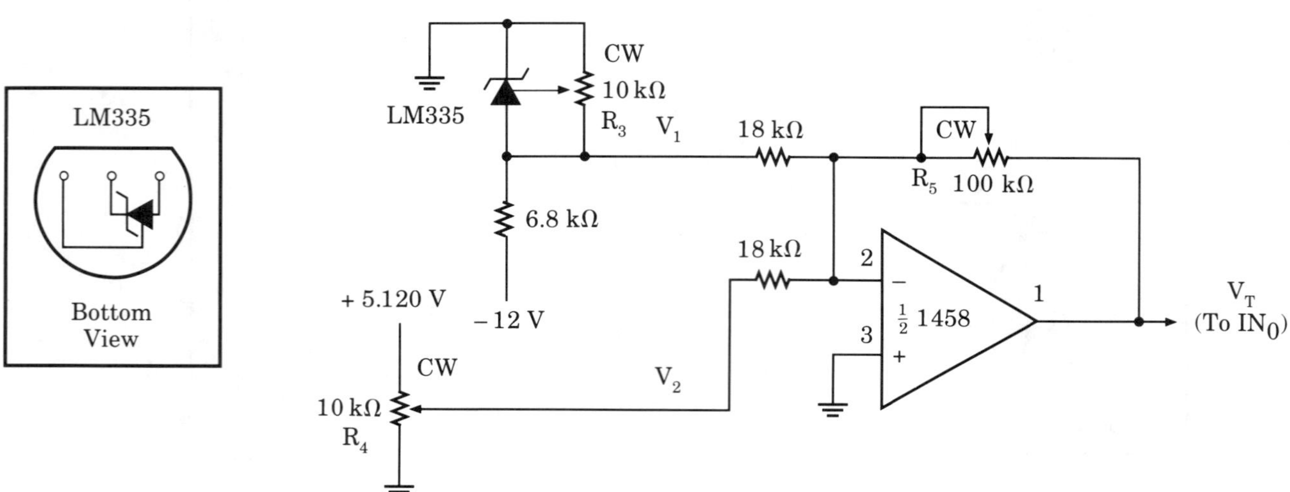

FIGURE 27.2
Temperature Sensor Circuit

8-bit digital output from the A/D converter in the accumulator. Finally, enter the following main program to call the A/D conversion subroutine and display the results:

```
UPDDT    EQU 036EH     ;SDK-85 DISPLAY SUBROUTINE ADDRESS
REPEAT:  CALL CONVERT  ;PERFORM A CONVERSION
         CALL UPDDT    ;DISPLAY THE RESULT
         JMP REPEAT    ;CONTINUE FOREVER
```

Vary R_2 to change the input voltage and note the displayed results. The display should produce values between 00H and FFH, with each 20 mV input change causing a 1-bit change in the digital output. Verify this relationship by recording the digital output values for these input voltages:

0.000 V
0.020 V
1.28 V
2.55 V
2.56 V
3.84 V
5.08 V
5.10 V

Compare the observed digital output values with the results produced using the equation

$$D_{out} = \frac{(256)(V_{IN})}{V_{REF}}$$

Move the wiper of R_2 to the IN_1 input on the ADC0809. Modify your CONVERT subroutine to convert input channel 1, run the test program, and check the results. Repeat these testing procedures for each of the remaining input channels.

2. Measuring Temperature with the A/D Converter

Build a temperature probe by soldering 24 in. (61 cm) wires to each of the three leads on the LM335. Protect the solder joints on the two outer leads with small-diameter heat-shrink tubing. Seal the entire LM335 assembly near one end of a 6 in. (15 cm) long piece of 1/4 in. diameter heat-shrink tubing. This seal should permit the temperature probe to be immersed in water.

Construct the temperature measurement circuit shown in Figure 27.2. Measure the ambient room temperature T_A with a laboratory thermometer, then adjust R_3 to produce the appropriate voltage at V_1. Next, adjust R_4 to produce -2.554 V at V_2. Finally, adjust R_5 to produce a voltage

$$V_T = (T_A)(20 \text{ mV})$$

Write a program to continually read and display the temperature (in BCD form) in degrees Fahrenheit. Since the output of the ADC0809 is in binary form, the conversion to BCD must be done in software.

Test your temperature measurement system over a wide range of temperatures, and compare each reading with a laboratory thermometer. Immerse the probe and the laboratory thermometer in an ice bath (a container full of ice cubes with water added) and note the results. Immerse the probe and thermometer carefully in boiling water to test the response of the circuit at the upper temperature limit.

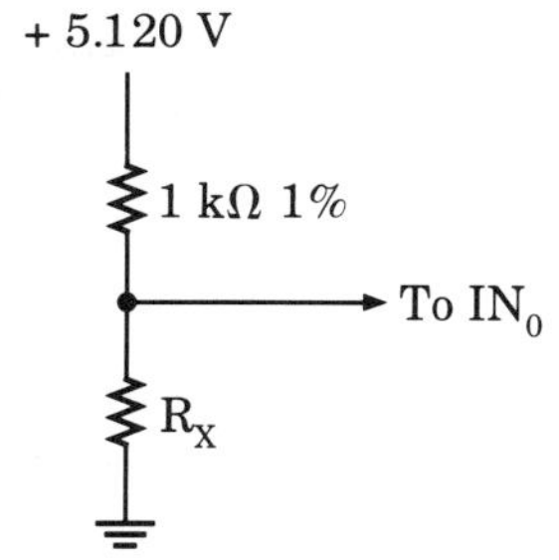

FIGURE 27.3
Ohmmeter Circuit

Additional Activities

1. An electronics company uses an 8085-based microcomputer to test all 5%-tolerance resistors as they are received from the resistor supplier. Develop this digital ohmmeter application using the A/D converter hardware (see Figure 27.1) and the voltage divider circuit shown in Figure 27.3. Your system should test 470, 1000, and 4700 Ω 5% resistors. The display should show 0470, 1000, and 4700, respectively, to indicate that the measured resistor is one of the given values and is in tolerance. The display should show EEEE to indicate that the measured resistor is not in tolerance.
2. Design a digital thermostat for a residential heating and air conditioning system. The system should include three analog input signals: an upper temperature limit, a lower temperature limit, and the measured room temperature. Use the LM335 temperature sensor to measure the room temperature; use two potentiometers to produce the temperature limit signals.

   Use three LED indicators to simulate outputs from the system. The first LED should be on to indicate that the temperature is in the acceptable operating range. The second LED should be on to indicate that the temperature is too low and the electric heating system is on. The third LED should be on to indicate that the temperature is too high and the air conditioning system is on.

Review Questions

1. Compute the digital output word produced by the A/D converter circuit (see Figure 27.1) if V_{REF} is 3.000 V and V_{IN} is 2.344 V.
2. What is the resolution of a 10-bit A/D converter circuit if the reference voltage is 4.000 V?
3. What will voltage V_1 be in Figure 27.2 if the temperature is 99°F?
4. How should the temperature measurement circuit (see Figure 27.2) be adjusted to produce a 20 mV/°C output voltage?

EXPERIMENT 28

Interfacing Project— A Slide Gate Controller

Objectives

Microcomputers are often used in industry to control mechanical systems. A typical application is the slide gate, a mechanism used to control the flow of material out of a storage bin. A microcomputer-based system can control the position of the slide gate to accurately regulate the flow of material. After completing this experiment, you will be able to

- Design and build the hardware needed to control a mechanical slide gate
- Design software to simultaneously scan a keyboard, refresh a display, and position a stepper motor
- Write control software to position the slide gate mechanism to within 0.1% of the fully open position

Reference Reading

Review Experiments 12, 13, 19, and 21.

Materials Needed

8085 single-board computer, including expansion memory (2K × 8) and download connection to a personal computer
Breadboard
3-digit, 7-segment LED display hardware
16-key keyboard hardware
Stepper motor and driver circuit components
Other components as needed for your hardware design

Discussion

A slide gate is a mechanism used to control the flow of material out of a storage bin. In grain-handling systems, for example, a slide gate is used to allow grain to flow from a storage bin into a truck or railroad car. Slide gates are also used in food processing plants to regulate the quantity of dry ingredients flowing into blending systems.

A typical slide gate mechanism is shown in simplified form in Figure 28.1. The motor turns a threaded screw, which in turn linearly moves the slide gate. The fixed guide shaft keeps the slide gate aligned as the screw is turned by the motor. The slide gate position is accurately controlled by rotating the motor a specified number of turns.

Many companies use slide gates that are manually controlled. The slide gate drive motor is turned on by the operator, who then waits until the gate has opened far enough before turning the motor off. Precision control of the gate position is difficult using this manual approach. The number of motor shaft revolutions must be carefully monitored to position the gate accurately. Control of this type is possible using a position feedback signal; as an alternative, a stepper motor can precisely turn the screw shaft the required number of turns. In this experiment, you will precisely position the slide gate with a computer-controlled stepper motor.

Procedure

1. Slide Gate Control System Requirements

A grain-handling systems manufacturer is adapting a manually operated slide gate for computer control. The modified slide gate mechanism is driven by a stepper motor that opens the gate by 1% of the fully open gate position when the drive motor rotates one full turn in the counterclockwise direction. The gate closes by 1% when the motor rotates one full turn in the clockwise direction.

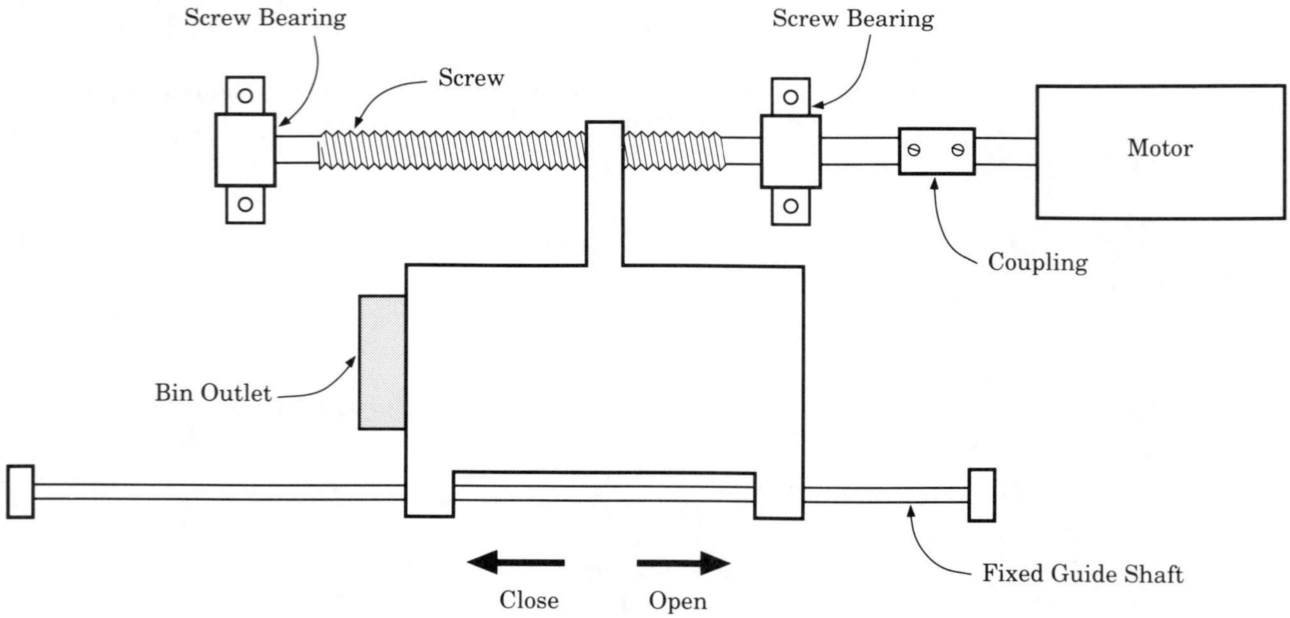

FIGURE 28.1
Slide Gate Mechanism

As a consultant to this company, your job assignment is to design and build a microcomputer-controlled slide gate position control system. The company has supplied a block diagram (Figure 28.2) to illustrate the design requirements. In addition, the specifications that follow define the functions of the proposed automatic slide gate system.

- The position of the slide gate must be controllable from the fully closed position to 99.9% of the fully open position. The system operator must enter a 3-digit position value between 00.0 and 99.9 to specify a new gate position.
- A 3-digit LED display indicates the current position (between 00.0 and 99.9) of the slide gate.
- When the system control software is first executed, the display should show "---" to indicate that the system is functioning. This display pattern is also the prompting message that tells the user to enter a new position value.
- A 3-digit position value between 00.0 and 99.9 is entered by pressing two digit keys, the decimal point key, then the third digit key. Leading and trailing zeros must be typed as the position value is entered. Finally, the ENTER key is pressed to move the gate to the new position.
- Pressing the CLEAR key during the position entry sequence should change the display to "---" to prompt the user to reenter the desired value.
- The system must include an emergency stop feature to allow the user to stop the gate at any time. This feature is to be activated by pressing the STOP key. The motor should stop the gate at the next 0.1% increment.
- The display should continually show the current position of the slide gate. When the gate reaches the target position, or when the gate stops after the STOP key is pressed, the position value should remain on the display. To enter a new position, the user must first press the CLEAR key to display the "---" prompting message.

2. Slide Gate Control System Hardware Design
The company uses several 8085-based single-board computers in other areas of the company. Company officials recommend that you design the slide gate controller so that one of the existing computers can be used. After reviewing the proposed design requirements, you have agreed to design the slide gate control system consisting of these subsystems:

- 8085-based single-board computer
- 16-key keyboard for command entry
- 3-digit, 7-segment LED display
- Stepper motor and driver circuitry

The keyboard, display, and stepper motor circuits are to be interfaced to available I/O port lines on the single-board computer. Complete the hardware design phase of the project by drawing a complete schematic diagram showing these interconnections.

3. Control Software Design
The software design phase is probably the most crucial portion of any interfacing project; this slide gate control application is no exception. By paying particular attention to design details at this stage of the project, you will spend much less time debugging and rewriting software later.

Begin the design of the slide gate control software by flowcharting the logic for the entire system. Use a modular design approach to make the program more

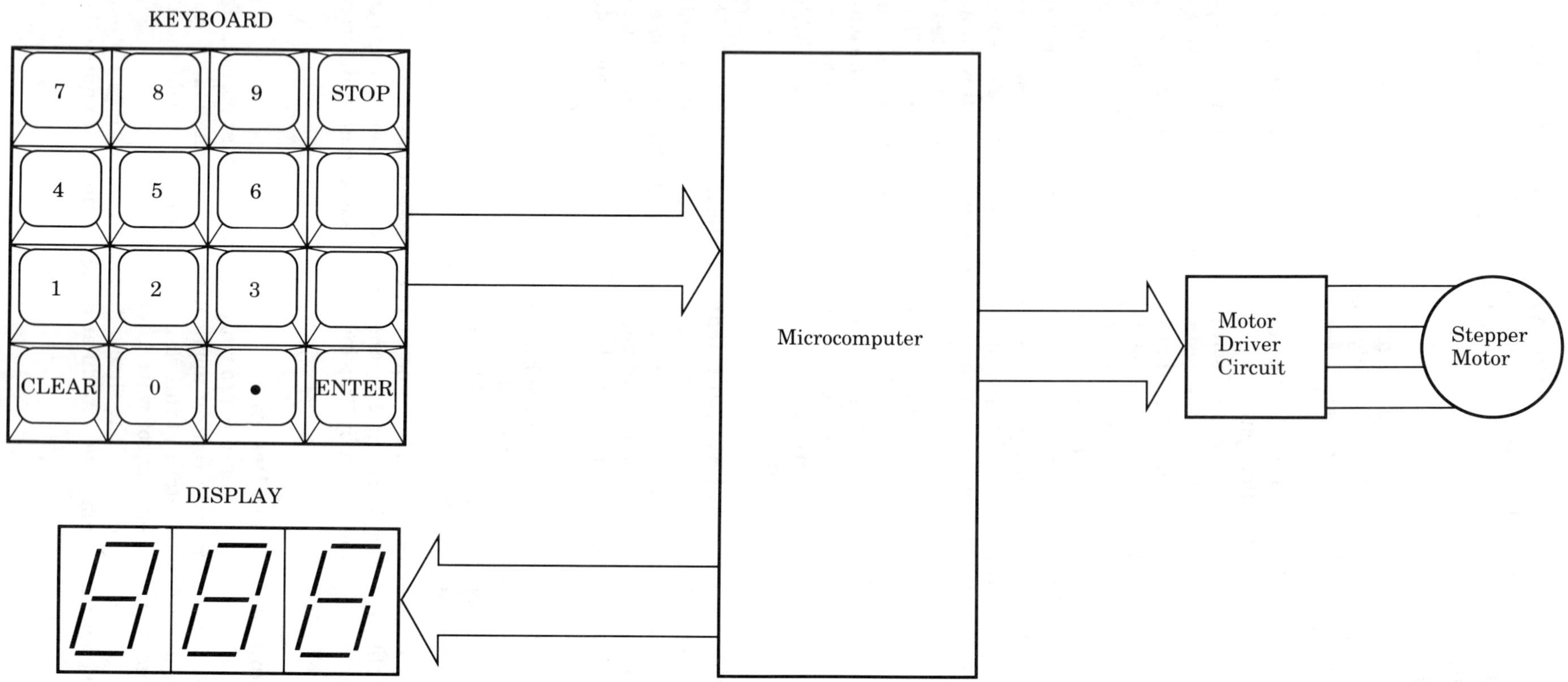

FIGURE 28.2
Slide Gate Controller Block Diagram

readable and to simplify your future testing and debugging tasks. Remember that small, individual subroutines are much easier to test than one large program.

The control system software should be as user friendly as possible. For example, the program should ignore invalid key entry sequences, such as pressing the ENTER key before all position digits are entered. Similarly, the keyboard and display sections of the program should work in harmony with each other; the display refreshing should continue, even when a key is pressed.

4. Hardware Construction and Testing

Construct and test each hardware subsystem separately before integrating them into a system. Test the keyboard wiring, the display driver circuitry, and the stepper motor hardware. Write simple test programs to check each subsystem; these programs are useful for initial hardware diagnosis, as well as for future system debugging.

If you (or your instructor) are mechanically inclined, you can easily build a slide gate model using inexpensive components available at your local hardware store. Actually, system debugging may be easier *without* a slide gate mechanism to contend with. Prototype circuits and programs often cause hardware mechanisms (such as our slide gate) to self-destruct before all system "bugs" are removed.

Even without a slide gate model to control, you can still fully test your control software. Mount the stepper motor on a small panel with a calibrated dial, and attach a pointer knob to the stepper motor shaft. The motor shaft revolutions are easy to count with this simple approach (and there will be no broken slide gate models to repair).

5. System Testing

After testing all hardware subsystems, write and test software to control the entire system. Test all keyboard functions to ensure that they operate correctly. Test the operation of the slide gate by commanding it to open from a fully closed position (0.00) to position 20.0. The shaft should rotate exactly 20 revolutions counterclockwise, then stop. The LED display should display the correct shaft position during and after the shaft movement.

Next, enter position 15.5 on the keyboard. The display digits should indicate the correct movement of the motor shaft as it rotates clockwise 4.5 turns.

Enter the gate position 00.0. The motor should rotate clockwise 15.5 turns, then stop at the fully closed position. Enter gate position 99.9 and note the results.

Check the performance of the CLEAR key, which cancels the position entry sequence and changes the display to "---" to prompt the user to reenter the desired value. Verify that the system does not "lose its place" when this key is pressed.

Test the action of the STOP button while the motor is turning. The motor should stop at the next 0.1% increment. Make sure the gate movement can restart correctly after the motor stops in this manner.

Additional Activities

1. The central computer in a food processing plant controls several slide gates located in remote areas of the plant. Design and build a serial interface to allow the central computer to control your slide gate controller system.

   Use an 8251A USART and associated components to allow the slide gate control system to communicate serially. Control the position of the slide gate by sending it command codes from a personal computer. Write software in BASIC to produce these command codes; add software to the single-board computer to control the USART and accept the commands from the personal computer.

2. Add limit switches at the fully open and the fully closed slide gate positions. These switches serve as safety limits to prevent damage to the gate mechanism if a system malfunction occurs. Also, the switch at the fully closed position allows the system to locate a known position when the system is first initialized or after a power outage occurs.

   Incorporate these limit switches into your software. Also, define a CLOSE switch on the keyboard matrix to close the gate on demand. Write control software that will return the gate to the closed position when this key is pressed.

EXPERIMENT 29

Interfacing Project— The Digital Storage Oscilloscope

Objectives

A digital storage oscilloscope uses analog-to-digital and digital-to-analog digital conversion techniques to sample and display signal waveforms on a display screen. Although commercial digital storage oscilloscopes are quite complex and expensive, a simple version can be designed around an 8085-based single-board computer using only a few dollars' worth of components. After completing this experiment, you will be able to

- Design the hardware needed to make a simple digital storage oscilloscope
- Design software to control the operating modes of the digital storage oscilloscope
- Sample, store, then reconstruct analog signal waveforms using your digital storage oscilloscope system

Reference Reading

Review Experiments 17, 26, and 27.

Materials Needed

8085 single-board computer with download connection to personal computer
Breadboard with logic switches
Digital voltmeter
Oscilloscope
12 V dual power supply
Other components as needed for your hardware design

Discussion

Digital Storage Oscilloscope Features

A/D and D/A converters are often used in digital recording applications. Audio recording studios use digital recording techniques to sample and store music. Meteorologists use digital data loggers to monitor and record atmospheric conditions. Geologists use similar instruments to record seismic disturbances. In the electronics laboratory, digital storage oscilloscopes sample, store, process, and then display electrical signal waveforms. This experiment focuses on the design and implementation of a simple digital storage oscilloscope to demonstrate basic digital recording concepts.

The digital storage oscilloscope is shown in block diagram form in Figure 29.1. The heart of the system is a microcomputer, complete with microprocessor, memory, and I/O capabilities. Analog signals are digitized periodically by an A/D converter and stored in RAM. The microcomputer can then process the digital information in one of several ways before displaying it. Digital filtering techniques can remove unwanted noise signals from the captured data. The microcomputer can determine peak, average, and RMS values of complex waveforms. The microcomputer can even store data externally on a floppy disk or tape cartridge so that signal processing can be completed on a larger computer system at a more convenient time.

A simple digital storage oscilloscope can be developed around an 8085-based single-board microcomputer. In addition to the microcomputer, the memory and data conversion circuits explored in previous laboratory experiments are all that is needed to complete the design. Although commercial digital oscilloscopes are much faster and much more versatile than the system you are about to develop, the basic concepts are identical. After completing this project, you should be able to apply basic digital data-recording techniques to many other applications.

Procedure

1. Digital Storage Oscilloscope Specifications

The digital storage oscilloscope must meet these design specifications:

- Two analog input channels (A and B) to record and display unipolar waveforms in the 0 to +5 V range, using a 10 kHz sample rate
- Variable trigger-level control potentiometer
- SAMPLE push-button switch to initiate data-recording cycle
- Display mode switches to allow display of channel A, channel B, both channels A and B (dual-trace mode), or channel A added to channel B (A + B mode)
- Peak waveform voltage (in millivolts) displayed on the 4-digit LED readout of the microcomputer

The variable trigger-level control causes the system to trigger and begin sampling only when the input waveform reaches a certain signal magnitude. The signal on channel A is the trigger source when in the channel A, dual-trace, or A + B mode. Channel B is the trigger source when the system is in the channel B mode.

Input channels A and B each can store 1024 analog signal samples in data RAM. In the channel A or channel B mode, the system will sample the selected input channel 1024 times, beginning when the SAMPLE button is pressed. All 1024 samples are then output repetitively through the D/A converter to the display screen.

The dual-trace mode, similar to the chop mode found on most standard oscilloscopes, reads and records one sample of the signal on channel A, then does the same for channel B. This process continues until each channel has been sampled 1024 times. The system then alternately outputs to the display one sample from

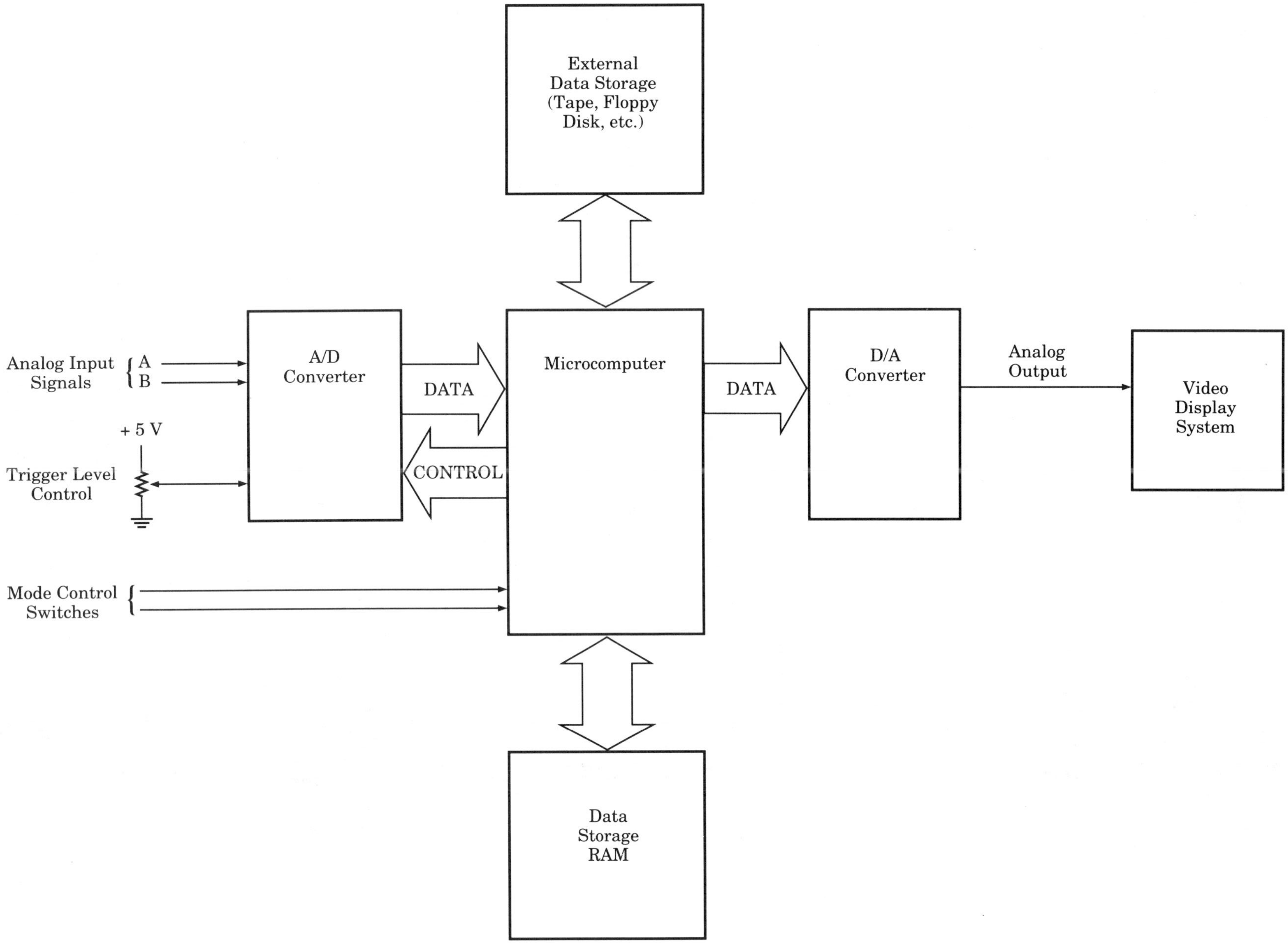

FIGURE 29.1
Digital Storage Oscilloscope Block Diagram

signal A, then one sample from signal B, and so on, until all data samples have been displayed. The results are scaled to show channel A on the upper half of the screen and channel B on the lower half.

In the A + B mode, the two input signals are added to form a composite signal. To fit the range of the 8-bit data conversion hardware, both input sample magnitudes are divided by 2 before being added. The resulting waveform is then displayed on the screen.

2. Digital Storage Oscilloscope Hardware Design
The digital storage oscilloscope hardware is to consist of the following subsystems:

- 8085-based single-board computer
- Standard oscilloscope to serve as a video display
- ADC0809 8-channel A/D converter
- MC1408 D/A converter
- 8K × 8 RAM memory for program and data storage

Draw a complete circuit diagram, including all necessary hardware components. Your circuit should input the A and B signals through two of the A/D converter input channels. The variable trigger-level control voltage can be read by a third analog input channel.

Use two microcomputer input port bits to define the operating mode (channel A, channel B, dual-trace, or A + B mode). Drive an interrupt input with the SAMPLE push-button switch. You may need to condition this switch signal to be compatible with the available interrupt input line.

3. Control Software Design
The control software for the digital storage oscilloscope should initialize all hardware, then proceed to the data input and output tasks. When the control program is executed, it should initialize all I/O hardware and clear the data storage memory by placing 00H in each location of the channel A and channel B data storage RAM.

After the system is initialized, the program should enter the data display mode, in which data values are continually sent to the D/A converter. Sampling is performed on an interrupt-driven basis, under the control of the SAMPLE push-button switch. Figure 29.2 summarizes in flowchart form the overall program logic for the system.

4. Hardware Construction and Testing
Construct and test each hardware subsystem separately before integrating them into the system. Test the A/D converter, the D/A converter, and the RAM memory hardware. Also, test the mode selection and SAMPLE switch input circuitry. Write simple test programs to check each subsystem; these programs will be useful for initial hardware diagnosis, as well as for future system debugging.

5. Software Development and System Testing
Add details to the flowchart (see Figure 29.2) to describe the sample and display mode logic. Next, write software to control the digital storage oscilloscope; use a modular program design approach to facilitate testing and debugging. Test the system initialization, data sampling, and data display sections of the program separately. After all software modules are functional, you are ready to combine them to test the entire system.

Test your digital storage oscilloscope using an appropriate signal source. Set a laboratory function generator to produce a 50 Hz sinusoidal output. Adjust the

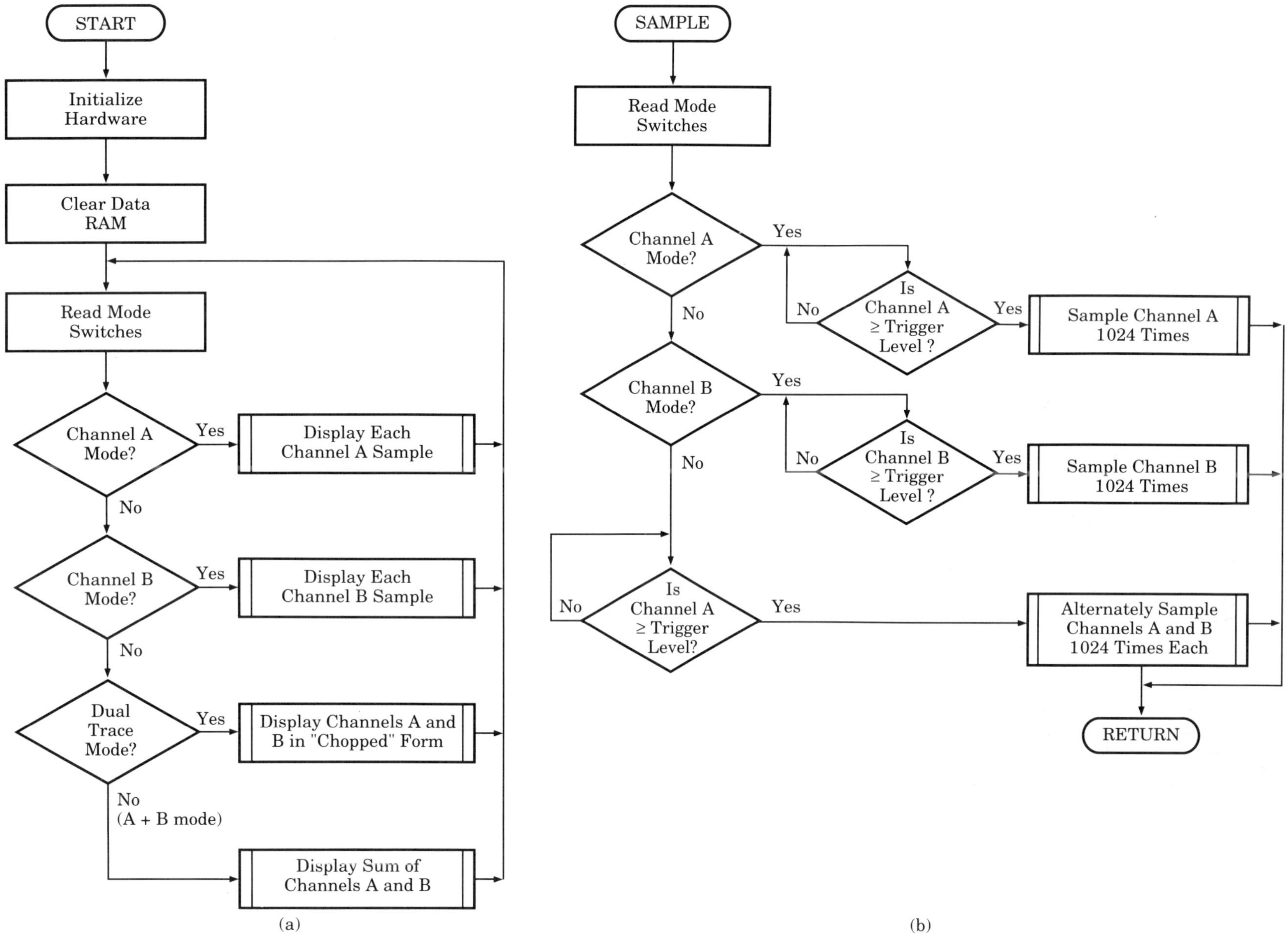

FIGURE 29.2
Flowcharts for (a) Main Program and (b) Interrupt Service Routine Used To Sample Data

offset control on the function generator so that the output voltage swings from +1 to +4 V. This signal must not go negative or higher than +5 V; otherwise, the ADC0809 A/D converter will be damaged. Connect the signal generator to the channel A input of your digital storage oscilloscope system.

Select the channel A mode on your digital storage oscilloscope system, and adjust the trigger-level control to +3 V. Execute your control program; the initial display produced by the system should be a straight line at 0 V (remember that no samples have been made yet). Press the Sample button to sample the 50 Hz input signal. Your system should sample the input signal and display the results on the oscilloscope screen. Also, the LED display on the single-board computer should show the peak voltage value, in millivolts.

Test the channel B, dual-trace, and A + B modes. Vary the trigger-level control and note the change in the displayed waveform. Sample sinusoidal, triangular, and rectangular waveforms of different frequencies. Determine the maximum frequency that your digital storage oscilloscope system can sample.

Additional Activities

1. Add signal-conditioning hardware to the digital storage oscilloscope system to allow audio signals from a microphone to be recorded. The signal-conditioning circuit should include a level shifter to move the bipolar audio signal from the microphone into the 0 to +5 V range acceptable by the A/D converter. Use the D/A converter to output the digitized audio signal to an audio amplifier and loudspeaker.
2. Add an 8251A USART to the digital storage oscilloscope system. Also, add control software to the single-board computer to upload the sampled data to a personal computer. Write a BASIC program for the personal computer to plot the sampled data values on the computer screen and on a dot-matrix printer.
3. Adapt the digital storage oscilloscope hardware for use as a digital temperature recorder. Write and test control software to automatically record the ambient temperature at 1-minute intervals. "Plot" the resulting temperature readings on an oscilloscope using the D/A converter.

EXPERIMENT 30

Interfacing Project—The Complete 8085 Microcomputer

Objectives

Building a complete microprocessor-based system, starting with the microprocessor integrated circuit itself, is the best way to integrate important microprocessor architecture, programming, and interfacing concepts. Successful development of a microprocessor-based system also requires considerable debugging and troubleshooting expertise. After completing this experiment, you will be able to

- Interface an 8085 microprocessor to memory and I/O devices
- Design and build a microprocessor-based system to perform a specific task
- Test 8085-based hardware using in-circuit emulation techniques

Reference Reading

Gaonkar, Ramesh S. *Microprocessor Architecture, Programming, and Applications with the 8085/8080A*. 2nd ed. Columbus, OH: Merrill, 1989. Sections 3.1 and 17.4–17.6.

The MCS-80/85 Family User's Manual. Santa Clara, CA: Intel Corp., 1986. Pages 6–10 to 6–23 and A1–1 to A1–19.

Materials Needed

8085 single-board computer
Breadboard
EPROM programmer
EPROM ultraviolet eraser

Microprocessor development system with in-circuit emulation (optional)
Oscilloscope
Digital voltmeter
Frequency counter
Logic probe
Logic analyzer
8085A-5 microprocessor
6264LP (150 ns) 8K × 8 RAM
2764 (450 ns) 8K × 8 EPROM
6.144 MHz crystal
Other components as needed for your hardware design

Discussion

Any microcomputer system consists of a microprocessor integrated circuit, memory devices, peripheral devices, and (of course) software. You will design and build a complete 8085-based microcomputer project in this experiment, using the concepts explored in previous laboratory exercises. As you design, build, and test your microcomputer project, you will encounter many of the challenges experienced by designers in industry.

"Bringing up" a new microcomputer system for the first time can be a very rewarding experience; unfortunately, it can also be quite frustrating at times. A systematic approach to the design, construction, and testing of this project will minimize your frustration level. The following sections describe some suggested procedures that will guide you as you complete this project.

Procedure

1. Definition of the Project Requirements
The first step in the development of a microprocessor-based project is the definition of the system requirements. The designer must define the functional requirements of the system before beginning the more detailed circuit design and software design tasks. Block diagrams and general flowcharts are used at this stage to describe the overall system.

Write a proposal describing an 8085-based application project. Include an analysis of all system input and output requirements. As a minimum, your project should use these components:

- 8085 microprocessor
- 8K × 8 RAM
- 8K × 8 EPROM
- General-purpose peripheral device (8255A or 8155)

In addition to these components, the project can include other peripheral devices such as keyboards, LED displays, programmable timers, USARTs, stepper motors, and transducers. (Check with your instructor concerning the availability of these items.)

Submit your proposal to your instructor for review and approval before proceeding.

2. System Hardware Design
After all system requirements are defined, draw a schematic diagram showing all hardware interconnections. Figure 30.1 illustrates the 8085 microprocessor signal

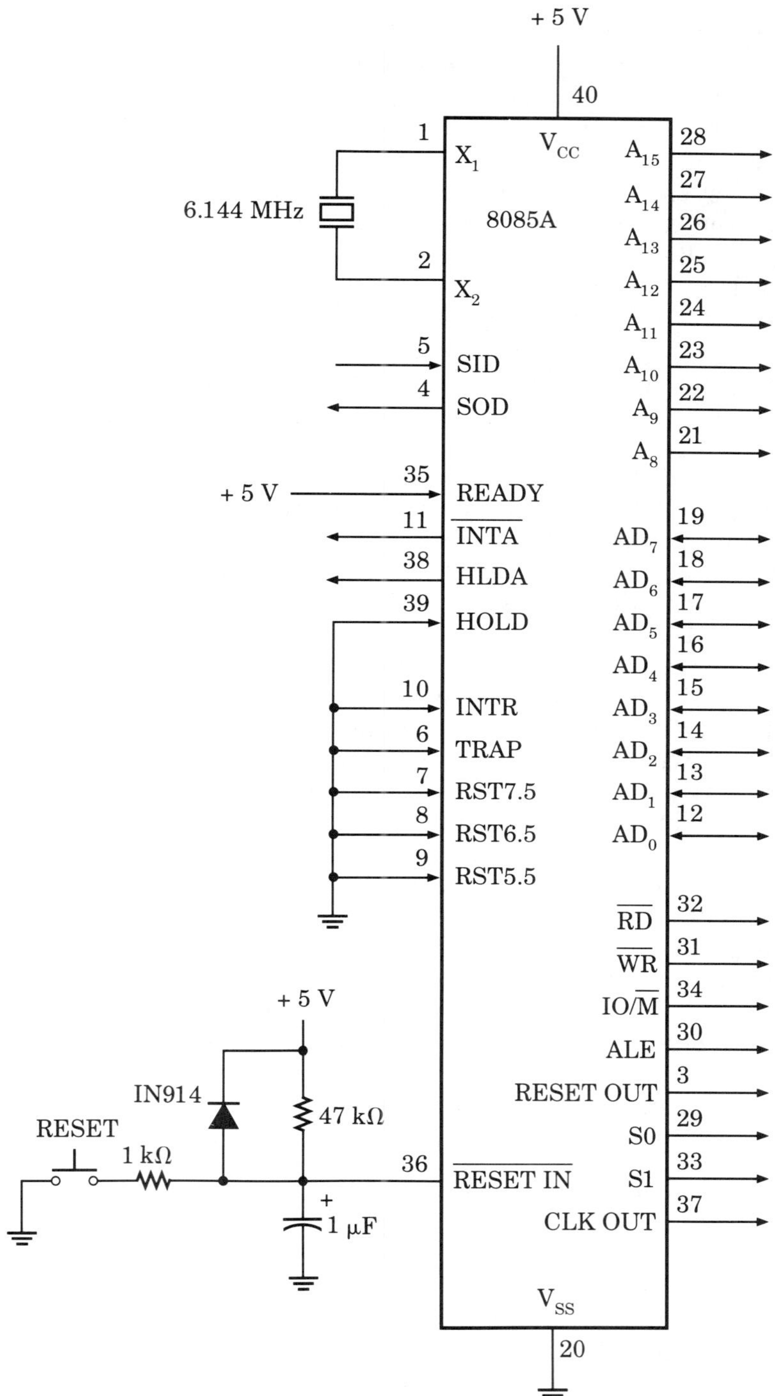

FIGURE 30.1
8085 Microprocessor Connections

connections. The TRAP, INTR, RST7.5, RST6.5, RST5.5, HOLD, and READY lines are tied to logic levels that disable these functions to facilitate initial hardware testing.

3. System Hardware Testing

Build and test the system hardware in a modular fashion. The 8085 microprocessor will be the *last* component connected to the system; all memory and I/O functions will be tested first using *in-circuit emulation* techniques. A microprocessor development system (if available) or your 8085-based single-board computer will be used to test each subsystem in the project. Eventually, all subsystems will be tested in unison before finally installing the 8085 microprocessor.

Build and test the RAM and EPROM hardware, including the necessary address decoding. Connect the in-circuit emulator cable to your prototype circuit. If you are using the single-board computer for in-circuit emulation, connect the necessary address, data, and control lines from the computer to your prototype. You may also need to change certain address decoder connections temporarily so that no addressing conflicts exist between the single-board computer and your prototype circuit.

Adapt the memory-testing techniques in Experiment 17 to test the memory circuit. Store the memory-testing programs in an EPROM; these programs may be useful for diagnostic purposes at a later time.

Build and test the I/O circuits used in your project. Test each circuit and save all diagnostic programs in EPROM for future use.

Finally, after all memory and I/O circuits are functional, remove the in-circuit emulation connections from your prototype. Install the 8085 microprocessor and connect it to the memory and I/O circuitry. Carefully check all wiring at least twice. Verify that *every* connection to the 8085 is correct.

Write a *simple* test program to send a binary count sequence to an 8-bit output port. Keep this test program simple; the goal is to test your prototype hardware, not your test program! Program an EPROM with this test program and install it in your prototype circuit.

Recheck all wiring, then turn on the system power supply. Monitor the least significant output port line with an oscilloscope to see if the expected square wave is present. If it is, check the other seven output port lines. If the 8-bit port is producing a binary count sequence, you have succeeded!

If the 8-bit port is not producing the expected output, press the RESET push-button switch (the power-on reset circuit may not have worked when power was first applied). If the system still does not function, do not be too disappointed; it is not unusual for prototype microcomputer systems to just "sit there" after power is first applied to them. If your circuit is in this category, try these tests:

- Check all wiring again. Be sure the address bus, data bus, and control signals properly connect the 8085 to the memory and I/O circuitry.
- Recheck your test program. Are you sure that the program as written outputs a square wave to the output port?
- Make sure that your test program is actually programmed into the EPROM and that the EPROM is installed correctly in the prototype.
- Measure the V_{cc} and GND voltages on the 8085 using a digital voltmeter. These values should be within the specified tolerances.
- Check the RESET IN signal by pressing the RESET push-button switch. The signal should go low and then return to a high level.
- Measure the voltage on the TRAP, HOLD, and READY lines. These lines must be at the appropriate logic level to allow the system to function properly.
- Monitor the CLK (OUT) line with an oscilloscope. You should see a 3.072 MHz signal.
- Check the ALE, $\overline{RD}$, $\overline{WR}$, and IO/$\overline{M}$ signals with a logic probe or oscillo-

scope. Each signal should be active to indicate that instructions are being fetched and executed properly.

- Check all address and data lines. If any bit seems to be stuck high or low when it should not be, trace that line to find the problem.
- Check the appropriate address decoder outputs to see if the EPROM and the output port device are being selected.

If you still have not found the problem using these preliminary tests, you might try substituting a known-good 8085 for the one in your prototype. As a last resort, attach the logic analyzer to your prototype system and trace various machine cycles (see Experiment 16).

After your complete microcomputer hardware system is functional, proceed with the development of software for your project. Develop the software on a microprocessor development system (if available) or on your single-board microcomputer. Use in-circuit emulation techniques whenever possible to allow efficient testing and debugging of the software as it operates the hardware of the prototype system. Without in-circuit emulation, you must store the prototype software in an EPROM, plug the EPROM into the hardware, and test the results. This entire process must be repeated to make any software modifications. Although this technique has been used to develop many microprocessor-based systems, it does not efficiently use a system designer's time.

After completing all hardware and software design changes, store the final version of the software in an EPROM. Thoroughly test all functions of your project, and then demonstrate the finished product to your instructor. You both can be proud of what you have accomplished!

APPENDIX A

Table of ASCII Codes

TABLE A.1
Table of ASCII Codes

GRAPHIC OR CONTROL	ASCII (HEXADECIMAL)
NUL	00
SOH	01
STX	02
ETX	03
EOT	04
ENQ	05
ACK	06
BEL	07
BS	08
HT	09
LF	0A
VT	0B
FF	0C
CR	0D
SO	0E
SI	0F
DLE	10
DC1 (X-ON)	11
DC2 (TAPE)	12
DC3 (X-OFF)	13
DC4 (~~TAPE~~)	14
NAK	15
SYN	16
ETB	17
CAN	18
EM	19
SUB	1A
ESC	1B
FS	1C
GS	1D
RS	1E
US	1F
SP	20
!	21
"	22
#	23
$	24
%	25
&	26
'	27
(	28
)	29
*	2A
+	2B
,	2C
–	2D
.	2E
/	2F
0	30
1	31
2	32
3	33
4	34
5	35
6	36
7	37
8	38
9	39
:	3A
;	3B
<	3C
=	3D
>	3E
?	3F
@	40
A	41
B	42
C	43
D	44
E	45
F	46
G	47
H	48
I	49
J	4A
K	4B
L	4C
M	4D
N	4E
O	4F
P	50
Q	51
R	52
S	53
T	54
U	55
V	56
W	57
X	58
Y	59
Z	5A
[	5B
\	5C
]	5D
∧ (↑)	5E
– (←)	5F
`	60
a	61
b	62
c	63
d	64
e	65
f	66
g	67
h	68
i	69
j	6A
k	6B
l	6C
m	6D
n	6E
o	6F
p	70
q	71
r	72
s	73
t	74
u	75
v	76
w	77
x	78
y	79
z	7A
{	7B
|	7C
} (ALT MODE)	7D
~	7E
DEL (RUB OUT)	7F

SOURCE: Reprinted by permission of Intel Corporation, copyright 1979.

APPENDIX B

8085 Instruction Set Summary

TABLE B.1
8080A/8085 Instruction Set Index

Instruction		Code	Bytes	T States		Machine Cycles
				8085A	8080A	
ACI	DATA	CE data	2	7	7	F R
ADC	REG	1000 1SSS	1	4	4	F
ADC	M	8E	1	7	7	F R
ADD	REG	1000 0SSS	1	4	4	F
ADD	M	86	1	7	7	F R
ADI	DATA	C6 data	2	7	7	F R
ANA	REG	1010 0SSS	1	4	4	F
ANA	M	A6	1	7	7	F R
ANI	DATA	E6 data	2	7	7	F R
CALL	LABEL	CD addr	3	18	17	S R R W W*
CC	LABEL	DC addr	3	9/18	11/17	S R•/S R R W W*
CM	LABEL	FC addr	3	9/18	11/17	S R•/S R R W W*
CMA		2F	1	4	4	F
CMC		3F	1	4	4	F
CMP	REG	1011 1SSS	1	4	4	F
CMP	M	BE	1	7	7	F R
CNC	LABEL	D4 addr	3	9/18	11/17	S R•/S R R W W*
CNZ	LABEL	C4 addr	3	9/18	11/17	S R•/S R R W W*
CP	LABEL	F4 addr	3	9/18	11/17	S R•/S R R W W*
CPE	LABEL	EC addr	3	9/18	11/17	S R•/S R R W W*
CPI	DATA	FE data	2	7	7	F R
CPO	LABEL	E4 addr	3	9/18	11/17	S R•/S R R W W*
CZ	LABEL	CC addr	3	9/18	11/17	S R•/S R R W W*
DAA		27	1	4	4	F
DAD	RP	00RP 1001	1	10	10	F B B
DCR	REG	00SS S101	1	4	5	F*
DCR	M	35	1	10	10	F R W
DCX	RP	00RP 1011	1	6	5	S*
DI		F3	1	4	4	F
EI		FB	1	4	4	F
HLT		76	1	5	7	F B
IN	PORT	DB data	2	10	10	F R I
LXI	RP,DATA16	00RP 0001 data16	3	10	10	F R R
MOV	REG,REG	01DD DSSS	1	4	5	F*
MOV	M,REG	0111 0SSS	1	7	7	F W
MOV	REG,M	01DD D110	1	7	7	F R
MVI	REG,DATA	00DD D110 data	2	7	7	F R
MVI	M,DATA	36 data	2	10	10	F R W
NOP		00	1	4	4	F
ORA	REG	1011 0SSS	1	4	4	F
ORA	M	B6	1	7	7	F R
ORI	DATA	F6 data	2	7	7	F R
OUT	PORT	D3 data	2	10	10	F R O
PCHL		E9	1	6	5	S*
POP	RP	11RP 0001	1	10	10	F R R
PUSH	RP	11RP 0101	1	12	11	S W W*
RAL		17	1	4	4	F
RAR		1F	1	4	4	F
RC		D8	1	6/12	5/11	S/S R R*
RET		C9	1	10	10	F R R
RIM (8085A only)		20	1	4	–	F
RLC		07	1	4	4	F
RM		F8	1	6/12	5/11	S/S R R*
RNC		D0	1	6/12	5/11	S/S R R*
RNZ		C0	1	6/12	5/11	S/S R R*
RP		F0	1	6/12	5/11	S/S R R*
RPE		E8	1	6/12	5/11	S/S R R*
RPO		E0	1	6/12	5/11	S/S R R*
RRC		0F	1	4	4	F
RST	N	11XX X111	1	12	11	S W W*
RZ		C8	1	6/12	5/11	S/S R R*
SBB	REG	1001 1SSS	1	4	4	F
SBB	M	9E	1	7	7	F R
SBI	DATA	DE data	2	7	7	F R

TABLE B.1 (Continued)
8080A/8085 Instruction Set Index

INR	REG	00SS S100	1	4	5	F*
INR	M	34	1	10	10	F R W
INX	RP	00RP 0011	1	6	5	S*
JC	LABEL	DA addr	3	7/10	10	F R/F R R†
JM	LABEL	FA addr	3	7/10	10	F R/F R R†
JMP	LABEL	C3 addr	3	10	10	F R R
JNC	LABEL	D2 addr	3	7/10	10	F R/F R R†
JNZ	LABEL	C2 addr	3	7/10	10	F R/F R R†
JP	LABEL	F2 addr	3	7/10	10	F R/F R R†
JPE	LABEL	EA addr	3	7/10	10	F R/F R R†
JPO	LABEL	E2 addr	3	7/10	10	F R/F R R†
JZ	LABEL	CA addr	3	7/10	10	F R/F R R†
LDA	ADDR	3A addr	3	13	13	F R R R
LDAX	RP	000X 1010	1	7	7	F R
LHLD	ADDR	2A addr	3	16	16	F R R R R

SHLD	ADDR	22 addr	3	16	16	F R R W W
SIM (8085A only)		30	1	4	–	F
SPHL		F9	1	6	5	S*
STA	ADDR	32 addr	3	13	13	F R R W
STAX	RP	000X 0010	1	7	7	F W
STC		37	1	4	4	F
SUB	REG	1001 0SSS	1	4	4	F
SUB	M	96	1	7	7	F R
SUI	DATA	D6 data	2	7	7	F R
XCHG		EB	1	4	4	F
XRA	REG	1010 1SSS	1	4	4	F
XRA	M	AE	1	7	7	F R
XRI	DATA	EE data	2	7	7	F R
XTHL		E3	1	16	18	F R R W W

Machine cycle types:
F four clock period instr fetch
S six clock period instr fetch
R Memory Read
I I/O read
W Memory Write
O I/O write
B Bus idle
X Variable or optional binary digit
DDD Binary digits identifying a designation register B = 000, C = 001, D = 010, Memory = 110
SSS Binary digits identifying source register E = 011, H = 100, L = 101, A = 111
RP Register Pair BC = 00, HL = 10
DE = 01, SP = 11

*5-clock period instruction fetch with 8080A.

†The longer machine cycle sequence applies regardless of condition evaluation with 8080A.

•An extra READ cycle (R) will occur for this condition with 8080A.

TABLE B.2

8085 Instructions in Operation Code Sequence

OP CODE	MNEMONIC	OP CODE	MNEMONIC	OP CODE	MNEMONIC	OP CODE	MNEMONIC	OP CODE	MNEMONIC	OP CODE	MNEMONIC
00	NOP	2B	DCX H	56	MOV D,M	81	ADD C	AC	XRA H	D7	RST 2
01	LXI B,D16	2C	INR L	57	MOV D,A	82	ADD D	AD	XRA L	D8	RC
02	STAX B	2D	DCR L	58	MOV E,B	83	ADD E	AE	XRA M	D9	—
03	INX B	2E	MVI L,D8	59	MOV E,C	84	ADD H	AF	XRA A	DA	JC Adr
04	INR B	2F	CMA	5A	MOV E,D	85	ADD L	B0	ORA B	DB	IN D8
05	DCR B	30	SIM	5B	MOV E,E	86	ADD M	B1	ORA C	DC	CC Adr
06	MVI B,D8	31	LXI SPD16	5C	MOV E,H	87	ADD A	B2	ORA D	DD	—
07	RLC	32	STA Adr	5D	MOV E,L	88	ADC B	B3	ORA E	DE	SBI D8
08	—	33	INX SP	5E	MOV E,M	89	ADC C	B4	ORA H	DF	RST 3
09	DAD B	34	INR M	5F	MOV E,A	8A	ADC D	B5	ORA L	E0	RPO
0A	LDAXB	35	DCR M	60	MOV H,B	8B	ADC E	B6	ORA M	E1	POP H
0B	DCX B	36	MVI M,D8	61	MOV H,C	8C	ADC H	B7	ORA A	E2	JPO Adr
0C	INR C	37	STC	62	MOV H,D	8D	ADC L	B8	CMP B	E3	XTHL
0D	DCR C	38	——	63	MOV H,E	8E	ADC M	B9	CMP C	E4	CPO Adr
0E	MVI C,D8	39	DAD SP	64	MOV H,H	8F	ADC A	BA	CMP D	E5	PUSH H
0F	RRC	3A	LDA Adr	65	MOV H,L	8G	SUB B	BB	CMP E	E6	ANI D8
10	——	3B	DCX SP	66	MOV H,M	91	SUB C	BC	CMP H	E7	RST 4
11	LXI D,D16	3C	INR A	67	MOV H,A	92	SUB D	BD	CMP L	E8	RPE
12	STAX D	3D	DCR A	68	MOV L,B	93	SUB E	BE	CMP M	E9	PCHL
13	INX D	3E	MVI A,D8	69	MOV L,C	94	SUB H	BF	CMP A	EA	JPE Adr
14	INR D	3F	CMC	6A	MOV L,D	95	SUB L	C0	RNZ	EB	XCHG
15	DCR D	40	MOV B,B	6B	MOV L,E	96	SUB M	C1	POP B	EC	CPE Adr
16	MVI D,D8	41	MOV B,C	6C	MOV L,H	97	SUB A	C2	JNZ Adr	ED	——
17	RAL	42	MOV B,D	6D	MOV L,L	98	SBB B	C3	JMP Adr	EE	XRI D8
18	——	43	MOV B,E	6E	MOV L,M	99	SBB C	C4	CNZ Adr	EF	RST 5
19	DAD D	44	MOV B,H	6F	MOV L,A	9A	SBB D	C5	PUSH B	F0	RP
1A	LDAXD	45	MOV B,L	70	MOV M,B	9B	SBB E	C6	ADI D8	F1	POP PSW
1B	DCX D	46	MOV B,M	71	MOV M,C	9C	SBB H	C7	RST 0	F2	JP Adr
1C	INR E	47	MOV B,A	72	MOV M,D	9D	SBB L	C8	RZ	F3	DI
1D	DRC E	48	MOV C,B	73	MOV M,E	9E	SBB M	C9	RET Adr	F4	CP Adr
1E	MVI E,D8	49	MOV C,C	74	MOV M,H	9F	SBB A	CA	JZ	F5	PUSH PSW
1F	RAR	4A	MOV C,D	75	MOV M,L	A0	ANA B	CB	——	F6	ORI D8
20	RIM	4B	MOV C,E	76	HLT	A1	ANA C	CC	CZ Adr	F7	RST 6
21	LXI H,D16	4C	MOV C,H	77	MOV M,A	A2	ANA D	CD	CALL Adr	F8	RM
22	SHLD Adr	4D	MOV C,L	78	MOV A,B	A3	ANA E	CE	ACI D8	F9	SPHL
23	INX H	4E	MOV C,M	79	MOV A,C	A4	ANA H	CF	RST 1	FA	JM Adr
24	INR H	4F	MOV C,A	7A	MOV A,D	A5	ANA L	D0	RNC	FB	EI
25	DCR H	50	MOV D,B	7B	MOV A,E	A6	ANA M	D1	POP D	FC	CM Adr
26	MVI H,D8	51	MOV D,C	7C	MOV A,H	A7	ANA A	D2	JNC Adr	FD	——
27	DAA	52	MOV D,D	7D	MOV A,L	A8	XRA B	D3	OUT D8	FE	CPI D8
28	——	53	MOV D,E	7E	MOV A,M	A9	XRA C	D4	CNC Adr	FF	RST 7
29	DAD H	54	MOV D,H	7F	MOV A,A	AA	XRA D	D5	PUSH D		
2A	LHLD Adr	55	MOV D,L	80	ADD B	AB	XRA E	D6	SUI D8		

D8 = constant, or logical/arithmetic expression that evaluates to an 8-bit data quantity.
D16 = constant, or logical/arithmetic expression that evaluates to a 16-bit data quantity.
Adr = 16-bit address.

APPENDIX C

Required Equipment and Supplies

Equipment

8085-based single-board microcomputer
Personal computer with parallel printer port and one serial port, with cables to connect parallel printer port and serial port to breadboard
Cross assembler software
RS-232C ASCII video terminal
Breadboard unit with +5 V power supply, eight logic switches, eight LED indicators, and two debounced switches
3 1/2 digit digital multimeter (4 1/2 digit instrument is preferred for A/D and D/A converter work)
Dual-trace oscilloscope (10 MHz bandwidth or higher)
Frequency counter (0–10 MHz)
Function generator (0–1 MHz)
Dual 0–15 V, 2 A power supply
Logic probe
Logic analyzer
EPROM programmer
EPROM ultraviolet eraser

Integrated Circuits

741 operational amplifier
74LS04 hex inverter
Two 7406 hex inverters (open collector)
74LS74 dual D flip-flop
74LS90 BCD counter
74LS93 binary counter
Two 74123 dual retriggerable monostable multivibrators

74LS138 3-to-8 decoder
74LS148 priority encoder
74LS240 octal inverting buffer
74LS244 octal 3-state buffer
74LS374 octal D latch
8085A-5 microprocessor
8155 programmable RAM, I/O, and timer device
8251A USART
8255A programmable peripheral device
8253A programmable interval timer
6264LP (150 ns) 8K × 8 RAM
2764 (450 ns) 8K × 8 EPROM
ADC0809 A/D converter
MAX232 RS-232C driver/receiver
MC1408 (or DAC0808) D/A converter
LM335 temperature sensor
LM336-5.0 precision voltage reference
LM1458 dual operational amplifier

Other Active Devices

Four MAN72A common-anode 7-segment LED displays
Four 4N26 optocouplers
Four TIP102 NPN Darlington transistors
TIP106 PNP Darlington transistor
2N2222 NPN transistor
Four 2N2907 PNP transistors
Four 1N914 diodes
Four 1N4004 diodes

Resistors

Two 10 Ω, 10 W resistors
Nine 100 Ω, 1/4 W resistors
Eight 220 Ω, 1/4 W resistors
1 kΩ, 1/4 W resistor
2.2 kΩ, 1/4 W resistor
Two 2.4 kΩ, 1/4 W resistors
Four 3.3 kΩ, 1/4 W resistors
Three 3.9 kΩ, 1/4 W resistors
Four 5.6 kΩ, 1/4 W resistors
Two 6.8 kΩ, 1/4 W resistors
Four 10 kΩ, 1/4 W resistors
Two 18 kΩ, 1/4 W resistors
1.8 MΩ, 1/4 W resistor
Three 10 kΩ, 10-turn potentiometers
100 kΩ, 10-turn potentiometer

Capacitors

47 pF ceramic disk capacitor
Ten 0.01 μF ceramic disk capacitors
Three 0.1 μF ceramic disk capacitors
Five 10 μF, 16 V capacitors

Other Components

16-key keyboard (4 × 4 matrix)
Small 8 Ω speaker
6-position SPST DIP switch
#47 6.3 V lamp
6.144 MHz crystal
Small permanent-magnet DC "toy" motor
Stepper motor (Superior Electric MO61-FD302 or similar type)
Laboratory thermometer (Fahrenheit scale)

APPENDIX
D

Using the 8085 Cross Assembler

References

Gaonkar, Ramesh S. *Microprocessor Architecture, Programming, and Applications with the 8085/8080A*. 2nd ed. Columbus, OH: Merrill, 1989. Section 1.2 and Chapter 11.

User's manual for your 8085 cross assembler program.

Discussion

The process of converting assembly language mnemonics (source code) into binary machine language (object code) is called *assembling* the program. We can manually assemble a program using the 8085 instruction set tables. This procedure is tolerable for very small programs; for larger, more complex programs, we must use a faster approach. A special software package called a *cross assembler* can assemble 8085 programs for us. The cross assembler not only eliminates the drudgery of manually looking up operation codes, but also provides these additional benefits:

- Symbolic labels can be used for memory addresses.
- Data constants can be given symbolic label names.
- All address operands are automatically computed.
- Literal ASCII characters can be entered. The cross assembler "looks up" the ASCII codes for us.
- Space can be reserved in memory for data storage.
- A well-organized listing is produced that encourages better program documentation.
- A data file is produced that can be transmitted to an 8085-based microcomputer for debugging.

A word processor program or text editor program can create the assembly language source program. Most word processors are capable of producing a source file that is compatible with 8085 cross assemblers. The word processor can create a new program file, insert or delete instructions, and move groups of program instructions within the file. It can also merge several small program modules into a larger program.

The source program file is cross-assembled after it is created by the word processor or text editor. Cross assemblers for the 8085 are available from several companies. Since each of these cross assemblers requires its own unique set of operating commands, only the features common to all cross assemblers are discussed here. Your instructor can supply the details needed for using the particular editor and cross assembler programs available to you.

The following sections describe many of the standard 8085 cross assembler features.

Data Constants

Specify numeric constants in either hexadecimal, binary, or decimal form using the H, B, or D suffixes, respectively. For example, each of the following values represents the same numeric quantity:

3EH represents a hexadecimal value.
62D represents a decimal quantity. (Decimal is also assumed if no suffix letter is given.)
00111110B represents a binary value.

Some cross assemblers require all numeric constants to begin with a digit between 0 and 9. For example, the hexadecimal number D7H must be entered as 0D7H.

The assembler interprets characters enclosed by single quotes (apostrophes) as literal ASCII values. For example, MVI B, 'A' is interpreted as MVI B,41H. Note that 41H is the hexadecimal representation of the ASCII character A.

Labels

Labels must begin in column one of the source program line and must be followed by a colon. The maximum allowable label length varies, but is typically eight characters. Labels must begin with an alphabetic character, but the remaining characters may be alphabetic or numeric. Examples of permissible labels include:

MESSAGE:
SUB1A:
LOOP123:

Comments

Insert comments liberally in each assembly language program to document the program logic. Comments are preceded by a semicolon (;). The assembler interprets an entire line as a comment if a semicolon is placed in column 1.

Assembler Directives

An assembler directive (also known as a pseudo-operation code) is not an executable instruction, but is a command that is understood by the cross assembler program. Here are some common assembler directives:

ORG	Defines the origin, or beginning address, of a program or subroutine.
EQU	Equates a label with a numeric constant.
DB	Define Byte. This directive is used to place a data string into memory.

DW Define Word. This directive is similar to DB, but places two bytes at a time into memory.
DS Define Storage. Reserves a specified number of bytes in memory. Used for reserving space for data values.
END Must be the last item in the source program file. This tells the cross assembler that no more instructions are to be assembled.

The following sample program illustrates the use of each of the commonly used assembler features. The assembler listing Figure D.1 is typical of the "list file" output generated when this sample program is cross-assembled.

```
;*************************************
;***** PROGRAM FILENAME: MEMFILL.SRC                *****
;***** PROGRAMMER: JOHN DOE                         *****
;***** DATE: NOVEMBER 12, 1999                      *****
;***** DESCRIPTION: FILLS MEMORY ARRAY WITH         *****
;*****    SPECIFIED BYTE.                           *****
;*************************************

          ORG  2000H

FILLBYTE  EQU  10101010B    ;BYTE TO PLACE INTO ARRAY
COUNT     EQU  32D          ;BYTE COUNTER

          MVI  A, FILLBYTE  ;INITIALIZE DATA VALUE
          LXI  H,ARRAY      ;INITIALIZE MEMORY POINTER
          MVI  B,COUNT      ;INITIALIZE LOOP COUNTER
LOOP:     MOV  M,A          ;STORE BYTE IN MEMORY
          INX  H            ;INCREMENT ARRAY POINTER
          DCR B             ;SEE IF FINISHED
          JNZ               ;IF NOT, REPEAT FOR NEXT BYTE
          RST 1             ;ELSE, QUIT

;*************************************
;***** DATA STORAGE AREA                            *****
;*************************************

          ORG 205H

ARRAY:    DS 32D           ;RESERVE 32-BYTE DATA SPACE
MESSAGE:  DB 'ABC 123', 53H,27H
YEAR:     DW 2001H

          END
```

This program stores the binary value 10101010 in each location in the address range 2050H–206FH. The data values defined by the DB and DW directives are not used in this program; they are included only to demonstrate the syntax of these directives.

```
                              ;***********************************************************************
                              ;***** PROGRAM FILENAME:  MEMFILL.SRC                              *****
                              ;***** PROGRAMMER:  JOHN DOE                                       *****
                              ;***** DATE:  NOVEMBER 12, 1999                                    *****
                              ;***** DESCRIPTION:  FILLS MEMORY ARRAY WITH SPECIFIED BYTE.       *****
                              ;***********************************************************************

2000                                    ORG 2000H

A         A 00                FILLBYTE  EQU 10101010B  ;BYTE TO PLACE INTO ARRAY ELEMENTS
2         0 00                COUNT     EQU 32D        ;BYTE COUNTER

2000      3E AA                         MVI A,FILLBYTE ;INITIALIZE DATA VALUE
2002      21 50 20                      LXI H,ARRAY    ;INITIALIZE MEMORY POINTER
2005      06 20                         MVI B,COUNT    ;INITIALIZE LOOP COUNTER
2007      77                  LOOP:     MOV M,A        ;STORE BYTE IN MEMORY
2008      23                            INX H          ;POINT TO NEXT LOCATION
2009      05                            DCR B          ;SEE IF FINISHED
200A      C2 07 20                      JNZ LOOP       ;IF NOT, REPEAT FOR NEXT BYTE
200D      CF                            RST 1          ;ELSE, QUIT

                              ;***********************************************************************
                              ;***** DATA STORAGE AREA                                           *****
                              ;***********************************************************************

2050                                    ORG 2050H

2050                          ARRAY:    DS 32D         ;ALLOCATE 32 BYTES FOR DATA STORAGE
2070      41 42 43 20         MESSAGE:  DB 'ABC 123',53H,27H
2074      31 32 33 53
2078      27
2079      01 20               YEAR:     DW 2001H

207B                                    END
```

FIGURE D.1
Cross Assembler Listing File

APPENDIX E

SDK-85 Microcomputer Connector Details

TABLE E.1
Bus Expansion Connector J1 Pin Assignments

ASSIGNMENT	PIN	PIN	MARKING	ASSIGNMENT	I/O
GND	1	2	—	OPEN	–
GND	3	4	CLK	Buffered CLK	O
GND	5	6	S1	Buffered S1	O
GND	7	8	S0	Buffered S0	O
GND	9	10	ALE	Buffered ALE	O
GND	11	12	HLDA	Buffered HLDA	O
GND	13	14	HOLD	Buffered HOLD	I
GND	15	16	INTA/	Buffered $\overline{\text{INTA}}$	O
GND	17	18	INTR	INTR	I
GND	19	20	RST 6.5	Buffered RST 6.5	I
GND	21	22	RST	Buffered RESET OUT	O
GND	23	24	RST IN/	$\overline{\text{RESET INPUT}}$	I
GND	25	26	D7	Buffered D7	I/O
GND	27	28		Buffered D6	I/O
GND	29	30		Buffered D5	I/O
GND	31	32	— DATA BUS —	Buffered D4	I/O
GND	33	34		Buffered D3	I/O
GND	35	36		Buffered D2	I/O
GND	37	38		Buffered D1	I/O
GND	39	40	D0	Buffered D0	I/O

SOURCE: Reprinted by permission of Intel Corporation, copyright 1978.

TABLE E.2
Bus Expansion Connector J2 Pin Assignments

ASSIGNMENT	PIN	PIN	MARKING	ASSIGNMENT	I/O
GND	1	2	RDY	READY	I
GND	3	4	WR/	Buffered $\overline{WR}$	O
GND	5	6	RD/	Buffered $\overline{RD}$	O
GND	7	8	IO/$\overline{M}$	Buffered IO/$\overline{M}$	O
GND	9	10	A15	Buffered A15	O
GND	11	12	ADDRESS BUS	Buffered A14	O
GND	13	14		Buffered A13	O
GND	15	16		Buffered A12	O
GND	17	18		Buffered A11	O
GND	19	20		Buffered A10	O
GND	21	22		Buffered A9	O
GND	23	24		Buffered A8	O
GND	25	26		Buffered A7	O
GND	27	28		Buffered A6	O
GND	29	30		Buffered A5	O
GND	31	32		Buffered A4	O
GND	33	34		Buffered A3	O
GND	35	36		Buffered A2	O
GND	37	38		Buffered A1	O
GND	39	40	A0	Buffered A0	O

SOURCE: Reprinted by permission of Intel Corporation, copyright 1978.

TABLE E.3
I/O Port Connector J3 Pin Assignments

ASSIGNMENT	PIN	PIN	MARKING	ASSIGNMENT
P1-6*	1	2	PORT 1	P1-7
P1-4	3	4		P1-5
P1-2	5	6		P1-3
P1-0	7	8		P1-1
P0-6	9	10	PORT 0	P0-7
P0-4	11	12		P0-5
P0-2	13	14		P0-3
P0-0	15	16		P0-1
P9-6	17	18	PORT 9	P9-7
P9-4	19	20		P9-5
P9-2	21	22		P9-3
P9-0	23	24		P9-1
P8-6	25	26	PORT 8	P8-7
P8-4	27	28		P8-5
P8-2	29	30		P8-3
P8-0	31	32		P8-1
GROUND	33	34		GROUND

*Note:
1. Pn-m stands for PORT n Bit m (e.g. P9-6 means PORT 9H Bit 6).
2. Ports 0 & 1 are Ports A and B of 8355 (A14).
3. Ports 8 & 9 are Ports A and B of 8755 (A15).

SOURCE: Reprinted by permission of Intel Corporation, copyright 1978.

TABLE E.4
I/O Port Connector J4 Pin Assignments

ASSIGNMENT	PIN	PIN	MARKING	ASSIGNMENT
P23H-4	1	2	PORT 23H	P23H-5
P23H-2	3	4		P23H-3
P23H-0	5	6		P23H-1
P22H-6	7	8	PORT 22H	P22H-7
P22H-4	9	10		P22H-5
P22H-2	11	12		P22H-3
P22H-0	13	14		P22H-1
P21H-6	15	16	PORT 21H	P21H-7
P21H-4	17	18		P21H-5
P21H-2	19	20		P21H-3
P21H-0	21	22		P21H-1
OPEN	23	24		OPEN
GROUND	25	26		GROUND

Note: Port 21H is Port A, Port 22H is Port B, Port 23H is Port C of 8155 (A16).

SOURCE: Reprinted by permission of Intel Corporation, copyright 1978.

TABLE E.5
I/O Port and Timer Connector J5 Pin Assignments

ASSIGNMENT	PIN	PIN	MARKING	ASSIGNMENT
P2BH-4	1	2	PORT 2BH	P2BH-5
P2BH-2	3	4		P2BH-3
P2BH-0	5	6		P2BH-1
P2AH-6	7	8	PORT 2AH	P2AH-7
P2AH-4	9	10		P2AH-5
P2AH-2	11	12		P2AH-3
P2AH-0	13	14		P2AH-1
P29H-6	15	16	PORT 29H	P29H-7
P29H-4	17	18		P29H-5
P29H-2	19	20		P29H-3
P29H-0	21	22		P29H-1
Timer $\overline{\text{OUT}}$	23	24	TIMER $\overline{\text{OUT}}$/IN	Timer In
GROUND	25	26		GROUND

Note: Port 29H is Port A, Port 2AH is Port B, Port 2BH is Port C of expansion RAM 8155 (A17).
Timer is on the same 8155 (A17).

SOURCE: Reprinted by permission of Intel Corporation, copyright 1978.

APPENDIX F

SDK-85 Microcomputer Monitor Subroutines

The SDK-85 monitor program contains several subroutines available to the user for data input and output processing. The following summary describes several of the most useful subroutines.* Consult the *SDK-85 System Design Kit User's Manual* for additional subroutine information; that document also contains a complete source listing of the SDK-85 monitor program.

Subroutine Name: UPDAD
Calling Address: 0363H
Description: Updates address field of display.
Inputs: Contents of DE are displayed. Register B controls decimal point (DP) at right edge of field: (B) = 01 turns on DP, (B) = 00 turns off DP.
Outputs: None
Registers Modified: A, B, C, D, E, H, L, and flags

Subroutine Name: UPDDT
Subroutine Calling Address: 036EH
Description: Updates data field of display.
Inputs: Contents of accumulator are displayed. Register B controls decimal point (DP) at right edge of field: (B) = 01 turns on DP, (B) = 00 turns off DP.
Outputs: None
Registers Modified: A, B, C, D, E, H, L, and flags

Subroutine Name: RDKBD
Calling Address: 02E7H
Description: Waits until key is pressed, then returns the key code. For

*SOURCE: Subroutine descriptions adapted from material copyrighted by Intel Corporation.

RDKBD to work properly, first unmask the RST 5.5 interrupt as follows:

```
MVI A,08H
SIM
```

Inputs: None
Outputs: Accumulator returns key code:

Key Pressed	*Value Returned*	*Key Pressed*	*Value Returned*
0	00H	B	0BH
1	01H	C	0CH
2	02H	D	0DH
3	03H	E	0EH
4	04H	F	0FH
5	05H	EXEC	10H
6	06H	NEXT	11H
7	07H	GO	12H
8	08H	SUBST MEM	13H
9	09H	EXAM REG	14H
A	0AH	SINGLE STEP	15H

Registers Modified: A, H, L, and flags

Subroutine Name: OUTPT
Subroutine Calling Address: 02B7H
Description: Outputs characters to display.
Inputs: Accumulator selects field: (A) = 00 selects address field, (A) = 01 selects data field. Register B controls decimal point (DP) at right edge of field: (B) = 01 turns on DP, (B) = 00 turns off DP. HL contains starting address of character array to be displayed.
Outputs: Characters on selected display digits:

Character Displayed	*Hexadecimal Value Pointed to by HL*	*Character Displayed*	*Hexadecimal Value pointed to by HL*
0	00	b	0B
1	01	C	0C
2	02	d	0D
3	03	E	0E
4	04	F	0F
5	05	H	10
6	06	L	11
7	07	P	12
8	08	I	13
9	09	r	14
A	0A	S	05
		Blank	15

Registers Modified: A, B, C, D, E, H, L, and flags

WE VALUE YOUR OPINION—PLEASE SHARE IT WITH US

Merrill Publishing and our authors are most interested in your reactions to this textbook. Did it serve you well in the course? If it did, what aspects of the text were most helpful? If not, what didn't you like about it? Your comments will help us to write and develop better textbooks. We value your opinions and thank you for your help.

Text Title ______________________________ Edition ________

Author(s) ______________________________

Your Name (optional) ______________________________

Address ______________________________

City ____________________ State ________ Zip ________

School ______________________________

Course Title ______________________________

Instructor's Name ______________________________

Your Major ______________________________

Your Class Rank _______ Freshman _______ Sophomore _______Junior _______ Senior

_______ Graduate Student

Were you required to take this course? _______ Required _______Elective

Length of Course? _______ Quarter _______ Semester

1. Overall, how does this text compare to other texts you've used?

   _______ Superior _______Better Than Most _______ Average _______Poor

2. Please rate the text in the following areas:

	Superior	*Better Than Most*	*Average*	*Poor*
Author's Writing Style	_______	_______	_______	_______
Readability	_______	_______	_______	_______
Organization	_______	_______	_______	_______
Accuracy	_______	_______	_______	_______
Layout and Design	_______	_______	_______	_______
Illustrations/Photos/Tables	_______	_______	_______	_______
Examples	_______	_______	_______	_______
Problems/Exercises	_______	_______	_______	_______
Topic Selection	_______	_______	_______	_______
Currentness of Coverage	_______	_______	_______	_______
Explanation of Difficult Concepts	_______	_______	_______	_______
Match-up with Course Coverage	_______	_______	_______	_______
Applications to Real Life	_______	_______	_______	_______

3. Circle those chapters you especially liked:
   1 2 3 4 5 6 7 8 9 10 11 12 13 14 15 16 17 18 19 20
   What was your favorite chapter? _______
   Comments:

4. Circle those chapters you liked least:
   1 2 3 4 5 6 7 8 9 10 11 12 13 14 15 16 17 18 19 20
   What was your least favorite chapter? _______
   Comments:

5. List any chapters your instructor did not assign. ______________________________

6. What topics did your instructor discuss that were not covered in the text? ______________________________

   ____

7. Were you required to buy this book? _______ Yes _______ No

   Did you buy this book new or used? _______ New _______ Used

   If used, how much did you pay? ___________

   Do you plan to keep or sell this book? _______ Keep _______ Sell

   If you plan to sell the book, how much do you expect to receive? ___________

   Should the instructor continue to assign this book? _______ Yes _______ No

8. Please list any other learning materials you purchased to help you in this course (e.g., study guide, lab manual).

   ____

9. What did you like most about this text? ______________________________

   ____

10. What did you like least about this text? ______________________________

    ____

11. General comments:

May we quote you in our advertising? _______ Yes _______ No

Please mail to: Boyd Lane
College Division, Research Department
Box 508
1300 Alum Creek Drive
Columbus, Ohio 43216

Thank you!